Conceptual Art in a Curatorial Perspective

Appropriated detail from image note 101, p. 135, Mel Bochner, *Working Drawings and Other Visible Things on Paper Not Necessarily Meant to Be Viewed as Art*, 1966, at the School of Visual Arts, New York.

Appropriated detail from image note 101, p. 135, Mel Bochner, *Working Drawings and Other Visible Things on Paper Not Necessarily Meant to Be Viewed as Art*, 1966, at the School of Visual Arts, New York.

Appropriated detail from image note 101, p. 135, Mel Bochner, *Working Drawings and Other Visible Things on Paper Not Necessarily Meant to Be Viewed as Art*, 1966, at the School of Visual Arts, New York.

Appropriated detail from image note 101, p. 135, Mel Bochner, *Working Drawings and Other Visible Things on Paper Not Necessarily Meant to Be Viewed as Art*, 1966, at the School of Visual Arts, New York.

Nathalie Zonnenberg

VIS-À-VIS

Valiz

Conceptual Art in a Curatorial Perspective

Between Dematerialization and Documentation

For my father, in memoriam
"You should write a book," he said

Contents

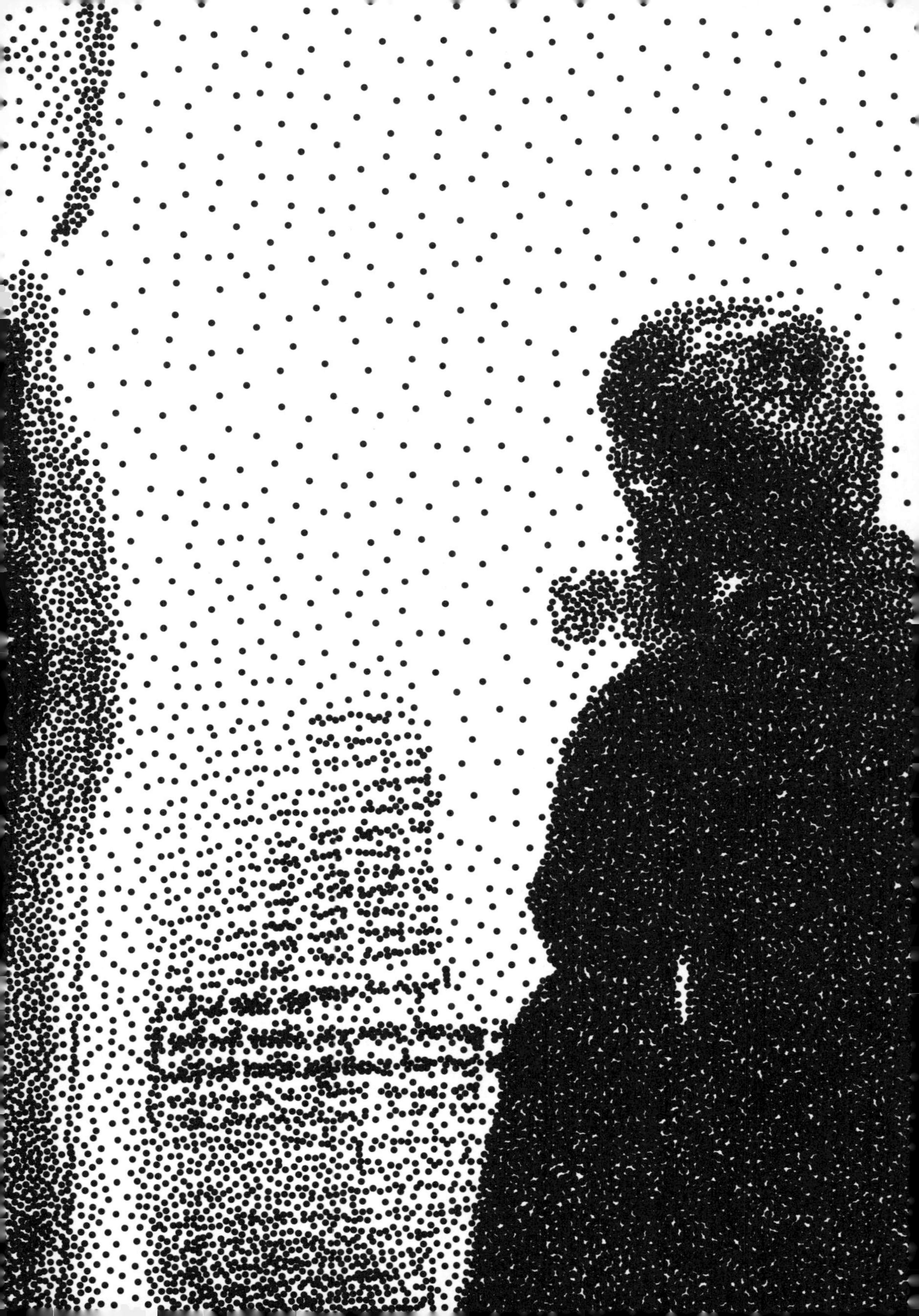

Introduction

The impossibility of reclaiming the volitivity of perceptual change leaves art historical explanations to pick the bones of dead forms. In this sense, all art dies with time and is impermanent whether it continues to exist as an object or not.
— Robert Morris[1]

1 Robert Morris, "Notes on Sculpture Part 4: Beyond Objects," *Artforum* vol. 8, no. 8 (April 1969), p. 53.

2 Prior to the exhibitions in the gallery space, Art & Project distributed the bulletin in order to announce these exhibitions, but more often than not the bulletin also functioned as an alternative space for the activities of the artists they affiliated with that did not fit the traditional format of exhibition.

In 1969 Dutch artist Jan Dibbets conceived and developed a project which can be regarded as exemplary for the paradoxical condition of many works of conceptual art. *Project for Art & Project* anticipated the fifteenth exhibition of the Amsterdam "avant-garde gallery" Art & Project and used the distributive format of the gallery's invitation, the so-called bulletin, to construct a work that would eventually reveal the network involved in the production, distribution, and collection of conceptual art in the late 1960s.[2] The bulletin was sent to a mailing list of about 400 addressees with the request to return one side to the gallery, after which each returned bulletin would be marked on a map by a straight line from the

Image appropriated from John Baldessari, *I Will Not Make Any More Boring Art*, Mezzanine Gallery, Nova Scotia College of Art and Design, 1971. See also p. 45.

home of the addressee to the location of the gallery in Amsterdam. In addition to this, the addressees were invited for the opening of the exhibition (of the work) that would take place at the closing day of the project.[3] The work had at least two different formats of presentation: while the first consisted of the exhibition of the 196 returned bulletins and their additional markings on four maps in the gallery (Amsterdam, the Benelux, Europe, and the world),[4] the second appeared in the 1970 July/August issue of *Studio International*[5] in printed format—representing the returned bulletins with a list of names.[6]

Among the addressees who returned the bulletin to the gallery were not only Dibbets's conceptual artist peers but also important critics, curators, dealers, and, most importantly, collectors (of a new type) interested in conceptual art. It may thus come as no surprise that the exhibited work in the gallery was subsequently acquired by the collector couple Herman and Henriëtte van Eelen.[7] The eventual sale can be considered an essential part of the work, successfully closing the cycle of production, distribution, and collection in which conceptual art operated in the late 1960s. In this respect Dibbets's *Project* has become a historical document, effectively illustrating the process of commodification that conceptual art was subjected to since its beginnings—something of which the artist seemed well aware when he conceived the project.[8] Ironically, the sale of Dibbets's *Project* as an autonomous work of art at the same time contradicts the very principles of conceptual art that were trying to counter the process of commodification. In another respect, the work is also illustrative of the dilemma of exhibiting conceptual art. Although Dibbets has always lightly objected to being ascribed as a "conceptual artist," *Project for Art & Project* could be defined as a textbook example of a conceptual artwork, which in its

3 The closing day of the project was on Tuesday, December 16, 1969, from 8 to 9 p.m. See Jan Dibbets, *Art & Project Bulletin* 15 (November 1969).

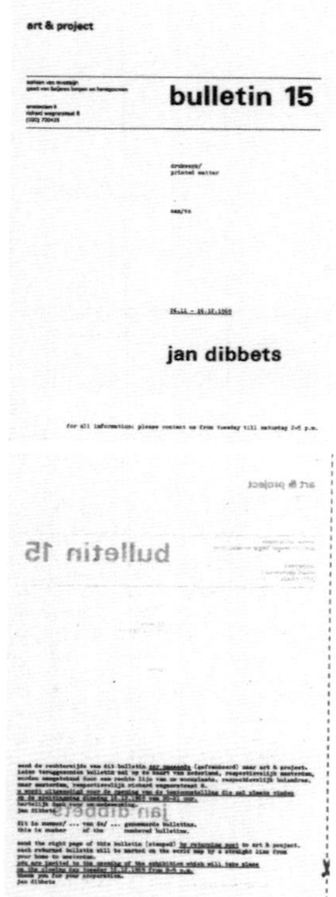

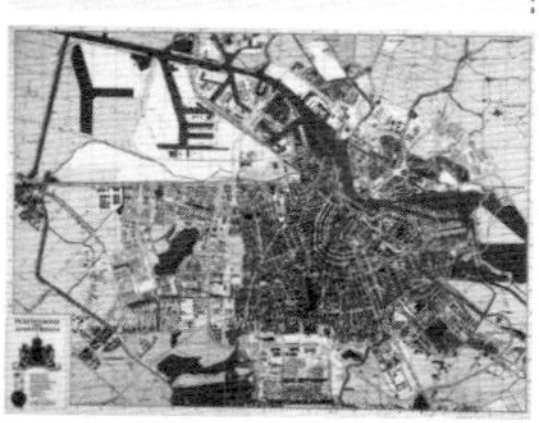

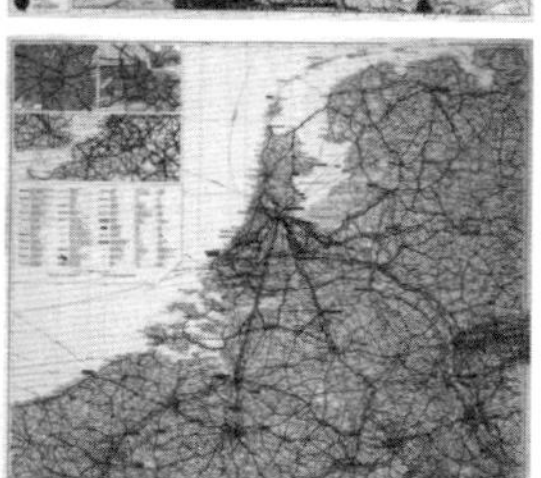

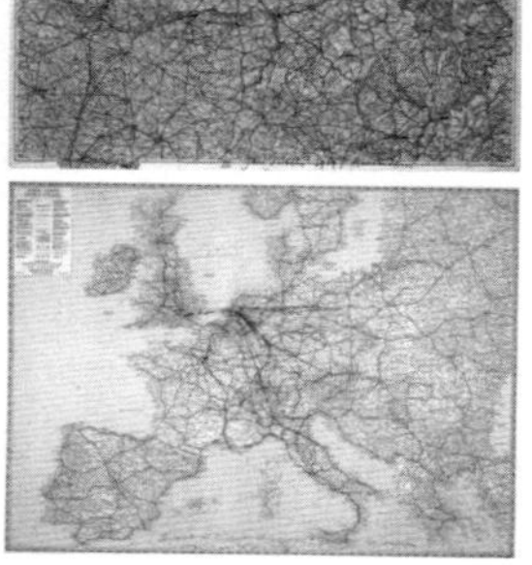

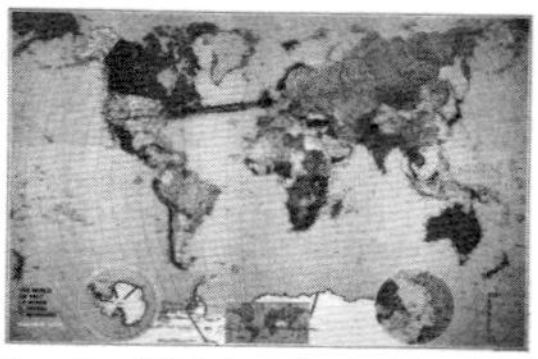

4 Jan Dibbets, *Project for Art & Project* (bulletin and maps), 1969.

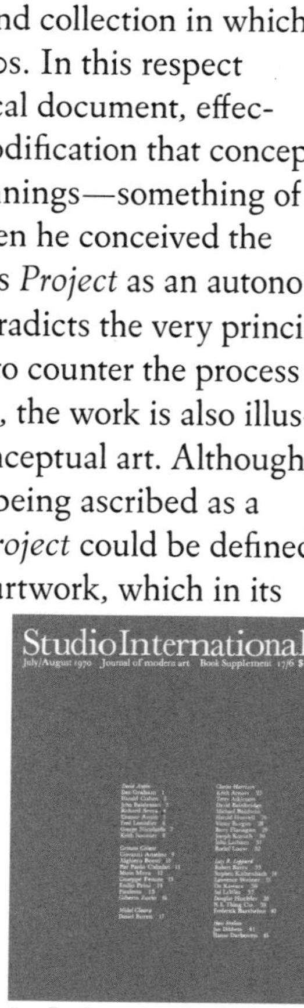

5 Book supplement of the July/August 1970 issue of *Studio International*, curated by Seth Siegelaub.

execution is negating or frustrating a definite format of exhibition.

When I co-curated the exhibition REDONE: *Conceptual Art from the Collection* with Toos van Kooten at the Kröller-Müller Museum in Otterlo in 2008, I was personally confronted with the dilemma of how to (re-)exhibit Dibbets's *Project*.[9] The Kröller-Müller Museum acquired the Van Eelen collection in 2006, and this was the first time that Dibbets's work was to be re-exhibited in a public context.[10] The four different maps with markings were separately framed behind thin Perspex, and the collection of 196 returned bulletins was kept in a simple cardboard box with no further instructions. It was thus of primary concern to anticipate the contextual implications this documentary type of work would acquire within a spatial presentation. Whereas the bulletins were organized according to the four geographic categories, we decided to display them in vitrines that were placed directly below the framed maps on the wall, in such a way that a large part of the names on the papers would be exposed—in order to generate an understanding of the relationship between the different parts of the project. The work was hereafter included in the exhibition *In & Out of Amsterdam: Travels in Conceptual Art 1960–1976*,[11] curated by Christophe Cherix at the Museum of Modern Art in New York (2010), where it occupied a central position.[12] Unfortunately, since the addressees and stamps of the different locations were not visible there, the larger implications of Dibbets's work were not conveyed to the public. The bulletins were all stocked together and displayed at some distance from the maps, as a result of which the correlation between the maps and bulletins was lost.

It is hard to argue that the documents within the collection of the Kröller-Müller Museum representing Dibbets's

6 For this specific issue of *Studio International* the New York curator-dealer Seth Siegelaub was invited to "curate" an exhibition in the magazine. He in turn invited a number of other curators, of which Hans Strelow selected the work by Dibbets.

7 The personal relationship with the artists and the specific interaction of each acquisition were more important for the Van Eelens than the (art historical) value of the works. Birgit Pelzer has pointed out that, for Belgium collectors Herman and Nicole Daled, "Buying works by living artists offered a way to escape the passive role assigned to art audiences. This insistence on action, on 'doing,' entered into a dialogue with art production at a time when the latter, crucially, viewed itself as a testing ground for thought." Birgit Pelzer, "Synchronies: A Journey of Discovery through Herman and Nicole Daled's Collection and Archives—1966–1978," in *A Bit of Matter and A Little Bit More: The Collection and Archives of Herman and Nicole Daled 1966–1978*, eds. Patrizia Dander and Ulrich Wilmes, exh. cat. Munich (Haus der Kunst) 2010, p. 17. Among the addressees who returned the bulletin were John Baldessari, Stanley Brouwn, On Kawara, Sol LeWitt, Ger van Elk, Daniel Buren, Piero Gilardi, Gerry Schum, and Lawrence Weiner; Wim Beeren, René Bloch, Cor Blok, Willi Bongard, Michel Claura, Konrad Fischer, Rudi Fuchs, Bernd Lohaus, Barbara Reise, Seth Siegelaub, Hans Strelow, John Wendler, and White Wide Space; and Martin and Mia Visser, Herman Daled, and Herman van Eelen.

8 In an interview conducted with Dibbets in 2010, he explained that he came up with the idea for the work to "test" whether what he thought of the system of art at the time was really true. See Nathalie Zonnenberg, "The Amsterdam Connection: In Conversation with Jan Dibbets and Ger van Elk," *Metropolis M* no. 4 (August/September 2010), pp. 52–62 and 112–115, <www.metropolism.com/magazine/2010-no4/de-amsterdam-connectie>. Dibbets's viewpoint at the time can be regarded as rather opportunistic, as he said in 1968: "Sell my work? To sell isn't part of the art. Maybe there will be people idiotic enough to buy what they could make themselves. So much the worse for them." See Lucy R. Lippard, "Escape Attempts," in Ann Goldstein and Anne Rorimer, *Reconsidering the Object of Art 1965–1975* (Los Angeles: Museum of Contemporary Art/Cambridge, MA: MIT Press, 1995), p. 28.

9 This exhibition was the result of a seminar with BA students that I initiated and coordinated at the VU University in Amsterdam, and which studied a large amount of conceptual artworks from the collection of the museum. See <http://krollermuller.nl/exposition/archive#2008> (28-09-2016).

10 The collection Van Eelen-Weeber contains thirty-five conceptual artworks from 1965 to 1973, as well as a few precursors like Yves Klein, Piero Manzoni, and Barnett Newman. The works have been brought together in a relatively short period of time, in close contact with the artists and their galleries. See <http://krollermuller.nl/exposition/archive#2006> (28-09-2016).

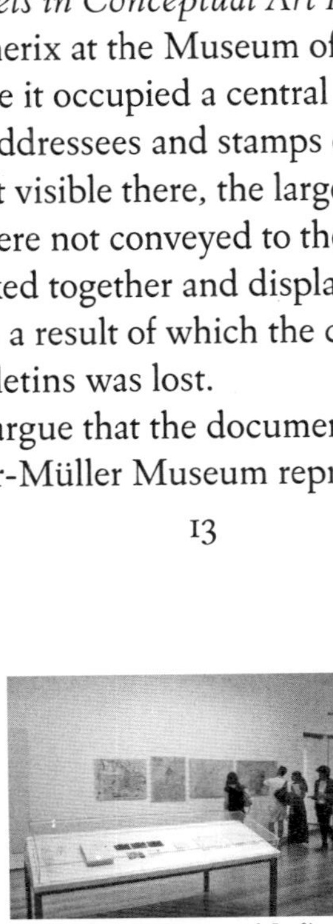

11 Installation view of *In & Out of Amsterdam* at MoMA, New York, 2010, with Jan Dibbets *Project for Art & Project*.

12 Christophe Cherix, *In & Out of Amsterdam: Travels in Conceptual Art 1960–1976*, exh. cat. New York (Museum of Modern Art) 2010. This noteworthy exhibition was based on a gift of conceptual works from the collection of the Dutch Art & Project gallery and credited the influence of Dutch art institutions in the development of conceptual art.

Project comprise an autonomous artwork; the various elements of the project need to be contextualized within an exhibitionary setting to make sense. In contrast, the publication of Dibbets's *Project* within the context of the *Studio International* journal offered a more appropriate format to display the several parts of the project as a whole; it used modest referential information to disclose the main purpose of the work. In the journal the unaddressed bulletin was published on one page, followed by the list of addressees, "by number of bulletin and name of person responding," and by the four maps, two on a page, simply referenced as "maps of responses" from Amsterdam, the Benelux, Europe, and the world.[13] The assembly of all the information involved in the project did not constitute an autonomous work of art any more than the original documents; it was merely a mode of distributing information to anyone who purchased the journal. By directly conveying the project's information in a publication, however, the journal effectively disclosed Dibbets's proposition as no other format could.

The above case elucidates the difficulties in the exhibition of works of conceptual art that are preserved within collections of public (and private) museums of modern and contemporary art. One of the main objectives of conceptual art was to criticize and subvert the commercial system of (contemporary) art that relegates the artwork to a plain commodity. Many works that were conceived at the time and applied a "dematerialization of art as object" were nevertheless sold and thus commodified.[14] This outcome is interpreted in two conflicting ways. Whereas some regard it as "a failure," others hold it as the "open-ended assignment" of conceptual art as a movement.[15] Since the latter option intrigues me as a practicing curator, I decided to explore how historical works of

13 Book Supplement of *Studio International* 17, no. 6 (July/August 1970), p. 42.

14 See Lucy R. Lippard and John Chandler, "The Dematerialization of Art," *Art International* vol. 12, no. 2 (February 1968), pp. 31–36.

15 See Michael Newman, "Conceptuele kunst van de jaren zestig tot negentig: Een onaf project?," *Kunst & Museumjournaal* vol. 7, nos. 1–3 (1996), pp. 101–112.

conceptual art should be approached within a contemporary exhibitionary context—starting from the knowledge that the etymological origin of "to curate" is "to take care" (*curare*). My aim is to define what should be considered the "original artwork," and to examine to what extent the sustained exhibition of such work—which is, after all, the task of public collections—conflicts with the intentions of the protagonists of the historical "movement." Would it be better to accept the documentary status of many works of conceptual art and present these in books and publications, as was initially thought to be the proper place for them? Or, if the exhibition in a spatial configuration is nevertheless compulsory, what other formats of display would be appropriate to effectively disclose these works?

Instead of answering these questions in the format of a manual or instruction book—based on my own practice or experiments within curation—the thesis that I present focuses on the historical reassessment of the conundrum of exhibition within conceptual art and the role that curators assumed in this regard. The French art historian Jean-Marc Poinsot argued that works of art do not only exist by means of their art historical disclosure, but additionally and especially by their continued exhibition.[16] To study the history of conceptual art's exhibition, therefore, can provide insight into the complexities and paradoxes of conceptual art's "ontological condition," as well as into the artistic and curatorial strategies that should be taken into consideration in support of the present and future exhibition of conceptual art.

As Sophie Richard demonstrated in her published dissertation *Unconcealed: The international network of conceptual artists 1967–1977: Dealers, exhibitions and public collections* (2010), "Conceptual Art" developed out of several (individual) artists' practices simultaneously emerging in the

16 See Jean-Marc Poinsot, *Quand l'oeuvre a lieu: L'art exposé et ses récits autorisés* (Geneva: Mamco; Villeurbanne: Institut d'art contemporain & Art édition, 1999).

United States and Europe, establishing collaborations and relationships among each other and with affiliated curators, dealers, and collectors, which in turn became an "international" network.[17] Within this network diverse positions and opinions have been decisive for the eventual framing of conceptual art as an art historical category. Consequently, there is not one overall theory of conceptual art but many, most of which are based on either theoretical reflections or formalist art historical affirmations.[18] I do not intend to add another definition of conceptual art to these theories; rather, I will use the existing array of literature to contextualize the complexity of the conundrum I intend to examine. Whereas the artists, theorists, and exhibitions of conceptual art that I evaluate will not differ much from those canonized, my analysis of the problems arising within historical examples of exhibitions of conceptual art attempts to provide a different perspective on the legacy of conceptual art.

Although my method of research is primarily art historical, I will approach the dilemma of (re-)exhibiting works of conceptual art from the perspective of a curator. As I am active as an exhibition curator within the field of art institutions and museums, I tend to encounter and examine works of art from this position. Accordingly, this book focuses on the properties of an exhibition as a means to communicate artworks to an audience, including the spatial, temporal, and relational considerations that such an enterprise entails. To this end, I will reconstruct curatorial methods and strategies that have allowed the conceptual work of art to be exhibited in the first place. Additionally, I will relate these methods and strategies to the historical and more recent discourses on conceptual art, revealing inconsistencies but also opportunities inherent to the exhibition practice of conceptual art. With this double approach, I aim to present a curatorial perspective

17 Sophie Richard, *Unconcealed: The International Network of Conceptual Artists 1967–77: Dealers, Exhibitions and Public Collections*, ed. Lynda Morris (London: Ridinghouse, 2009).

18 See, for example, Michael Newman and Jon Bird, eds., *Rewriting Conceptual Art* (London: Reaktion Books, 1999); Alexander Alberro and Blake Stimson, eds., *Conceptual Art: A Critical Anthology* (Cambridge, MA: MIT Press, 1999); and Peter Osborne, *Conceptual Art* (London and New York: Phaidon Press, 2002).

that concentrates on the communicative or public rationale of conceptual artworks rather than their theoretical affirmations—although these aspects cannot be entirely separated within conceptual art.[19]

The discipline of curation has become increasingly theoretical in recent years, producing a discourse of its own that has entered, and might even have come to dominate, the discourse of contemporary art in general.[20] Arguably, present-day curatorial discourse is indissolubly connected to conceptual art. The processes of "demystification" that artists (in close collaboration with curators) generated in the late 1960s established a shift in the conditions of art production that is often referred to as the "linguistic turn."[21] According to curator and theorist Paul O'Neill, conceptual art's demystification of "the hidden structures of the art world" (i.e., the role of the museum, the role of the collector, and the influence of the exhibition space on the production of artworks) anticipated a "curatorial turn" within the practice and discourse of art in the early 1990s.[22] This turning point is not only evidenced by the recent development of the practice of exhibition-making into a more discursive and professional discipline, institutionalized in educational and training programs, but also by the large amount of critical and scholarly literature produced on the methods, theories, and histories of contemporary exhibition-making.[23]

While the study of and writing on exhibitions and curating has come to dominate the general art discourse since the 1990s, it has also forced the academic discipline of art history to broaden its scope. According to art historian and professor of museum studies Bruce Altshuler, the curatorial boom of the late 1980s and 1990s runs parallel to an expanding interest in social and institutional histories within art history,

19 Boris Groys argued that conceptual art has made artistic practice meaningful and communicative again; in his perspective the "linguistic turn" meant that art had begun to be used as language, rather than using language itself, with a communicative and even educative purpose. Boris Groys, "Global Conceptualism Revisited," *e-flux journal* no. 29 (November 2011), <www.e-flux.com/journal/global-conceptualism-revisited/> (24-1-2015).

20 Groys even acclaimed that contemporary art is primarily to be understood as an exhibition practice, blurring the boundaries between the roles of artist and curator. Boris Groys, "Politics of Installation," *e-flux journal* no. 2 (January 2009), <www.e-flux.com/journal/politics-of-installation/> (24-1-2015).

21 See, for example, Newman and Bird 1999, p. 2.

22 See Paul O'Neill, "The Curatorial Turn: From Practice to Discourse," in *The Biennial Reader*, eds. Elena Filipovic et al. (Ostfildern: Hatje Cantz Verlag, 2010), p. 241. Originally published in Judith Rugg and Michele Sedgwick, eds., *Issues in Curating Contemporary Art and Performance* (Chicago: University of Chicago Press, 2007), pp. 13–28. O'Neill more specifically refers to the discourse generated by Seth Siegelaub and the artists he affiliated with (Barry, Huebler, Kosuth, and Weiner) in New York in the late 1960s.

23 See Bernd Klüser and Katharina Hegewisch, *Die Kunst der Ausstellung: Eine Dokumentation dreissig exemplarischer Kunstausstellungen dieses Jahrhunderts* (Frankfurt: Insel-Verlag, 1991); Reesa Greenberg et al., eds., *Thinking about Exhibitions* (London and New York: Routledge, 1996); Bruce Altshuler, *Salon to Biennial: Exhibitions that Made Art History, Volume 1: 1863–1959* (London: Phaidon Press, 2008), and Bruce Altshuler, *Biennials and Beyond: Exhibitions that Made Art History, 1962–2002* (London: Phaidon Press, 2013); Terry Smith, *Thinking Contemporary Curating* (New York: Independent Curators International, 2012).

"prompted by the postmodern questioning of grand narratives, by postcolonial studies, and by multiculturalist demands for inclusion of the previously excluded."[24] Altshuler also claimed that this development was in fact a response to the groundbreaking 1989 exhibition *Magiciens de la terre* at the Centre Pompidou in Paris. Likewise, within the research and literature on conceptual art, exhibitions have played significant roles, such as the 1999 exhibition *Global Conceptualism* at the Queens Museum in New York, which called attention to a more global perspective on conceptual art.[25] In turn, the study of such exhibitions, published in the Exhibition Histories series by Afterall Books since 2010, for example—including case studies of the exhibitions *When Attitudes Become Form, Op losse schroeven,* Lucy Lippard's "Numbers Shows," the Third Havana Biennial, and *Magiciens de la terre,* among others—offers important points of reference for my own elaborations.

Positioning my study within this specific field of exhibition history and theory, I will not so much focus on artists' oeuvres or individual works of art—even if not explicitly avoiding this—but turn my attention towards the multifaceted context of the exhibitionary setting. Exhibitions are marked by artistic or aesthetic strategies, and perhaps even moreso by institutional or socioeconomic strategies. This realization requires that some refinements on the narrative of conceptual art need to be made. While the art historical canonization of conceptual art—concentrating on artists' discourse and oeuvres—is on its way to completion, even in those regions that were formerly not part of the Western art historical hegemony, it is my opinion that the current (art historical) assignment concerning the study of conceptual art is twofold.[26] First, it is necessary to analyze the paradoxical relationship between the discourse and practice of conceptual

24 Bruce Altshuler, "A Canon of Exhibitions," *Manifesta Journal* no. 11 (2010–2011), p. 6.

25 The exhibition *Global Conceptualism: Points of Origin, 1950s–1980s* at the Queens Museum in New York in 1999 presented many conceptual practices outside the New York and American-European circles of conceptual art, including those in Japan, Central and Eastern Europe, Russia, Latin America, and Australia.

26 The history of conceptual practices outside the United States and Western Europe has increasingly been canonized in the past fifteen years. See, for example, Dubravka Djuric and Misko Suvakovic, eds., *Impossible Histories: Historical Avant-gardes, Neo-avant-gardes, and Post-avant-gardes in Yugoslavia, 1918–1991* (Cambridge, MA: MIT Press, 2003); Laura Hoptman and Tomas Pospiszil, eds., *Primary Documents: A Sourcebook for Eastern European Art Since the 1950s* (New York: Museum of Modern Art, 2002); and Boris Groys, *History Becomes Form: Moscow Conceptualism* (Cambridge, MA: MIT Press, 2010).

art that contributed to the allegedly failed self-imposed assignment. Second, it should be questioned to what extent the notion of this "failure" is related not simply to the increased commercialization of the art world but rather to a deficient understanding of the conceptual work of art by museums and art institutions—especially with regard to the question of how to exhibit these works in a contemporary perspective.

In order to contribute to the above research desiderata, I will first reevaluate several theories and definitions of conceptual art from the (historical) literature in chapter one; more specifically, the notions of "dematerialization," "primary and secondary information," and "art documentation," respectively framed by Lucy Lippard (1968), Seth Siegelaub (1972), and Boris Groys (1997). These particular notions can be considered imperative for the ontological condition of the conceptual artwork in regard to its exhibition, and will be used as a theoretical framework to assess three case studies of conceptual art exhibitions from the late 1960s to the present in the subsequent three chapters.

The first part of chapter one expands on "The Principle of Dematerialization" through an analysis of the ideological stance of the artists involved in relation to applied formats of exhibition and the larger system of art's production, distribution, and collection. Lippard's rather broad definition of conceptual art as "work in which the idea is paramount and the material form is secondary, lightweight, ephemeral, cheap, unpretentious and/or 'dematerialized'" might seem highly inadequate to use as a theoretical framework to analyze the ontological implications of the conceptual work of art.[27] Yet Lippard worked as a critic and curator in close collaboration with conceptual artists, and approached this type of art with respect to its material form—even if this was exactly what

27 Lucy R. Lippard, "Escape Attempts," in Goldstein and Rorimer 1995, p. 17.

was being problematized. While she soon agreed with her critics that a "piece of paper or a photograph is as much an object, or 'material,' as a ton of lead," the notion of dematerialization continued to be addressed in the literature on conceptual art.[28] It can even still be considered relevant to determine to what extent the traditional understanding of a work of art is challenged by conceptual practices, both in its ontological condition and material formation, and in relation to its exhibition.

The second part of chapter one, entitled "Primary and Secondary Information," examines the strategies of conceptual artists to present their work outside the realm of the leading art institutions, using in particular the format of the publication. It was the contention of Seth Siegelaub, curator and dealer of the New York conceptual artists Robert Barry, Douglas Huebler, Joseph Kosuth, and Lawrence Weiner, that the specific, idea-based character of conceptual art utterly fit into the format of the publication as a new "space" to show art.[29] Furthermore, the publication was a means to surpass the existing market strategies of art at the time and develop a new system of art distribution that would be based on royalties. The Artist's Reserved Rights Transfer and Sale Agreement (1971)[30] developed by Siegelaub in collaboration with lawyer Robert Projansky was another attempt to protect the rights of conceptual artists and guarantee an income for their "immaterial work."[31] The idea was never effectively realized. In fact, the contract also facilitated the trade of conceptual works via the existing market system, and many indistinct documents of conceptual art ended up in private and public collections around the world, where they are considered and treated as original artworks. From an "art as information," conceptual art thus turned into an "art as documentation." In this turn, conceptual artists' rejection of the art

28 Lucy R. Lippard, "Preface," in *Six Years: The Dematerialization of the Art Object from 1966 to 1972* (Berkeley and Los Angeles: University of California Press, 1997), p. 5. Previously published in New York: Praeger, 1973.

29 Siegelaub regarded the nature of conceptual artists as one unrelated to space. However, none of the artists he worked with agreed. See RoseLee Goldberg, "Space as Praxis," *Studio International* 190, no. 977 (September/October 1975), p. 130.

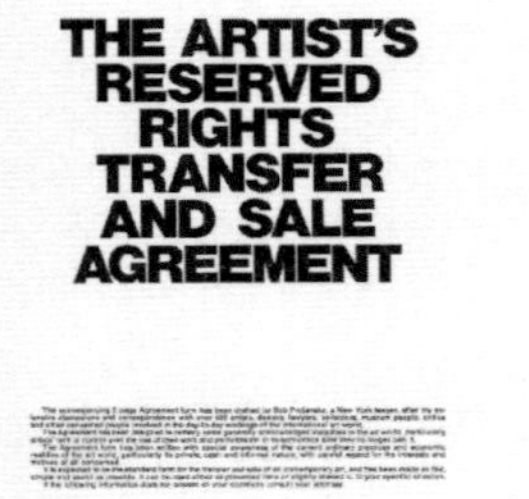
THE ARTIST'S RESERVED RIGHTS TRANSFER AND SALE AGREEMENT

30 Seth Siegelaub and Robert Projansky, The Artist's Reserved Rights Transfer and Sale Agreement, 1971.

31 Here I am referring to Maurizio Lazzarato's concept of "immaterial labor" (i.e., labor as service). See Maurizio Lazzarato "Immaterial Labour," in *Radical Thought in Italy*, ed. Paolo Virno and Michael Hardt, trans. Paul Colilli and Ed Emory (Minneapolis: University of Minnesota Press, 1996), pp. 132–146. Although not a definition used by the practitioners of conceptual art in the 1960s, this term is anticipating recent discussions on, and reevaluations of conceptual art, for example, by Jan Verwoert, who regards conceptual art not as a new method of work that changed the role of the artist into an office worker, as had been asserted by Benjamin Buchloh, but about the "rejection of work." Jan Verwoert, lecture on the occasion of the presentation of Camiel van Winkel's book *During the Exhibition the Gallery Will Be Closed: Contemporary Art and the Paradoxes of Conceptualism* (Amsterdam: Valiz, 2012), Stedelijk Museum Amsterdam, December 9, 2012.

object as a commodity, paradoxically enough, has been commodified.

The third part of chapter one, "Art Documentation," further analyzes the commodified work of conceptual art that is often captured in documents and certificates. The definition of art documentation by the Russian-German philosopher Boris Groys accurately describes the current ontological condition of historical works of conceptual art as "documents referring to art without being art itself."[32] These documents, however, can be considered the only "originals" of conceptual artworks that museums or private collectors own—originals, moreover, that require some sort of "reproduction." The diagrams and texts, instructions for events or projects, and proposed or imagined artworks can solely exist in the form of a plan to be produced (or not) within a specific spatiotemporal situation, or can allow for reexecution; that is, refabrication or reenactment in various time frames, spaces, and circumstances. In this respect the issue of originality is challenging the institutional system in which art operates to revise its methodologies. As I will argue, the custody of conceptual artworks in collections goes beyond the traditional museological responsibilities of maintenance, conservation, and presentation. It prompts some sort of "shared authorship."[33] Since the "receiver" of these works is no longer the well-informed participant involved in the small conceptual art circle of the late 1960s and early 1970s, to convey these works to a contemporary public may only be accomplished by the "delegated receivership of the curator," as Dutch art critic Camiel van Winkel puts it.[34]

The trajectory or (historical) analysis of conceptual art's condition discussed in the first chapter along with a reexamination of key theories and definitions serves as a theoretical

32 Boris Groys, *Art Power* (Cambridge, MA: MIT Press, 2008).

33 See also Poinsot 1999, p. 103.

34 See Camiel van Winkel, "Global Concept: Applications and Embodiments," in *A Book about Collecting and Exhibiting Conceptual Art after Conceptual Art*, eds. Sabine Folie, Georgia Holz, and Ilse Lafer (Cologne: Verlag der Buchhandlung Walther König, 2013), pp. 77–96, p. 95. Van Winkel argues that the curator receives the work on behalf of the public, reads, interprets, and examines it, and communicates the results back to the public.

framework to assess three exhibitions in the chapters that follow. These exhibitions serve as case studies for a reevaluation of the forms that have been assigned to conceptual artworks in different exhibitionary settings. When researching the many exhibitions with and of conceptual art from the early years to the present, at least three different time frames in which the curatorial perspective on conceptual art has changed considerably can be distinguished: the initial phase, when conceptual art was first exhibited in the late 1960s; a second phase in the early 1990s, when several exhibitions on the legacy of conceptual art were curated and its historicization started; and finally, current practices of remaking exhibitions that try to reactivate the legacy of conceptual art. The three selected cases, *Konzeption-Conception: Documentation of a To-day's Art Tendency* (1969), *L'art conceptuel, une perspective* (1989), and *When Attitudes Become Form: Bern 1969/Venice 2013* (2013), are key exponents of these respective phases. The distinct role of the curator and the applied curatorial methodologies within these respective exhibitions will be a main principle of examination. The intersection of historical research and curatorial discourse is used in order to analyze how curators in the past have applied curatorial methodologies and in turn gain insight into the theoretical but also practical ramifications of exhibiting conceptual works.

The selection of these three exhibitions of conceptual art is based upon several criteria, including the significance they have played in the manner in which conceptual art has been critically received and consequently art historically canonized. First of all, I have made my selection of case studies within the region of Western Europe. This was not only a practical choice—I am based in Europe and the access to these archives was more readily available to me than those in the United States—but also because conceptual art was received and exhibited by important public museums in Europe in a very early phase, as well as supported by several European collectors that were involved in the "movement" of conceptual art.[35] Furthermore, the three case studies show a clear historical development of the exhibition of conceptual art, which provides insight into how institutional and curatorial strategies added to the canonization of conceptual art that at the same time created problems in effectively disclosing the works involved.

Regarding the initial phase of conceptual art's exhibition, the spectrum of exhibitions that have contributed to the reception and acknowledgement of conceptual art as an art historical category is manifold. Meanwhile, through emerging curatorial research, some of these have become truly legendary, such as Harald Szeemann's *When Attitudes Become Form* (Kunsthalle Bern, 1969), Wim Beeren's *Op Losse Schroeven* (Stedelijk Museum Amsterdam, 1969), and Lucy Lippard's "Numbers Shows," respectively in Seattle (1969), Vancouver (1970), Buenos Aires (1970), and Valencia, California (1973), to name only a few.[36] In these years, however, there were almost no exhibitions that explicitly framed conceptual art as a movement or specific type of art and tried to determine its specific character. One of the exhibitions that did, and probably the first, was *Konzeption-Conception: Documentation of a To-day's Art Tendency* at the Städtisches Museum Schloss Morsbroich in Leverkusen in 1969, curated by the German art dealer Konrad Fischer and the director of the museum, art historian Rolf Wedewer.

While this exhibition is mentioned in various historical studies on conceptual art, in-depth study, let alone a factual description of the exhibition, is lacking. Moreover, since most of these sources refer to the catalogue, it was not even certain

35 See Richard 2009.

36 Christian Rattemeyer et al., *Exhibiting the New Art, 'Op Losse Schroeven' and 'When Attitudes Become Form' 1969* (London: Afterall Books, 2010); Cornelia Butler et al., *From Conceptualism to Feminism: Lucy Lippard's Numbers Shows 1969–74* (London: Afterall Books, 2012).

that a physical exhibition actually took place. I present a first reconstruction of the physical exhibition in Leverkusen in chapter two, and argue that it already brought to the fore the dilemma of exhibiting works of conceptual art in this early phase, confirming the mediatory role of the curator from the very beginnings of conceptual art.[37] Its key achievement was to make an exhibition specifically dedicated to conceptual art in order to grant the new type of art a place in the annals of art history. The critical reviews of this exhibition in the German press at the time hinted at the problem inherent to the exhibition of conceptual artworks, as well as the role of the publication as a means to appropriately communicate the new art tendency. Moreover, the substantial critical debate in the newspapers contributed to the "avant-garde quality" of conceptual art and anticipated subsequent theories on this type of art.[38]

More often than not, the critical attitude of the conceptual artists themselves has to a large extent added to the illustrious status of early exhibitions, which incorporated what has come to be called "institutional critique."[39] Hans Haacke's famous *MoMA Poll*,[40] included in the exhibition *Information* (1970) at the Museum of Modern Art in New York, as well as his censored exhibition *Shapolsky et al. Manhattan Real Estate Holdings, A Real Time Social System, as of May 1, 1971* at the Guggenheim Museum in New York, or Daniel Buren's censored contribution to the *Sixth Guggenheim International* (1971),[41] all provoked the institution. It was only in 1989 that Benjamin Buchloh acknowledged this kind of provocation as an important aspect of conceptual art in his catalogue essay "From the Aesthetic of Administration to Institutional Critique (Some Aspects of Conceptual Art 1962–1969)" for the Paris exhibition *L'art conceptuel, une perspective*.[42] This

37 While there was no photographic documentation of this exhibition, I based my reconstruction upon the extensive contemporary reviews in the German newspapers and historical documents regarding the organization of the exhibition that are available in the archives of the city of Leverkusen. I also made use of floor plans of the exhibition spaces of Museum Schloss Morsbroich in Leverkusen, which I visited, and historical documents on the *Prospect 69* exhibition, which was organized by Fischer around the same time as *Konzeption*. These documents are available in the archives of the Kunsthalle Düsseldorf, as well as the city of Düsseldorf.

38 Shortly after *Konzeption*, Klaus Honnef published his book *Concept Art* (Cologne: Phaidon Verlag, 1971), which is certainly highly influenced by Konrad Fischer's activities within the field of conceptual art, since he refers to several of Fischer's exhibitions.

39 See Benjamin H. D. Buchloh, "From the Aesthetic of Administration to Institutional Critique (Some Aspects of Conceptual Art 1962–1969)," in *L'art conceptuel, une perspective*, ed. Claude Gintz et al., exh. cat. Paris (Musée d'art moderne de la Ville de Paris) 1989, pp. 41–53.

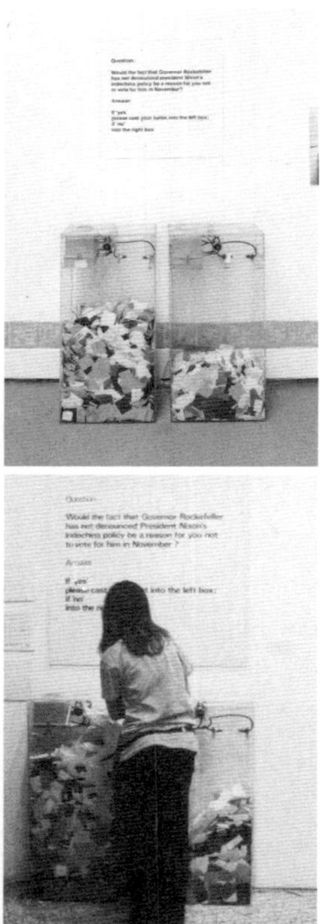

40 Hans Haacke, *MoMA Poll*, 1970.

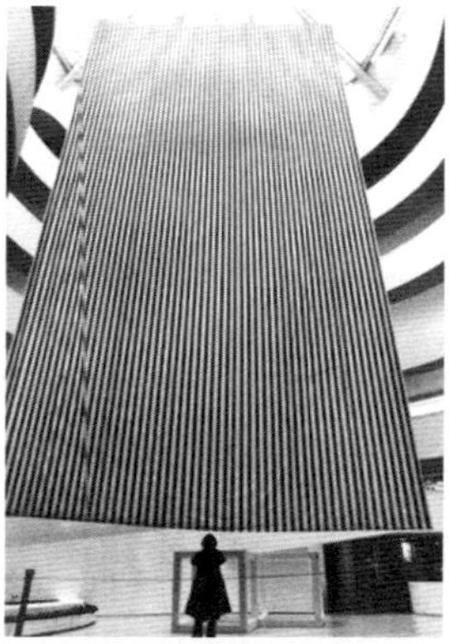

41 Daniel Buren, *Peinture-Sculpture* (Painting-Sculpture), contribution to the *Sixth Guggenheim International*, New York, 1971.

42 Buchloh 1989.

exhibition, initiated by the director of the Musée d'art moderne de la ville de Paris, Suzanne Pagé, and curated by art historian Claude Gintz, made a first attempt to reevaluate historical conceptual practices.

Organized exactly twenty years after *Konzeption*, the Paris exhibition is mentioned in many publications as a key exhibition of conceptual art, but has never been studied to substantiate this claim. As I argue in chapter three, *L'art conceptuel, une perspective* greatly contributed to the historical framing of conceptual art, especially through the comprehensive catalogue that included Buchloh's seminal text, which was subsequently revised and reprinted in 1990, in the winter issue of *October* journal.[43] The overall focus on the role of the catalogue, however, has overshadowed the importance of the actual exhibition in Paris. I will demonstrate that the exhibition process included valuable discussions with several of the participating artists about defining the "original" in their works, and the manner in which their historical works could be represented in a present time frame within the galleries of a museum. In my analysis, based on assessing the catalogue, correspondences, documents, and photographs concerning the exhibition—conserved in the archives of the Musée de l'art moderne—as well as an interview I conducted with curator Gintz in 2011, it becomes clear that many of the artists at the time did not have proper solutions for this problem.[44]

What is more, the critical attitude that some of the invited artists assumed (Michael Asher, Daniel Buren, Hans Haacke) was frustrated by museological restrictions that had to be taken into consideration by curator Gintz. While he was of the opinion that the importance of conceptual art within an art historical perspective was anticipated by the practices of a new generation of artists in the late 1980s who were reconsidering the artistic practices of the 1960s and 1970s in their own

43 Ibid. See also Benjamin H. D. Buchloh, "Conceptual Art 1962–1969: From the Aesthetic of Administration to the Critique of Institutions," *October* vol. 55 (Winter 1990), pp. 105–143.

44 Archives MAMVP (Box 524); Claude Gintz, in conversation with the author, Paris, December 3, 2011.

work, he was not able to address this specific aspect in his exhibition.[45] That conceptual artists' critique of institutions and the larger system of art prevented the acquisition of their works by important museum collections seems only logical. But the fact that the initial resistance of institutions like the Guggenheim Museum or the Museum of Modern Art in New York to engage with these critical practices had still not changed much by 1989 seems ironic.[46]

The variety of curatorial models developed since the 1990s offers broad potential for a less traditional manner of exhibiting works of art that have no permanent form. The flexible and open-ended exhibition project *Do it,* initiated by the Swiss curator Hans Ulrich Obrist in 1993, is a good case in point. Based on the idea of the musical score, Obrist initially invited twelve artists to send him instructions for works of art that were translated in nine languages and brought together in a publication, which could then be, and have been, (re-)enacted in different venues and settings all over the world.[47] The parallels with conceptual publication-exhibitions in the 1960s are no coincidence; in his curatorial practice, Obrist is highly influenced by the experimental practices of Seth Siegelaub, Pontus Hultén, and Harald Szeemann, among others, as can be read in the various interviews he conducted with these pioneering curators.[48]

In recent years the formula of reenacting works from the 1960 and 1970s has become a recurring genre within curatorial practice, and has even developed into the reproduction of entire historical exhibitions. Canadian art historian Reesa Greenberg has observed the trend of reconstructing historical exhibitions since the mid-1990s, and even distinguished different typologies within what she termed the "remembering exhibition."[49] Also, Australian art historian and critic Terry Smith coined a new curatorial genre, "recuration," in which

45 Here I refer to a group of American artists that is generally categorized as "neo-conceptual," including Peter Halley, Jenny Holzer, Jeff Koons, Barbara Kruger, Louise Lawler, Sherrie Levine, Richard Prince, and Cindy Sherman, among others. Gintz, in conversation with the author, 2011.

46 The Museum of Modern Art in New York was often the target of the critique of conceptual artists, which culminated in the early 1970s in the repeated demonstrations and actions of the Art Workers' Coalition. In 1992 and 1993 the Guggenheim Museum acquired a large amount of (post-)minimal and conceptual artworks from the collection of the Italian count Giuseppe Panza di Biumo. In 2010 the MoMA filled a gap in their collection with the acquisition of the collection of the Dutch gallerists Adriaan van Ravesteijn and Geert van Beijeren of Art & Project. The recent acquisitions of private collections of conceptual art in museums of contemporary art throughout the world is indicative of the role of the private collector in the survival of conceptual artworks.

47 Hereafter the project grew to more than 300 contributions of instruction works or unrealized projects or ideas, still ongoing. See Hans Ulrich Obrist, ed., *Do It: The Compendium* (New York: Independent Curators International, 2013).

48 Hans Ulrich Obrist, *A Brief History of Curating* (Zurich: JRP/Ringier, 2011).

49 Reesa Greenberg, "Remembering Exhibitions: From Point to Line to Web," *Tate Papers* no. 12 (2009), <www.tate.org.uk/research/tateresearch/tatepapers/09autumn/greenberg> (10-6-2011).

he specifically appraised the importance of including contemporary topics in the reconstructed exhibition.[50] While there are many exhibitions that have brought attention to historical projects by conceptual artists, and museums have acquired works and (private) collections of conceptual art, these works are still sparsely properly exhibited within a museological framework.

Yet some exhibitions have more specifically addressed the problem of originality or authenticity within conceptual art, like *In-Between Minimalisms & Free Sol LeWitt* at the Van Abbemuseum in Eindhoven in 2010, in which the Danish artists' collective Superflex reproduced a wall structure by Sol LeWitt[51] in order to distribute it in edition and make it available to a broader audience.[52] A more serious or even scholarly exhibition in this respect is the remake exhibition *When Attitudes Become Form: Bern 1969/Venice 2013* at the Fondazione Prada in Venice in 2013, which I will examine in chapter four. Since the original 1969 exhibition by Harald Szeemann is generally considered to be an exhibition of conceptual art, the remake in Venice offers a valuable contribution for a continued exhibition of conceptual art today. In its specific approach of "recurating" the historical event, including many works of conceptual art, within a different spatiotemporal framework, the remake offered a multifaceted methodology that was largely dedicated to the dilemma of reproducing works of art that aspired to dematerialization. The Fondazione Prada is not a public but rather a private museum, and accordingly does not necessarily need to adapt to general museum ethics. However, concerning the comprehensive care it has taken for many seminal works of conceptual art from important public collections, its approach can certainly be regarded as an exemplary method within museum practice, as I will argue.

50 See Terry Smith, *Thinking Contemporary Curating* (New York: Independent Curators International, 2012), p. 198.

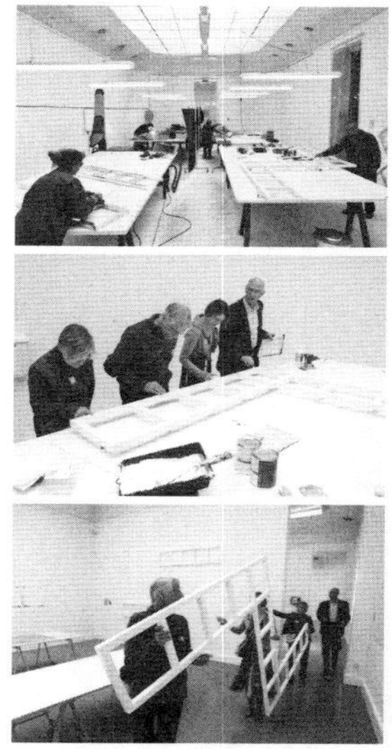

51 Superflex, *Free Sol LeWitt*, Van Abbemuseum, Eindhoven, 2010. Photo Bram Sayes.

52 Represented in his "Sentences" and "Paragraphs" as well as other texts. See Nathalie Zonnenberg, "Free Sol LeWitt and In-Between Minimalisms," *Manifesta Journal* no. 10 (2009–2010), pp. 98–103.

Since the first two case studies within this book are historical, these are examined in a more traditional art historical manner through the analysis of archival materials and the contemporaneous reception, as a way to archeologically reconstruct the supporting ideas and configuration of the original exhibitions. The case of *Attitudes,* however, is a present-day exhibition that in and of itself already included a reconstruction exercise, both in its reevaluation and reexecution of a historical exhibition. It could therefore be studied in different ways—both historically and from a current perspective. This resulted in a more art critical method of research and analysis in the fourth and final chapter, based upon my own critical assessment of the physical exhibition, on the one hand, and a reexamination of the historical exhibition in the context of current curatorial discourse on the other. I first visited and extensively examined the exhibition at the site in Venice, and subsequently evaluated my experience through the study of the catalogue and the reception of both the original and the remake exhibition in art historical literature and various international art magazines and journals.[53]

Although a study of exhibitions presumes the inclusion of photographic documentation of how these exhibitions were installed *pro tanto,* this book is deprived of visual information regarding my case studies. The choice to not include installation views of the three exhibitions under discussion is not merely prompted by practical considerations—photographs of the first two case studies are either absent or inaccessible—but essentially by my attempt to concentrate primarily on the methodology of a specific exhibition rather than its visual outcome. The fact that exhibitions of conceptual art are barely photographically documented might be attributed to many conceptual artists' persuasion that ideas or concepts should be chiefly conveyed by textual information and

53 See, for example, Rattemeyer et al. 2010.

cataloguing rather than by visual documentation.[54] Conversely, both the historical and remake exhibition in the third case study made extensive use of photographic documentation. In order to employ an unequivocal focus on the methodology of these specific (historical) curatorial practices, however, this book provides only sparse referential imagery in its margins. It is not my intention to prescribe a curatorial methodology for the continued exhibition of works of conceptual art, but to encourage innovative and experimental modes of curatorial research and practice within current museum practices—which, admittedly, are still very much dominated by a modernist understanding of art history.

To this end, this study first and foremost explores to what extent the critical approach of the "art object" within conceptual art practice, conflicting modernist tenets of originality, and market value were incorporated into historical moments of exhibiting conceptual art.

54 See Alexander Alberro and Patricia Norvell, *Recording Conceptual Art: Early Interviews with Barry, Huebler, Kaltenbach, LeWitt, Morris, Oppenheim, Siegelaub, Smithson, Weiner* (Berkeley, CA: University of California Press, 2001).

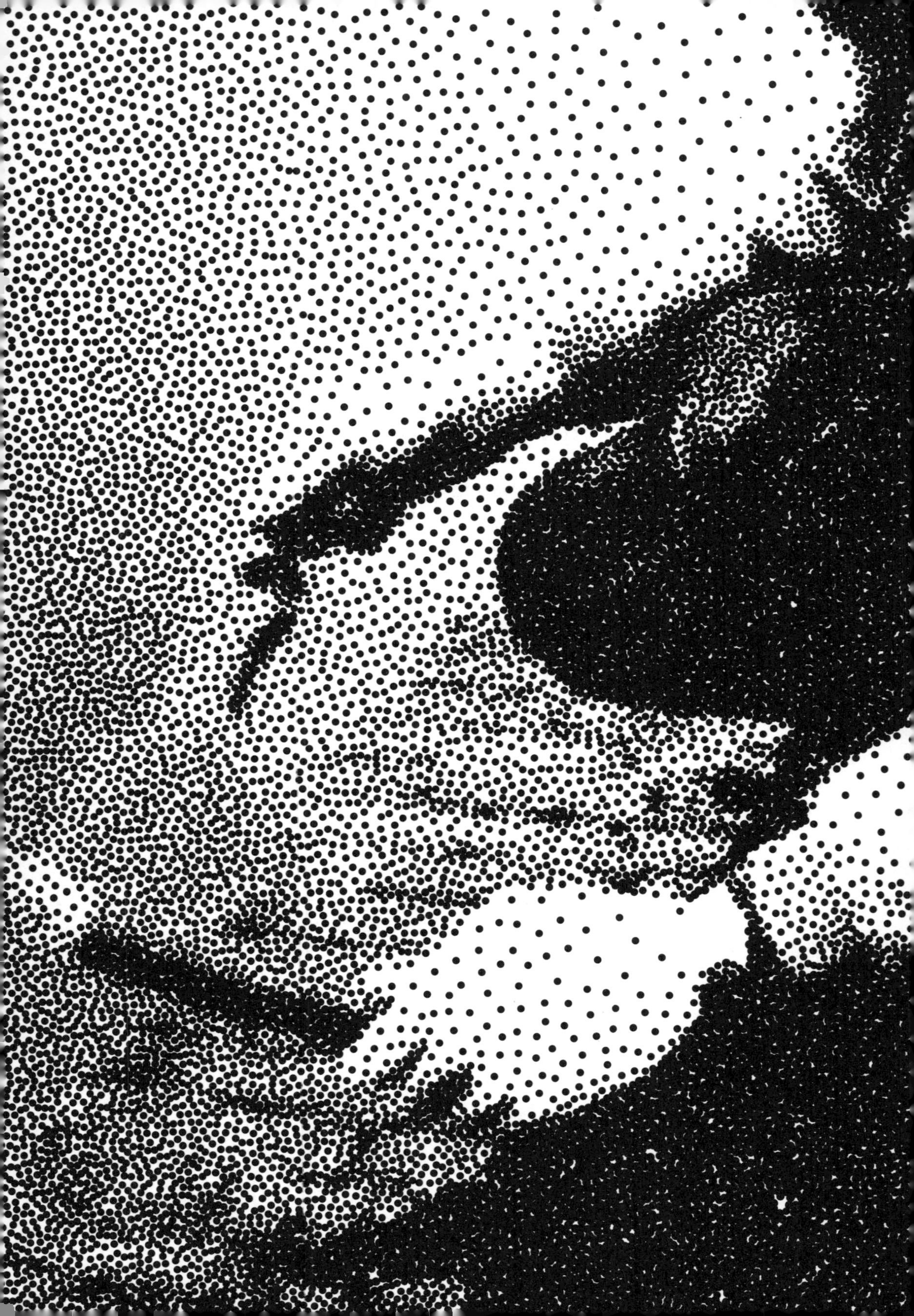

Chapter 1

A Trajectory of Conceptual Art's "Object"

(Between Dematerialization and Documentation)

The collector is someone who enters into a conspiracy with the artist that is beyond the issue of accessibility, an agreement that the sensibility is an important one. This agreement may be really what the owner has that is "original."
— Douglas Huebler[1]

1 Douglas Huebler, statement in *Prospect 69*, exh. cat. Düsseldorf (Kunsthalle Düsseldorf) 1969, p. 26.

Theories and Definitions of Conceptual Art

Conceptual art has generated its own specific discourses. Moreover, it brought about its own aesthetic theories—initiated by the artists involved and adapted by several like-minded artists, art professionals, and theorists who engaged with them. Artists' writings, such as Joseph Kosuth's "Art after Philosophy" (1969) and Sol LeWitt's "Paragraphs on Conceptual Art" (1967) and "Sentences on Conceptual Art" (1969), are generally regarded as most representative for conceptual aesthetics, and often read as manifestos for the "movement."[2] Kosuth's claim that conceptual artists act as theorists

2 Joseph Kosuth, "Art after Philosophy," *Studio International* vol. 178, no. 915 (October 1969), pp. 134–137; "Art after Philosophy: Part II: 'Conceptual Art' and Recent Art," *Studio International* vol. 178, no. 916 (November 1969), pp. 160–161; "Art after Philosophy: Part III, *Studio International* vol. 178, no. 917 (December 1969), p. 212; Sol LeWitt, "Paragraphs on Conceptual Art," *Artforum* vol. 5, no. 10 (Summer 1967), pp. 79–84; "Sentences on Conceptual Art," *0–9* no. 5 (January 1969), pp. 3–5. See, for example, Alexander Alberro, "Reconsidering Conceptual Art," and Blake Stimson, "The Promise of Conceptual Art," in Alberro and Stimson 1999, p. xx, and p. xli.

Image appropriated from Lawrence Weiner, The Residue of a Flare Ignited Upon a Boundary, 1969. See also p. 70.

and operate merely among themselves contributed to the reputation of conceptual art as being inaccessible to the public—a stigma that is still very active today. Whereas artists such as Kosuth were certainly excluding the larger public in claiming that "an audience separate from the participants doesn't exist," artists like LeWitt, but also Lawrence Weiner and Robert Morris, conversely acted in a manner to "engage the mind of the viewer."[3] Weiner, in his "Declaration of Intent" (1969), more explicitly addressed the role of the "receiver" in the (eventual) realization of the conceptual work, while LeWitt and Morris, departing from minimalist aesthetics and assuming the actual realization of the work, address the work's interaction with "space, light and the viewer's field of vision."[4]

These different attitudes also become visible in the early scholarly literature on conceptual art. The German art historian and critic Klaus Honnef was the first to survey the scope of conceptual art in his 1971 book *Concept Art*,[5] analyzing various artists' positions, as well as exhibitions of conceptual art both in Europe and the United States, and anticipating the framing of conceptual art as an art historical category.[6] Ursula Meyer's 1972 publication *Conceptual Art*[7] mainly followed Kosuth's stance on conceptualism, noting, among others, that the book had become an important new space to show art.[8] The German-born artist and sculpture professor explicitly referred to the notions of "primary and secondary information," coined by the New York curator-dealer Seth Siegelaub in an interview with Meyer included in her book, which differentiate between the conceptual work and its (format of) presentation. Meyer's publication was soon followed by Lucy Lippard's 1973 compilation book *Six Years: The Dematerialization of the Art Object from 1966 to 1972*.[9, 10] Lippard, who (together with John Chandler) had published the essay "The Dematerialization of Art" in 1968, further

3 Joseph Kosuth, "Introductory Note to Art-Language by the American Editor," (1968), p. 39, as cited in Alberro and Stimson 1999, p. xvii. Also Art & Language considered the artist's position as that of a theorist or philosopher, fully capable of explaining his own work. See David Bainbridge et al., *Art-Language: The Journal of Conceptual Art* vols. 1–4, nos. 1–4 (1969–1978); LeWitt 1967.

4 Lawrence Weiner, "Declaration of Intent," in *January 5–31, 1969*, ed. Seth Siegelaub, exh. cat. New York (Seth Siegelaub) 1969, n.p.; Robert Morris, "Notes on Sculpture II," *Artforum* vol. 5, no. 2 (October 1966), p. 21.

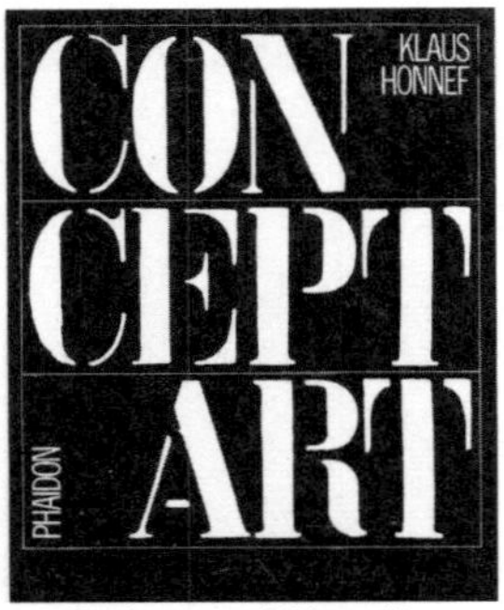

5 Book cover of Klaus Honnef's book *Concept Art*, 1971.

6 Honnef 1971. Honnef's book has been largely omitted in the early and more recent literature on conceptual art—possibly because it was never translated into English. In Lucy Lippard's extensive and varied compilation of "fragmented text, art works, documents, interviews, and symposia... in the Americas, Europe, England, Australia, and Asia," a reference to Honnef's 1971 book is missing.

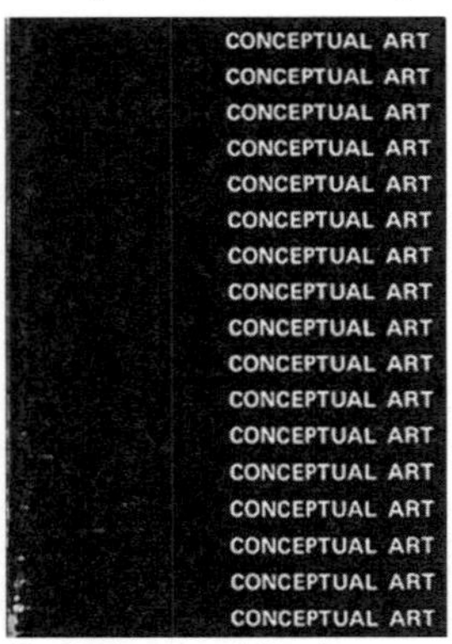

7 Book cover of Ursula Meyer's *Conceptual Art*, 1972.

8 Ursula Meyer, *Conceptual Art* (Toronto and Vancouver: Clarke, Irwin & Company Limited, 1972).

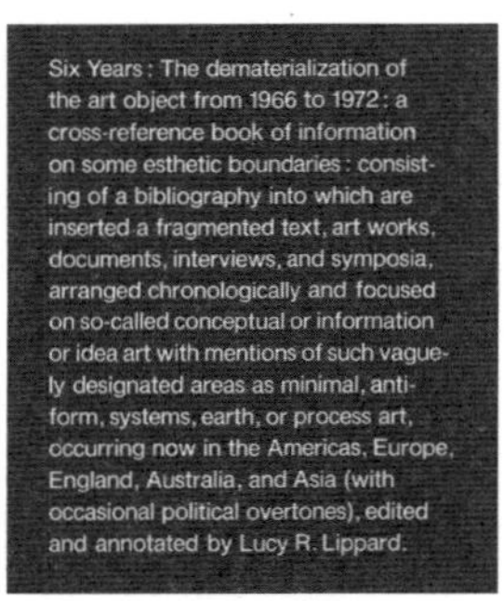

9 Book cover of Lucy Lippard's *Six Years*, 1973.

10 Lippard and Chandler 1968; Lippard 1973.

elaborated in *Six Years* on the notion of dematerialization to come to a broad definition of conceptual art. Processing the consequences of minimalism, most visible in the stance of conceptualism practiced by artists like LeWitt and Morris, Lippard referred to "a process of dematerialization, or a de-emphasis on material aspects (uniqueness, permanence, decorative attractiveness)" in her introduction to the book.[11]

While many throughout the years have pointed out the inaccuracy of the term, the notion of dematerialization nevertheless remained an important point of reference in the subsequent literature on conceptual art, whereas Siegelaub's complex notions of primary and secondary information were largely neglected. Parallel to the renewed interest in conceptual art within exhibition practice, a vast array of publications that reevaluate, rewrite, or reconsider the early literature of conceptual art has appeared since the 1990s, starting with Benjamin Buchloh's seminal essay "Conceptual Art 1962–1969: From the Aesthetic of Administration to the Critique of Institutions," first published in the catalogue of the Paris exhibition *L'art conceptuel, une perspective* (1989),[12] and subsequently in a somewhat revised form in *October* journal in 1990.[13] In his text, Buchloh ascribed the conceptual "movement" to the avant-garde tradition of Marcel Duchamp, a claim that was followed by many scholars. In juxtaposing various artists' positions, Buchloh sketches a sociopolitical development of conceptual art, which is most strongly expressed in the institutional critique applied by European artists like Daniel Buren, Hans Haacke, and Marcel Broodthaers.

In Alexander Alberro and Blake Stimson's 1999 *Conceptual Art: A Critical Anthology*, various early texts on conceptual art from both Europe and the United States are republished, and as such, acknowledge the simultaneous

11 Lippard 1973, p. 5.

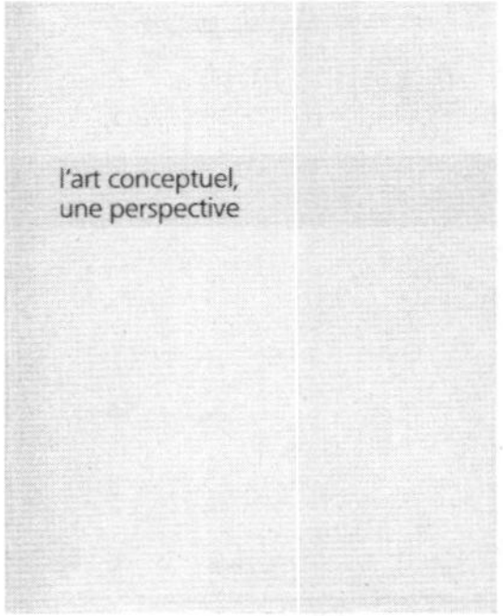

12 Book cover of *L'art conceptuel, une perspective*, 1989.

13 Benjamin H. D. Buchloh, "From the Aesthetic of Administration to Institutional Critique (Some Aspects of Conceptual Art 1962–1969)," in *L'art conceptuel, une perspective*, ed. Claude Gintz et al., exh. cat. Paris (Musée d'art moderne de la ville de Paris) 1989, pp. 41–53; Benjamin H. D. Buchloh, "Conceptual Art 1962–1969: From the Aesthetic of Administration to the Critique of Institutions," *October* vol. 55 (Winter 1990), pp. 105–143.

development of conceptual art on both sides of the Atlantic.[14] In his own contribution to this anthology, "Reconsidering Conceptual Art, 1966–1977," Alberro discusses different categories, or "genealogies" of conceptualism, which he terms "linguistic," "analytic," and "synthetic."[15] Differentiating between the conceptualism of Kosuth and the members of Art & Language group, on the one hand (linguistic), and the conceptual theory of Sol LeWitt and others on the other (analytic), Alberro defines a third, more radical and institutional critical model of conceptual art, which he refers to as "synthetic" (e.g., Buren, Haacke, but also several Latin American artists like Eduardo Costa, Hélio Oiticica, and Cildo Meireles).[16] Stimson, in his contribution, addresses the "promise" of conceptual art, which refers in particular to the redefinition of the social function of art.[17] This notion is comparable to Michael Newman's "open-ended assignment," presented in his 1996 text "Conceptuele kunst van de jaren zestig tot negentig: Een onaf project?" ["Conceptual art from the 1960s to the 1990s: an unfinished project?"].[18]

Newman is also the first to reassess Lippard's notion of dematerialization with respect to the broader context of institutional changes that have taken place at the threshold of the new millennium. In his subsequent publication, *Rewriting Conceptual Art* (1999), edited together with Jon Bird, conceptual art is first defined as a "linguistic turn" in modernist aesthetics and alternately regarded, by various authors, both as an art historical movement and a critique of the object.[19] The American art critic and historian Thomas McEvilley more distinctively explained conceptual art's critique of the object, again reassessing Lippard's notion of dematerialization, as a critique of modernism/formalism that paved the way for post-conceptualist (i.e., postmodernist) practices. In his book *The Triumph of Anti-Art: Conceptual and Performance*

14 Alberro and Stimson 1999.

15 Alexander Alberro, "Reconsidering Conceptual Art, 1966–1977," in Alberro and Stimson 1999, p. xvi–xxxviii.

16 Ibid., p. xxlv. Alberro defines the first category (Kosuth and the members of Art & Language group) as the dominant model of conceptualism; the other two categories he adapted from Kosuth, who followed Immanuel Kant's distinction between analytic and synthetic propositions.

17 Blake Stimson, "The Promise of Conceptual Art," in Alberro and Stimson 1999, pp. xxxviii–lii.

18 Newman 1996. Part of this issue was devoted to Siegelaub's project "The Context of Art," with contributions by many conceptual artists that reevaluated the legacy of conceptual art.

19 Newman and Bird 1999.

Art in the Formation of Post-Modernism (2005), the relevance of Lippard's early observations is redefined in a broader historical perspective.[20]

Peter Osborne's 2002 survey *Conceptual Art* more generally reexamined conceptual aesthetics within a global perspective, including both (Latin) American and (Eastern) European examples, as well as other genealogies of conceptual art.[21] The British philosopher and art historian claims that the questions raised by conceptual art still dominate the current discourse on art. He considers all contemporary art to therefore be essentially post-conceptual, an argument that was also made by the Dutch art historian and critic Camiel van Winkel in his published 2012 dissertation *During the Exhibition the Gallery Will Be Closed: Contemporary Art and the Paradoxes of Conceptualism*.[22]

While these latter, more theoretical writings on conceptual art fully acknowledge and underline the paradoxes of conceptual art and the impact that this type of art still has on current art practices, the actual implications of conceptual art's strategies for institutional or curatorial practice have hardly been addressed and studied. A sole exception is Jean-Marc Poinsot's book *Quand l'oeuvre a lieu: L'art exposé et ses récits autorisés* (1999), in which the consequences of conceptual strategies for the present-day status of these works within museum conservation and disclosure have been surveyed.[23] Poinsot analyzes the difficulties in defining the actual conceptual artwork and emphasizes the value of documentation and certificates to accomplish this. In this respect Boris Groys's notion of "art documentation," first coined in 1997 in the German version of his text "Art in the Age of Biopolitics," offers a useful definition to describe the complex status of conceptual artworks after their historical moment.[24] As the Russian-German philosopher states, "art documentation is by

20 Thomas McEvilley, *The Triumph of Anti-Art: Conceptual and Performance Art in the Formation of Post-Modernism* (Kingston, NY: McPherson & Company, 2005).

21 Osborne 2002.

22 Van Winkel 2012.

23 Poinsot 1999.

24 Boris Groys, "Art in the Age of Biopolitics: From Artwork to Art Documentation," in Groys 2008, p. 54. First published in Boris Groys, *Logik der Sammlung: Am Ende des Musealen Zeitalters* (Munich and Vienna: Carl Hanser Verlag, 1997).

definition *not* art; it merely *refers* to art, and in precisely this way it makes it clear that art, in this case, is no longer present and immediately visible, but rather absent and hidden."[25]

In the interviews that Patricia Norvell conducted in the late 1960s with several conceptual artists like Robert Barry, Douglas Huebler, and others, edited and published together with Alexander Alberro only in 2001, the problem of documentation, or the use of documents in order to elicit the public's participation, is explicitly emphasized.[26] Alberro's more recent publication, *Conceptual Art and the Politics of Publicity* (2003), thoroughly examined early documents and works of conceptual artists from the archives of Seth Siegelaub.[27] In this seminal publication on the practices and strategies of conceptual art in the late 1960s in New York, Alberro is the first to actually reevaluate Siegelaub's notions of primary and secondary information, which he applies as a coordinating definition for several conceptual models relating to site-specificity, linguistics, and dematerialization. In the examination of several works and projects that Siegelaub conducted with conceptual artists, Alberro intelligently demonstrates the contradictions of conceptual art with regard to the distinction between theory and practice.

Arguably, Lippard's thesis about the "dematerialization of the art object" marked the starting point for the definition of the conceptual artwork, a process that might initially have been directed against the commodification of art, but that eventually did not affect the supporting political system as intended/prescribed. Moreover, the critique of the object was best expressed through the frustration of the most visible format of presentation: the museum exhibition. Although not all of the artists who are considered conceptual would or did ascribe the sociopolitical implications of dematerialization, the nature

25 Ibid., p. 53.

26 Alberro and Norvell 2001.

27 Alexander Alberro, *Conceptual Art and the Politics of Publicity* (Cambridge, MA: MIT Press, 2003).

of, and the manner in which, many works of conceptual art relate to the broader aspects of time and place is paramount to the understanding of their exhibition today. That the idea-based character of conceptual art is best exhibited or distributed by a publication or catalogue where primary and secondary information congregate, however, is something to reevaluate. This contention has not prevented the acquisition of many of these documents by private and public collections to be exhibited as such; the present status of these documents could thus be defined according to Groys's notion of art documentation.[28]

In addition, the determination of "originality" is an extremely complex one in the case of conceptual art; not only in terms of authorship or authenticity, but moreover in its ontological definition (i.e., the factual condition or "being" of the artwork). Rosalind Krauss's definition of the minimalist artwork, referring to its seriality, as "multiples without originals," is equally applicable to the conceptual work of art.[29] However, since the conceptual work of art is often contained in documentation and certifications, these documents—often lacking any other tangible material—are identified as the original work. Although the documentary status of many conceptual artworks has long been recognized, "to categorize art documentation as 'simple' artwork would be to misunderstand it by overlooking its originality, its identifying feature," as Groys remarks.[30]

In order to get to the core of my thesis, how to re-exhibit historical works of conceptual art, I will first try to to define the current ontological status of conceptual artworks in the subsequent parts of this chapter, and more specifically (re)-evaluate the notions of "dematerialization," "primary and secondary information," and "art documentation" respectively framed by Lippard (1968), Siegelaub (1972), and Groys

28 Groys 2008 (1997), p. 54.

29 Rosalind E. Krauss, "The Cultural Logic of the Late Capitalist Museum," in *October: The Second Decade, 1986–1996*, ed. Rosalind E. Krauss et al. (Cambridge, MA: MIT Press, 1997), p. 434.

30 Ibid.

(1997). While the first definition was reevaluated and theorized throughout the general historiography of conceptual art, the second only recently received proper theoretization in Alberro's account; the third, however, is an as yet unexploited definition that deserves further examination within the discourse of conceptual art, which I attempt to accomplish in the following elaborations.

The Principle of Dematerialization

In 1991 and 1992 the Solomon R. Guggenheim Museum acquired a large amount of (post-)minimal and conceptual artworks from the renowned collection of the Italian count Giuseppe Panza di Biumo.[31] This acquisition by one of the most established museums of contemporary art, at a time when conceptual art was beginning to be acknowledged as an art historical category, evidences the acceptance of conceptual artworks as collectable "objects." As common as this affirmation may seem today, at the time of purchase the museum took quite a risk in sparing no expense to obtain goods that were basically not there.[32] Many of the conceptual (but also minimal) artworks that Panza purchased over the years only existed in the form of certificates; documents of authenticity that are of little value in legal terms.[33] There are records of a few severe cases in which Panza had considerable disagreements with artists whose works he autonomously (re-)constructed in accordance with these certificates (Carl Andre and Dan Flavin, among others).[34] These cases illustrate the complexity of appropriately interpreting such documents—following the artist's intentions—as well as the undefined status of the works, which are now in the custody of the Guggenheim Museum.

31 Through purchases and gifts, the Guggenheim Museum New York acquired over 350 works of minimal, conceptual, post-minimal, and environmental art; an additional 335 works are on extended loan.

32 The Panza acquisition was estimated to have cost around $30 million, an amount that was collected through the sale of three important paintings from the collection: *Fugue* (1914) by Wassily Kandinsky, *Boy in Blue Jacket* (1916) by Amadeo Modigliani, and *Birthday* (1923) by Marc Chagall. See Grace Glueck, "Guggenheim to Sell 3 Works to Help Buy Others," *The New York Times*, March 23, 1990.

33 See Daniel McClean, "Authenticity in Art and Law: A Question of Attribution or Authorization?" in *In Deed: Certificates of Authenticity in Art*, eds. Susan Hapgood and Cornelia Lauf (Amsterdam: Roma Publications, 2011), p. 89. McClean asserts, "While the legal structure would seem to govern and regulate the art market like other aspects of society, the law is generally ambivalent toward intervening within the art system on questions of authenticity. At the root of this ambivalence is the belief that art is based upon subjective (aesthetic) judgment and that opinions concerning authenticity are necessarily prone to error..."

34 For a precise analysis of these cases, see Martha Buskirk, "Authorship and Authority," in *The Contingent Object of Contemporary Art* (Cambridge, MA: MIT Press, 2003), pp. 19–56.

That said, it is surprising that it took the museum almost twenty years to launch the Panza Collection Initiative (PCI) in 2010, dedicated to the long-term preservation and potential future exhibition of minimalist, post-minimalist, and conceptual art. As the museum stated in 2010, there is no true consensus on this subject. "Traditional curatorial and conservation practices are often inadequate in dealing with art that is ephemeral, variable, or fabrication-based in nature. Further, these unorthodox approaches to art making raise difficult conceptual, ethical, and legal questions regarding authenticity, ownership, and interpretive rights. The lack of a clear methodology for managing these issues has left the fate of many works of the era uncertain...."[35] This holds especially true for conceptual art. Whereas in the case of minimal art there is still a material object to be fabricated, in the case of conceptual art one has to deal with instructions or propositions for pieces that, following Lawrence Weiner's dictum, "may be fabricated," but "need not be built" at all.[36]

Interesting but equally ironic about this notice is that, more than forty years after Lippard concluded that an art "freed from the tyranny of a commodity status and market orientation" had failed, the commodified work of conceptual art that has transferred via the hands of the private collector to the museum collection is (again) stirring up conventional modes of art's production and exhibition.[37] What makes the initiative of the Guggenheim Museum challenging is that it reopened the 1990 dispute on the reestablishment of the "original artwork," which Rosalind Krauss has described in her renowned essay "The Cultural Logic of the Late Capitalist Museum."[38] As Krauss stressed, "We watch the activity of markets restructuring the aesthetic original, either to change it into an 'asset'... or to normalize a once-radical practice of challenging the very idea of the original through

35 The PCI concentrated on the work of four artists, two living and two deceased: Dan Flavin, Donald Judd, Bruce Nauman, and Lawrence Weiner, and stated, "Together these artists are represented in the collection by a total of ninety-four works. Each artist's practice poses its own demands regarding preservation and display, but the holdings of the four artists' works also collectively implicate many issues and practices that are broadly at stake for art throughout the period. The four case studies will be carried out through a set of consistent procedures: archival research; oral history interviews with the artists, artist estates, fabricators, former assistants, and other relevant parties; and the installation and physical examination of selected works." See <www.guggenheim.org/new-york/collections/conservation/conservation-projects/panza-collection-initiative> (6-10-2011).

36 Cited from Lawrence Weiner's famous *Declaration of Intent*: "The artist may construct the piece. The piece may be fabricated. The piece need not be built. Each being equal and consistent with the intent of the artist, the decision as to condition rests with the receiver upon the occasion of receivership." First published in exh. cat. New York 1969, n.p.

37 Lucy R. Lippard, "Postface," in Lippard 1973, p. 263.

38 Krauss et al. 1997, pp. 427–441.

a recourse to the technology of mass production."[39] While many pieces of conceptual art—diagrams and texts, instructions for events or projects, and proposed or imagined artworks—can be (re-)executed by others than the artist and reconstituted or readapted to different spaces and circumstances, or solely exist in the form of a plan to be produced at a later date, how to appropriately deal with these possibilities within an exhibitionary setting remains both an urgent and rousing question (at least for the curator).

When Lippard and Chandler wrote in 1968 that "a number of artists are losing interest in the physical evolution of the work of art… a trend appears to be provoking a profound dematerialization of art, especially of art as object, and if it continues to prevail, it may result in the object's becoming wholly obsolete," expectations of a radical shift in art's production, reception, and distribution were in the air.[40] The type of art addressed, then specified as "an ultra-conceptual art" or "idea art," was further explored by Lippard in the following years, and led to the compilation book *Six Years: The Dematerialization of the Art Object from 1966 to 1972*, in which she deliberately claims *not* to refer to a new art movement, but "to expose… the chaotic network of ideas in the air, in America and abroad, between 1966 and 1971."[41] She also acknowledges the inaccuracy of the term she coined in her earlier writing, but "for lack of a better term" continues "to refer to a process of dematerialization or a de-emphasis on material aspects (uniqueness, permanence, decorative attractiveness)."[42]

While many continued to criticize the term, I do not consider it to be a more or less accurate term or point of reference for the thesis I intend to present than the term "conceptual art" itself, which since its beginnings has been equally

39 Ibid., p. 430.

40 Lippard and Chandler 1968, as published in Alberro and Stimson 1999, p. 46.

41 Lippard 1973, p. 5.

42 Ibid.

criticized, but eventually evolved into an art historical category.[43] As an art historical category, "conceptual art" has been regarded in very specific or more widely encompassed definitions that consist of different models, lineages, or trajectories; consequently, to use it as a description of *one* specific type of art is highly problematic.[44] Because I would like to meet the persistent call of the late Seth Siegelaub—to consider conceptual art within "the broad social issues of [its] time," rather than to regard it in "a standard, conservative, hermeneutically-sealed, textbook-type history"—to explain conceptual art in a curatorial perspective also entails critically reassessing the theoretical concept of dematerialization.[45] Can dematerialization be explained beyond the obvious explications, such as the reduction of the visual elements of the artwork, or the unwillingness of artists to produce "any more objects" that support the market system of art, and get to the deeper implications of these actions within curatorial practice?[46]

Within art historical writing, dematerialization is generally described as a specific lineage of conceptual art, criticizing the traditional "objecthood" of the artwork or, more specifically, the art object as a commodity.[47] This lineage cannot be entirely separated from—and even merges with—other lineages that question the originality of work, place art at the threshold of information, or meld within the context of public spaces and publicity.[48] What is more, dematerialization explicitly refers to the changing status of the art object, which stands at the basis of the development of conceptual art and particularly relates to the problem of exhibiting works that are non-object.

In their 1968 essay, Lippard and Chandler place the trend of dematerialization at that time within a historical evolution of art, as described by the Russian-American composer

43 See Terry Atkinson, "Concerning the Article 'The Dematerialization of Art,'" letter to Lucy Lippard and John Chandler, November 2, 1968, in Alberro and Stimson 1999, pp. 52–58; Mel Bochner, "Excerpts from Speculation (1967–1970)," *Artforum* vol. 8, no. 9 (May 1970), pp. 70–73.

44 Following Peter Osborne's argumentation, "one should be wary of replacing too narrowly historical and critically sectarian a definition of conceptual art, such as Kosuth's 'purely conceptual art'... by the more general notion of 'conceptualism'—understood to denote a broad change in 'attitude' towards the art object as 'materially constituted and visually privileged.' For such an inclusive attitudinal definition marks out a terrain that almost all contemporary art inhabits: 'conceptual*ism*' is more or less coextensive with 'contemporary art.'" Osborne 2002, p. 18.

45 Seth Siegelaub, "Addendum," in exh. cat. Paris 1989, p. 257.

46 Huebler, in exh. cat. Düsseldorf 1969.

47 See Alberro, in Alberro and Stimson 1999, p. xvii.

48 Ibid.

Joseph Schillinger in his book *The Mathematical Basis of the Arts*. Following his schema, art has evolved into five zones, of which the last, the scientific, post-aesthetic "will make possible the manufacture, distribution and consumption of a perfect art product and will be characterized by a fusion of the art forms and materials, and finally, a 'disintegration of art,' the 'abstraction and liberation of the idea.'"[49] This vision on the arts of their time preliminarily included a utopian thinking that was related to the broader sociopolitical changes of the late 1960s.[50] More specifically, it elaborated on the parallel with the subsequent art historical framing of conceptual art as a further consequence of a development that was instigated by minimal art.

In the preface of *Six Years*, Lippard states that "'Eccentric abstraction,' 'Anti-Form,' 'Process Art,' 'Anti-Illusionism,' or whatever, did come about partly as a reaction against the industrialized geometry and sheer bulk of much minimal art. Yet minimal art was itself anti-formalist in its nonrelational approach, its insistence on a neutralization of 'composition' and other hierarchical distinctions."[51] In her attempt to describe an art in the process of dematerialization, Lippard refers to Sol LeWitt's premise that "the concept or idea was more important than the visual results of the system that generated the object," which undermined formalism by insisting on a return to content.[52] She discerns a variety of work that starts from the systematic serial drawings by LeWitt and temporary works by artists such as Carl Andre, Robert Morris, Bruce Nauman, and Robert Smithson, to "the accent or overlay of an art context, an art framework, or simply an art awareness, that is, the imposition of a foreign pattern or substance on existing situations or information (e.g., Barry, Dibbets, Huebler, Oppenheim, Smithson, Weiner and others)."[53]

49 Lippard and Chandler, in Alberro and Stimson 1999, p. 47.

50 The utopianism that Lippard and Chandler refer to in their essay is explained in Lippard's foreword to *Six Years* in regard to Richard Buckminster Fuller, who coined the term "ephemeralization," which refers to technological advancement by means of gradually diminishing the amount of materials and effort to accomplish an increasing use of functions. See, for example, Richard Buckminster Fuller, *Utopia or Oblivion: The Prospects for Humanity* (New York: Overlook Press, 1969).

51 Lippard 1973, p. 5.

52 Lippard later called Sol LeWitt her "major intellectual influence," in Lucy R. Lippard, "Escape Attempts," in Goldstein and Rorimer 1995, pp. 17–38, p. 19.

53 Lippard 1973, p. 5. As Jean Marc Poinsot commented, "Une partie importante du débat suscité par l'apparition de l'art conceptuel a tourné autour de sa dématérialisation, mais si l'on se reporte à la série d'exemples que Lucy Lippard et John Chandler citent dans leur texte *'The Dematerialization of Art'* il apparaît que la plupart des œuvres en question sont des objets, des œuvres, des expositions déniés tels un dessin effacé ou remplacé par une inscription au crayon très légère, un objet caché ou encore un signe sur quelque support que se soit qui recouvre ou jouxte ce dont il est le signe. Il n'y a pratiquement pas d'œuvre dans leur liste qui ne repose sur une réalité matérielle bien précise et si l'on examine avec soin l'activité des artistes conceptuels, force est de constater qu'elle ne peut être réduite à la diffusion d''informations' ou de concepts dont la seule dissémination se ferait par le processus dématérialisant du langage imprimé." Poinsot 1999, pp. 104–105.

As an exhibition curator, Lippard worked with many of these artists, and a shared fundamental issue that she recognized in their work was "a concern with the object"; either as a formal discourse on the work of art, to go beyond the physical relation to the object, or as a principled attitude. "Some artists now think it's absurd to fill up their studios with objects that won't be sold, and are trying to get their art communicated as rapidly as it is made."[54] Principally, Lippard thus regarded the rejection of the art object in a twofold manner: as a formal critique of the definition of the artwork, and as a more ideological critique on the system of art's distribution or trade.

As Thomas McEvilley argued, "Ephemeral works are in part an attempt to avoid the processes of commodification and fetishism in which artworks favoured by the formalist ideology seemed so deeply implicated."[55] Connected to a larger comment on capitalist society in which art was "bought and sold by the greedy sector that owned everything that was exploiting the world and promoting the Vietnam War," artists' political positioning, according to McEvilley, became an equivalent of their artistic attitude.[56] The anti-establishment attitude of artists devoted to dematerialization in the 1960s, as Siegelaub pointed out, has been largely marginalized in the historicization or canonization of conceptual art; but this attitude did found the artistic strategies behind the dematerialization of the art object that are still relevant today.[57] In contrast to conceptual art's first historicizers, McEvilley focused on the ideology or intentions behind conceptual art, distinguishing these as artistic strategies rather than art historical categories.[58] He stressed that "the complex of strategies forming Conceptual Art was first defined negatively.... Its early form was to a degree determined, or controlled, by the form of what it was criticizing."[59]

54 Ibid., pp. 6–7.

55 Thomas McEvilley, "Anti-Art as Cognition: Themes and Strategies," in McEvilley 2005, p. 93.

56 Lippard, in Goldstein and Rorimer 1995, p. 28.

57 Lippard recalls a commentary by Jan Dibbets that sketches the positioning of artists in the late 1960s: "Sell my work? To sell isn't part of the art. Maybe there will be people idiotic enough to buy what they could make themselves. So much the worse for them." Lippard, in Goldstein and Rorimer 1995, p. 28.

58 In his approach, McEvilley nonetheless duplicates his precursors in defining the dematerialization of the art object "an unrealizable ideal," but recognizes "a real meaning to the project." (p. 95) I am here only drawing from McEvilley's conception of dematerialization but have adjusted most of the works he refers to due to incomplete data and interpretations.

59 McEvilley 2005, p. 98.

When breaking with the tradition of modernist painting and sculpture and/or the formalist art of commodity-making, conceptual artists were producing declarations (about artistry) that became artworks; "demonstrations of a real seriousness about art in a broader or deeper sense."[60] McEvilley asserts, following the conceptual originators, that this attitude was anticipated by the prototype of Marcel Duchamp. Early examples of such works include Robert Morris's *Statement of Aesthetic Withdrawal* from 1963.[61] Morris sent this signed and notarized declaration to the head of MoMA's architecture department, architect Philip Johnson, after the acquisition of his work *Litanies* (1963),[62] which was exhibited in Morris's first solo show in the museum. When the artist had still not received his payment after six months, he responded with his *Statement*.[63] This critical approach to the system of art can also be discerned in Lawrence Weiner's famous "Declaration of Intent," first published in Seth Siegelaub's exhibition catalogue *January 5–31, 1969*, in which he, rather than producing or even conceiving an artwork, formulated the parameters to which it should conform.

Other, more persuasive, declarations include John Latham's 1966–1969 *Art and Culture*. Latham withdrew Clement Greenberg's acclaimed collected essays on modernist painting, *Art & Culture* (1961) from the library of St. Martins School of Art in London and, together with his students, chewed and then spit out a third of its pages, thus illustrating his aversion to Greenberg's specific modernist notion of the artwork.[64] In the same year, John Baldessari announced he would stop making work by his own hand and signature, which was followed by the burning and subsequent exhibition of the ashes of all his former paintings in 1970. Another seminal work by Baldessari that can be ascribed to the declaration is *I Will Not Make Any More*

60 Ibid.

61 Robert Morris, *Document*, 1963.

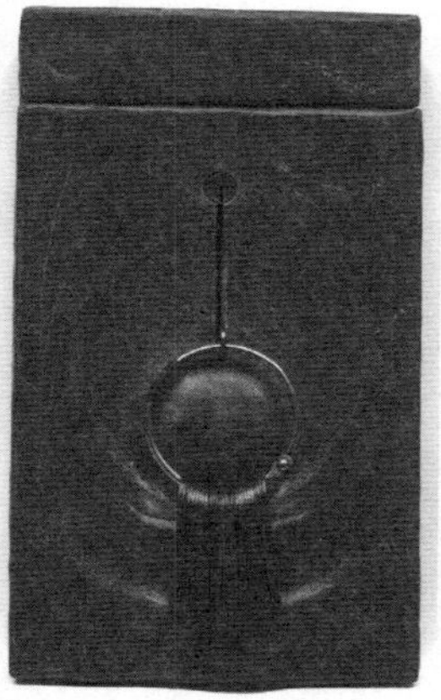

62 Robert Morris, *Litanies*, 1963.

63 The declaration reads, "The undersigned, ROBERT MORRIS, being the maker of the metal construction entitled LITANIES, described in the annexed Exhibit A, hereby withdraws from said construction all esthetic quality and content and declares that from the date hereof said construction has no such quality and content." See further Martha Buskirk, "Introduction," in Buskirk 2003, pp. 1–16.

64 This work can be regarded within what Peter Osborne has termed "the crisis of Greenbergian criticism" at the beginning of the 1960s; essentially a crisis in its medium-based conception of the artwork, its "specific" modernism, which simultaneously registered a crisis in the ontology of the artwork and established the conditions for the resolution of this crisis through the renovation of the romantic ideology of artistic intentionality in a radically new, critical-discursive guise. Peter Osborne, "Conceptual Art and/as Philosophy," in Newman and Bird 1999, pp. 47–65, p. 49.

Boring Art (1971),[65] the result of an invitation by the Nova Scotia College of Art and Design, which wanted to exhibit his work. When the Californian artist was not able to travel to Canada to install the exhibition, he sent the school a piece of paper with the aforementioned text, instructing it to recruit students in order to write the words "all over the walls of the gallery space" as an imposition.[66]

The negative designation of art or, to use the terminology of Peter Osborne, "the lineages of negation" that paved the way for conceptual art further expanded in the art institutions or systems in which art becomes manifest, and more particularly in the focus on the exhibition space.[67] "As the other side of dematerialization," McEvilley stressed, "Conceptual Art has analyzed the context in which the art object had once been contained, focusing on the system of market-related processes that surrounded it like a net."[68] Again, Duchamp and his insight that it was the institutional context that defined the work of art comes up as an inspiration, one that was further contextualized by Yves Klein in exhibiting the empty gallery of Iris Clert[69] in 1958.[70] According to McEvilley, it was Klein who first applied the term dematerialization to art.[71] He conceived the exhibition of an empty space—a gesture that he had applied several times—in traditional terms, calling them "invisible paintings and sculptures."[72]

The idea of emptiness is also a recurring theme within the work of Robert Barry. As one of the four artists associated with Siegelaub, he can be considered among the few "true conceptualists." In a symposium moderated by Siegelaub at Bradford College in 1968 he stated, "There is something about void and emptiness which I am personally very concerned with. I guess I can't get it out of my system. Just emptiness. *Nothing* seems to me the most potent thing in the

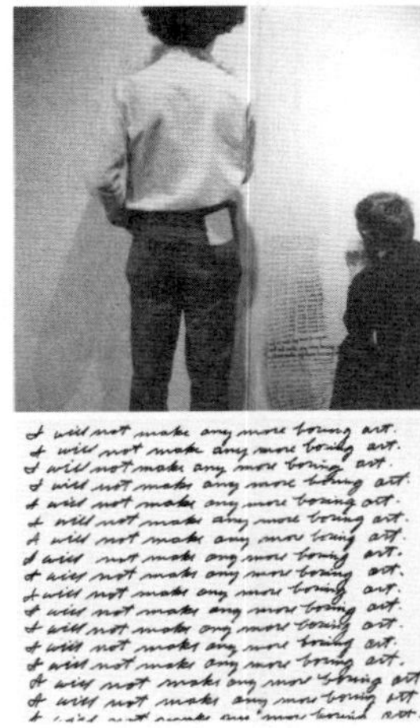

65 John Baldessari, *I Will Not Make Any More Boring Art*, Mezzanine Gallery, Nova Scotia College of Art and Design, April 1–10, 1971.

66 Baldessari committed another version of the piece to videotape. Like an errant schoolboy, he dutifully writes, "I will not make any more boring art," over and over again in a notebook for the duration of the tape. See <www.medienkunstnetz.de/works/i-will-not-make-any-more-boring-art/> (21-10-2011).

67 Osborne 2002, p. 18.

68 McEvilley 2005, p. 96.

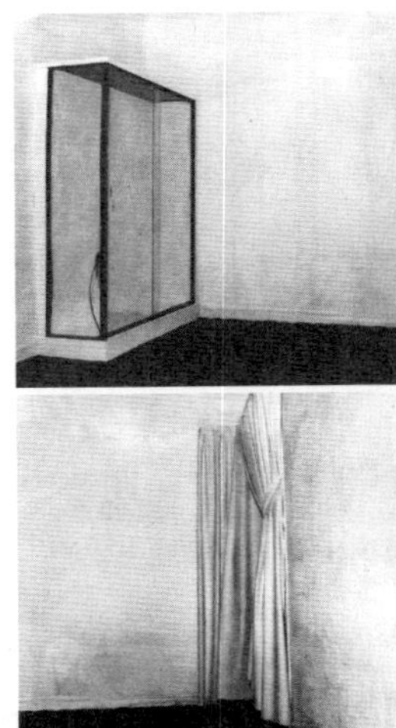

69 Yves Klein, *The Void* (Le vide), installation view at Iris Clert, Paris, 1958.

70 This exhibition by Klein, known under the title *The Void*, has recently gained importance through the exhibition *Vides (Voids)* at the Centre Pompidou in Paris, February 25–March 23, 2009.

71 Klein used the term "dematerialization" in regard to his "exhibition" of the color blue at the Galerie Iris Clert in 1958. See Yves Klein, "The Specialization of Sensibility in Raw Material State into Stabilized Pictorial Sensibility," in *Voids: A Retrospective*, ed. John Armleder and Matthieu Copeland, exh. cat. Paris (Centre Pompidou)/(Zurich: JRP/Ringier), 2009, pp. 51–55.

72 McEvilley 2005, p. 96.

world."[73] His *88mc Carrier Wave (FM)* and *1600kc Carrier Wave AM*, included in Siegelaub's *January 5–31, 1969* exhibition, consisted of transmitted carrier waves in an enclosed room, which would not be visible in any way and could only be determined by the caption on the wall describing the work. *Some places to which we can come, and for a while "be free to think about what we're going to do." (Marcuse)*, a project that Barry initiated in 1970, which is still in progress, anticipates the active role of the visitor in the (empty) exhibition space, using it as a place to meet and reflect.

The model of the empty exhibition space was further explored in Art & Language's *Air Conditioning Show*,[74] which was conceived in 1966 and first appeared as an article in *Arts Magazine* in 1967, but was only executed as an "exhibition" in 1972 in the Visual Arts Gallery in New York.[75] Art & Language stated that "any attempt at picturing (visualizing) the situation is merely evidence that the art-audience is stuck with its visual art-object. A question that might be asked here is, would there be a difference between a 'non-exhibition' model and a model that exhibits nothing?"[76] In this respect they ascribe to the fact that "it is obvious that the public nature of historical experience and its open-endedness (the two main types of reflexive relatedness) is reflected in language. This is to say that the lingual datum is basic to history."[77]

Expanding Art and Language's "non-exhibition model," Michael Asher's project in the Claire Copley Gallery in Los Angeles in 1974[78] more explicitly revealed the underlying political system of the institution. Asher removed the partition wall of the gallery behind which the office space was located, thus exposing the "financial centre" of the gallery. In the same year the artist had an exhibition at the Nova Scotia College of Art and Design, in which he did not modify

73 Robert Barry, in a symposium moderated by Seth Siegelaub at Bradford Junior College, Bradford, MA, in Lippard 1973, p. 40.

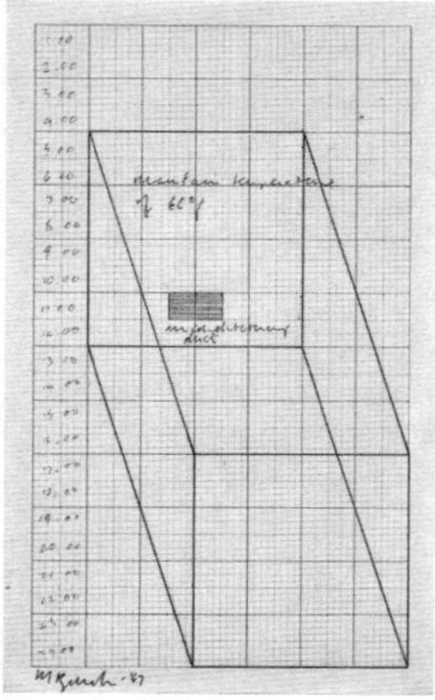

74a Art & Language, study for *The Air-Conditioning Show*, 1967.

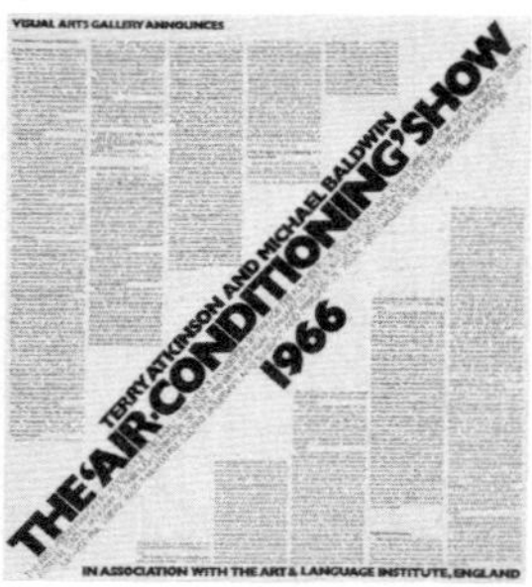

74b Art & Language, poster for *The Air-Conditioning Show*, 1971–1972.

75 See Michael Baldwin, "Remarks on Air-Conditioning: An Extravaganza of Blandness," in Alberro and Stimson 1999, pp. 32–34; first published in *Arts Magazine* 42, no. 2 (November 1967), pp. 22–23. The starting point of the text was to air-condition a volume of air through the gallery space.

76 Art & Language (Michael Baldwin and Terry Atkinson), "The Air-Conditioning Show, 1966," poster text, Visual Arts Gallery, New York, 1972, reprinted in exh. cat. Paris 2009, p. 68.

77 Ibid., p. 69.

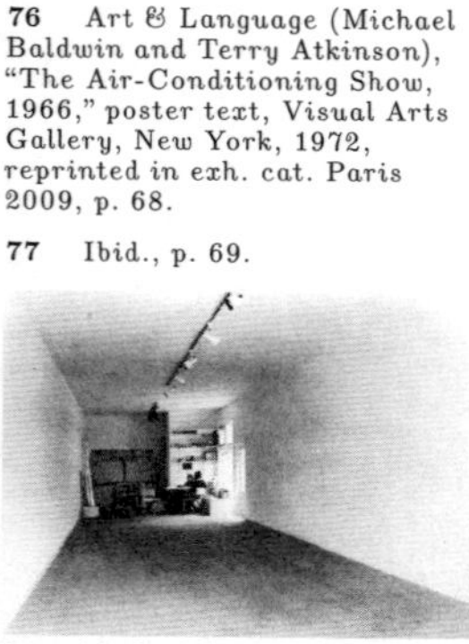

78 Michael Asher, *Untitled Intervention*, Claire Copley Gallery, Los Angeles, 1974.

anything, neither the space nor its architecture, and intervened in the existing situation only by not turning on the lights. In these works, dematerialization can be explained by the uniqueness of the projects' moment; their finite duration is a fundamental aspect to Asher's meaning of the work. He usually refuses to partake in the physical reexecution of former works because of the missing historical context, stating that his projects "have no objects, and present just the exhibition space, addresses specific questions or concerns about that space which are particular to its context."[79] Explicitly related to the context in which they are shown, the works cannot be re-exhibited; the survival of these works is merely secured in their documentation.

79 See Yesomi Umolu, "The Void as Dedication: Proceeding from a Space of Transgression to Veneration," <www.artandeducation.net/paper/the-void-as-dedication-proceeding-from-a-space-of-transgression-to-veneration/> (10-10-2011).

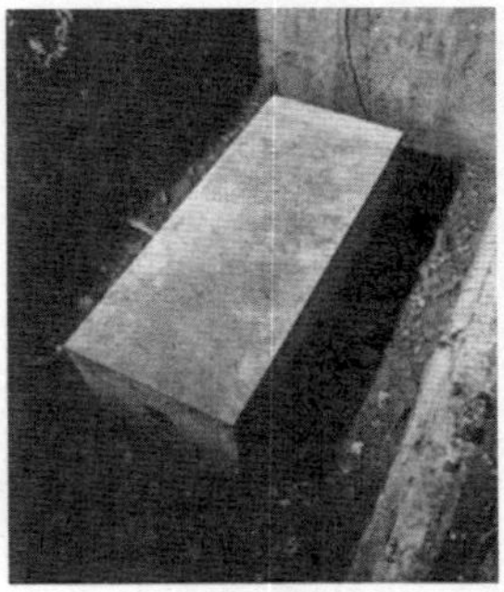

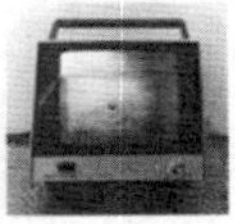

A subgenre that McEvilley discerns from Klein's exhibition of the empty gallery, related to immateriality and subtraction, is the empty or hidden piece. McEvilley finds examples of such works in Bruce Nauman's *Audio-Video Underground Chamber* (1972–1974)[80] and Robert Barry's *Closed Gallery Piece* (1969).[81] The latter exists in the distribution of the invitation card of a selected group of galleries containing the text "During the exhibition the gallery will be closed." According to McEvilley, the invitation card itself should be considered the piece, but since the context in which the sent invitation was functioning gives the piece meaning, the printed piece of paper as an autonomous work in an exhibition is not only ignoring the original intention of the work but also confusing the remaining document as a work. In his book *Quand l'œuvre a lieu. Art exposé et ses récits autorisés* the French art historian Jean-Marc Poinsot further elaborates on this problem: "One has to understand that the exhibition at issue here was not possible because the artists and the gallerists had already extended its definition in the bulletin [invitation card], and, because the bulletin as part of the exhibition

80 Bruce Nauman, *Audio-Video Underground Chamber*, 1972–1974.

81 Other than McEvilley describes, this work did not exist in a "sign on the door" at Art & Project in Amsterdam, but in the sent invitation card that reads, "During the exhibition the gallery will be closed." See *Art & Project Bulletin* 37, 1971.

returned the work tractable to the gallery as a sign captured in a syntagmatic [constituent] relation."[82] This implies that, since the exhibition of the piece was not tangible in the first place, the subsequent exhibition of the piece would not be possible as such.

Barry, but also Ian Wilson, has made several pieces in which the distributive format of the invitation card was used to suggest or occupy a mental space that captures the work. As Poinsot has pointed out, "'Models of exhibitions that do not exhibit anything' have played a very specific role within conceptual art; while the use of language, associated with the command of the surrounding reality taken in the field of the exhibition, was able to establish a dialectical and aesthetic approach to the contemporary practice of semiotic systems that circulates from the most elaborate languages to the most intangible realities, apparently without difficulties."[83] Other than Lippard, who at the time does not further specify or theoricize dematerialization, Poinsot proposed a broader definition of dematerialization that is appropriate to the majority of artworks developed in the late 1960s and early 1970s. He roughly defines dematerialization as "the end of painting and sculpture as exclusive materials in the division of the visual within artistic representation."[84] More specifically, he explains dematerialization as "the disappearance of the artifact as a permanent and exclusive guarantee of the totality of the artwork rather than the reduction of the artwork to an idea or similar reality. In other words, the artwork could exist in a form other than the object elaborated by the artist, fabricated under his direction, or chosen by him."[85]

Sol LeWitt's wall drawings, described in certificates, are clear examples of such works that have the possibility to be reexecuted at various spatial-temporal situations following his instructions—implementing the principle of dematerization.

82 Poinsot 1999, p. 112. ("Il faut comprendre ici que l'exposition en question n'était possible que parce que les artistes et les responsables de la galerie avaient déjà étendu sa définition à ce bulletin, et, que le bulletin comme partie de l'exposition rendait manipulable l'ouverture de la galerie comme signe pris dans une relation syntagmatique.")

83 Ibid., p. 116. ("Par contre, 'les modèles d'expositions qui n'exposent rien' ont joué un rôle très spécifique dans l'art conceptuel, car le recours au langage, associé à la maîtrise de la réalité environnante prise dans le champ de l'exposition, a pu établir une approche dialectique et esthétique de la pratique contemporaine des systèmes sémiotiques qui circule apparemment sans difficultés des langages les plus élaborés aux réalités les plus insaisissables.")

84 Ibid.

85 Ibid., p. 79 and p. 110 ("la fin du tableau et de la sculpture comme matière exclusive du découpage du visuel dans le signe artistique"; "Ce que recouvre la notion de dématérialisation est... la disparition de l'artefact comme garantie permanente et exclusive de l'intégrité de l'œuvre, plus que la réduction de l'œuvre à une idée ou à une réalité du même ordre. En d'autres termes, l'œuvre pouvait exister sous une forme autre qu'un objet élaboré par l'artiste, fabriqué sous son contrôle ou choisi par lui.") My translation. Poinsot's definition in fact opens up the discussion on dematerialization as an aspect that anticipates the ontological status of the conceptual artwork.

Although always in close collaboration with the LeWitt Estate they, as Lippard declared, "allow for infinite generalization, or variety."[86] Conversely, Ian Wilson's discussion pieces solely depend on the physical presence of the artist and, besides a written text that "a discussion with Ian Wilson has taken place," lack further indications for reexecution or representation. As I have come to the point where dematerialization is defined as a process that scrutinizes the artwork's traditional boundaries rather than actually eliminating its tangible form, works like Wilson's complicate a simple determination. Whereas they can be regarded as most successful in terms of effectively applying the principles of the conceptual assignment, they simultaneously make their continued existence in an exhibitionary or any communicable format to a large degree unattainable.[87]

Similar to Benjamin Buchloh's definition of conceptual art "from the aesthetic of administration to institutional critique," dematerialization can be defined as a development that commenced from the critique of the formalist art object or commodity to the critique of the entire system of art that supported this commodity.[88] But the exposure and critique of the underlying system of rules that defined art in a highly developed capitalist society was an act that inversely also needed the structures of this system to make its point. As Buchloh has stated, "one major paradox of all conceptual practices... [is] that the critical annihilation of cultural conventions itself immediately acquired the conditions of spectacle culture...."[89] Elaborating on the paradoxes that comprise conceptual art, one could argue that the fact that an art defined by dematerialization essentially lives on through the market-making of its residue is even a bigger paradox.[90]

As Michael Newman stressed, works that include a principle of dematerialization still need some sort of presentation

86 Lippard 1973, p. 5.

87 Although Ursula Meyer argued that "conceptual art emphasizes the elimination of the art-object," in referring to LeWitt's wall drawings she states, "Without the interference of objects Sol LeWitt gives a subtle emphasis to actual space through the direct application of his schematic drawings to the gallery wall." Likewise, "Mel Bochner's measurement series document and evaluate the space of galleries and museums. Daniel Buren's stripes applied to walls, doors and billboards create a focused tension with the environment." But she also mentions works that remained in a tangible form/object, such as Jan Dibbets's perspective corrections or Hanne Darboven's number constellations. In Meyer 1972, p. xiii.

88 Benjamin Buchloh, "From the Aesthetic of Administration to Institutional Critique (Some Aspects of Conceptual Art 1962–1969)," in exh. cat. Paris 1989, pp. 41–53; Also, according to Alexander Alberro, this strand of conceptualism became the dominant theoretical model of conceptualism, as an alternative to the initially dominant tautological model by Joseph Kosuth.

89 Ibid., p. 52. What is ironic about this statement is that Buchloh, who is examining conceptual art in a purely art historical, aesthetic framework, seems not to interpret the declarations made by conceptual artists within this very discourse *as artistic attitudes*, but rather places them in a philosophical or ontological discourse.

90 In the late 1960s Lippard stressed, "The artists who are trying to do non-object art are introducing a drastic solution to the problem of artists being bought and sold so easily, along with their art.... The people who buy a work of art they can't hang up or have in their garden are less interested in possession. They are patrons rather than collectors. That's why all this seems so inapplicable to museums, because museums are basically acquisitive." In 1995, in retrospect of her text on dematerialization, she refers to her perspective at the time as "utopian." Lippard 1973, p. 8.

to be an artwork or to function as an artwork. In order to provide this, many artists have produced notes, sketches, descriptions, and documentary materials. But although the necessity to demonstrate or communicate the work in one way or another meant that there were "traces that remained (as notes or sketches for the work or as documentation) that consequently could be made marketable"; if these remnants had not been collected, most of these works would no longer exist.[91] According to Newman, these "documentary works" have alternatively also proved successful in tackling the system of commodity-making, "in the sense that it escapes to the inherent formalism of the tautology and to the pursuit of pureness of the immaterial."[92]

Newman considers Michael Asher's documented architectural interventions in galleries or museums as a key example of such works, a type of conceptual art that he places within the category of "synthetic conceptualism." Remarkably, Newman considers this category contrasting to "analytic conceptualism," the traditional ("Kosuthian") definition of conceptual art, according to him, in which he specifically places works related to dematerialization.[93] The distinction between the two categories becomes even more confusing when Newman ascribes a second trend to this category, a type of work that "better succeeded in surpassing the gallery circuit" by using the magazine page as a place of distribution and consumption, such as Dan Graham's *Homes for America*[94] that was published in *Arts Magazine* in 1966.[95] While this type of conceptual art, according to Newman, was further explored in the advertisement pieces in public spaces executed by Hans Haacke, Victor Burgin, and others, it is also precisely the "information-type" of art, as emphasized by Seth Siegelaub in his early "catalogue-exhibitions," in which Kosuth has been ascribed a significant role.

91 See Michael Newman, "Conceptuele kunst van de jaren zestig tot negentig: Een onaf project?," *Kunst & Museumjournaal* vol. 7, nos. 1–3, 1996, p. 105. My translation.

92 Ibid. My translation.

93 Ibid., p. 103. Although this category is used by other historicizers of conceptual art, they do not ascribe the same features to it. See, for example, Ursula Meyer or Alexander Alberro.

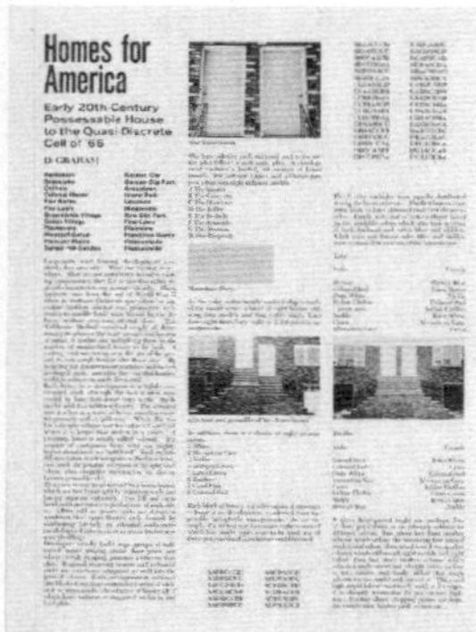

Homes for America
Early 20th Century Possessable House to the Quasi-Discrete Cell of '66

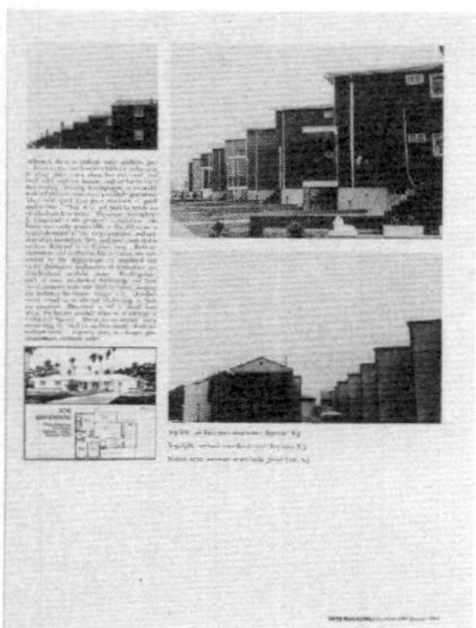

94 Dan Graham, *Homes for America*, published in *Arts Magazine*, 1966.

95 See *Arts Magazine* 41 (December 1966/January 1967).

While the notion of dematerialization has been deemed by many as a "piece of paper or a photograph is as much an object, or 'material,' as a ton of lead," the critique of the object within the discourse of conceptual art has been too easily surpassed by modernist principles that obstinately prevail within the today's market-driven system of the visual arts.[96] Whereas the distinctions or determination of different lineages of conceptual art has been a demanding art historical effort in the 1990s, this theoreticization or categorization of conceptual art has not brought any deeper insights into the museological or curatorial interpretation of such works. In contrast, the notion of dematerialization is applicable to any work of art that, within the sociohistorical context of the late 1960s and early 1970s, frustrated and intended to frustrate a traditional format of exhibition. The format of publication that conceptual artists often chose to "exhibit" or communicate their work was a consequence coherent to their positioning, and should be further examined within Siegelaub's notion of "Primary and Secondary Information."

96 See Lippard 1973.

Primary and Secondary Information

In 1972 Ursula Meyer stated, "Books have become an increasingly important medium for Conceptual Art, often taking the place of exhibitions. They have more permanence than transient shows in galleries."[97] According to Meyer's observations, which heavily lean on the ideas of Siegelaub, the traditional gallery (or exhibition) space, designed to exhibit objects, was no longer suitable for exhibiting the new art of "conceptions." Already in 1969 Siegelaub had described how he perceived the developments in the contemporary art of his time, saying, "Gradually there developed an 'art' which

97 Meyer 1972, p. xiii.

didn't need to be hung. An art wherein the problem of presentation paralleled one of the problems previously involved in the making and exhibition of a painting: i.e., *to make someone else aware that an artist had done anything at all*. Because the work was not visual in nature, it did not require the traditional means of exhibition, but a means that would present the intrinsic ideas of the art."[98]

As an independent curator-dealer, Siegelaub had been working since the late 1960s to provide new conditions of transmitting the new art to the audience, whereby the ideas of artists "may be made as widely available as possible without the risk of spurious identities becoming attached to them."[99] In order to do so, he considered the format of the catalogue/publication an accurate vehicle; a potential "exhibition space." "When art does not any longer depend upon its physical presence, when it becomes an abstraction, it is not distorted and altered by its reproduction in books. It becomes 'PRIMARY' information, while the reproduction of conventional art in books and catalogues is necessarily (distorted) 'SECONDARY' information. When information is PRIMARY, the catalogue can become the exhibition."[100]

It was Siegelaub's conviction that people are more likely to engage with art through printed media and conversation than by directly encountering an artwork. In the case of conceptual art, where the artwork concerns conceptions that are not connected to a physical presence, its intrinsic value is therefore principally not altered by the presentation in a book, according to Siegelaub.[101] The idea that conceptual art could be "communicated" to an audience through the printing and distributing of only its primary information was never fully accepted by the artists involved; however, it generated a pioneering model for presenting the newly established "dematerialized art" to an audience.[102] Siegelaub's notion of primary

98 Seth Siegelaub, in conversation with Charles Harrison, "On Exhibitions and the World at Large," *Studio International* vol. 178, no. 917 (December 1969), p. 202.

99 Ibid.

100 Siegelaub, in conversation with Ursula Meyer, in Meyer 1972, p. xiv.

101 Harrison 1969, p. 202.

102 In a radio symposium moderated by Siegelaub on WBAI-FM with Barry, Huebler, Kosuth, and Weiner, none of the artists agreed (except maybe Kosuth) on Siegelaub's statement that the fundamental nature of their work is that it does not relate to space. See Lippard 1973, pp. 127–133.

and secondary information is not completely unambiguous when applied to the different conceptual projects in and outside his own practice. I therefore want to examine the connotations of an information-based art and its ambiguous relation to the book/publication (i.e., to reevaluate the notion of primary and secondary information, and thereby stress the status of conceptual art as an art of representation rather than of presentation).

Whereas Newman places the trend of "exhibiting" concepts or conceptual art via the format of magazines or other publications as deliberately *opposed* to the trend of dematerialization, I propose regarding this as an aspect of the same progression—as it was initially conceived. As suggested by both Meyer and Siegelaub, it was exactly the dematerialized status of conceptual art that made it preeminently an art to be documented and (re-)presented in a book format. Furthermore, the focus on the book or publication as a way to communicate propositions, according to Meyer, was dictated by the theoretical examinations of the conceptual artists. While the conceptual artists provided their own theories, the writing of a "critical interpretation" of the work, "*different* from the artist's intention," was assumed to be unnecessary—essentially because it was "prejudicing information."[103]

The idea that the artists themselves are best equipped to explain their work, and therefore take over the position of the theorist/critic, was based upon the assumption that (conceptual) artists were thinkers rather than producers.[104] Meyer stressed that "attending to the critical function itself is the nature of Conceptual Art. There is no further need for critical interpretation of idea and intention already clearly stated."[105] Undoubtedly, she was referring to Kosuth's tautological/linguistic interpretation of conceptual art that "should express definitions about art or the formal consequences of these

103 Meyer 1972, p. *viii*.

104 Alexander Alberro referred to a reduced role of the artist as producer in relation to the model of conceptualism as defined by Hans Haacke. See Alexander Alberro, "Reconsidering Conceptual Art, 1966–1977," in Alberro and Stimson 1999, p. *xxiv*.

105 Ibid., p. *ix*.

definitions only."[106] Siegelaub's catalogue-exhibitions provided a proper format of presentation for Kosuth's linguistic model of conceptual art. In the exhibition catalogue of Siegelaub's *January 5–31, 1969*, Kosuth published a statement on the changed format of presentation of his dictionary-based works (*Art as Idea as Idea*), from the mounted photostats to spaces in newspapers and periodicals.[107] He explained:

> This way the immateriality of the work is stressed and any possible connections to painting are severed. The new work is not connected with a previous object—it's accessible to as many people as are interested, it's non-decorative—having nothing to do with architecture; it can be brought into the home or museum, but wasn't made with either in mind; it can be dealt with by being torn out of its publication and inserted into a notebook or stapled to the wall—or not torn out at all—but any such decisions is unrelated to the art. My role as an artist ends with the work's publication.[108]

Kosuth's statement is based upon a group of works that he himself categorized as "The Second Investigations" (1968–1969),[109] in which he proposed a confrontation between art and non-art systems and contexts, but it more generally illustrates the motivation of artists to present their work in the realm of the publication.[110]

The projects that various artists were developing in periodicals and other publications since the early 1960s, experimenting with the page as a site to merge idea and presentation, can be seen as a prelude to Siegelaub's catalogue projects.[111] The early magazine pieces by Dan Graham are among the first examples, in which the artist explored, as Anne Rorimer argues,"the page to cite itself as a site: that is, the content of the work and its context in a publication

106 Kosuth, cited in Honnef 1971, p. 41. My translation.

107 Honnef pointed out that Kosuth's theory cannot be separated from his artistic work; he considered the former much more convincing than the artistic projects that have been entitled "investigations" and should have an entirely abstract character, but instead are described as schoolmasterish and rather trivial testimonies. Honnef argued that it was only when Kosuth started to publish his art investigations in newspapers that he succeeded to get rid of the iconic image. (p. 43)

108 See Lippard 1973, pp. 72–73.

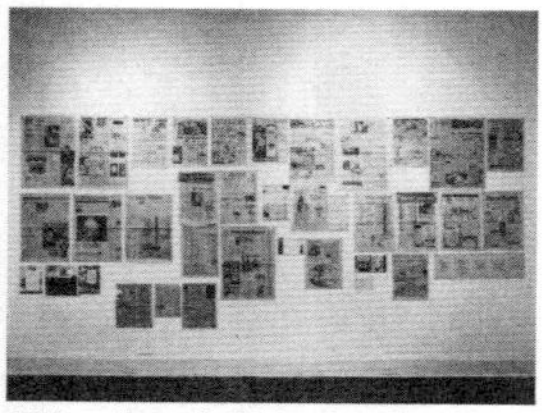

109 Joseph Kosuth, *The Second Investigations*, as exhibited at The Renaissance Society at the University of Chicago, 1976.

110 For more information on these works by Kosuth, see Anne Rorimer, "Siting the Page: Exhibiting Works in Publications: Some Examples of Conceptual Art in the USA," in Newman and Bird 1999, pp. 11–26, p. 17.

111 See, for example, Germano Celant, *Book as Artwork 1960–1972* (London: Nigel Greenwood Inc. Ltd., 1972), an accompanying exhibition in the Nigel Greenwood Gallery was curated by Lynda Morris.

coincide in so far as the former serves as a self-referential inventory of the latter."[112] Graham started with these works in 1965, right after the gallery that he briefly ran fell short, which, according to Rorimer, stipulated a "reaction against the gallery experience, but also... a response to contradictions [he] discerned in gallery artists."[113] In contrast to Kosuth, for whom the use of space in magazines and newspapers made it possible to avoid the creation of an autonomous object of commercial worth, it allowed Graham to circumvent the spaces in which art objects are sold. As Rorimer argues, "By placing works in magazines, he substituted the ideational space of the magazine page for that of the enterable exhibition space."[114]

Graham's piece *Figurative* (1965),[115] a cash register receipt arbitrarily placed between advertisements for Tampax and Warner's Bra and published in the March 1968 issue of *Harper's Bazaar*, functioned as a "sort of anti-ad [which] resists being merchandized as a precious and purchasable or saleable object, and replaces traditionally composed figuration with functioning numerical figures. Representational material and presentational method are thereby fused in that the work is to be seen simultaneously on the page and inside the magazine that contains it."[116] *Schema*,[117] produced as an independent publication in 1965, as well as a contribution to *Aspen Magazine* no. 5/6 in 1967, also defines the materially present page as the primary container of the work.[118] The piece consists of printed material and information on a page: a list of all the facts concerning the specific published format in which the page is bound, specifying numbers of adjectives, adverbs, nouns, and infinitives, in addition to type of paper stock, typeface, etc.

Graham's *Homes for America* was first realized as a slide show included in the exhibition *Projected Art* at the Finch College Museum of Art in New York (1966), before it was

112 Rorimer, in Newman and Bird 1999, p. 15.

113 Ibid., p. 19.

114 Ibid., p. 15.

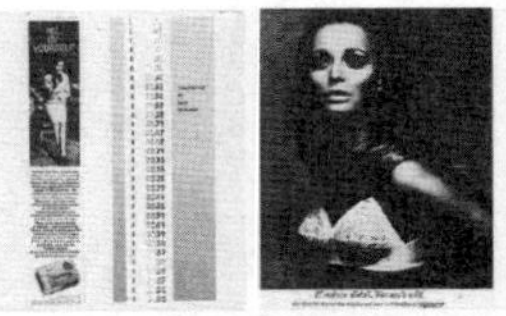

115 Dan Graham, *Figurative*, 1965, printed in *Harper's Bazaar*, 1968.

116 Rorimer, in Newman and Bird 1999, p. 16 also see: Anne Rorimer, "Reevaluating the Object of Collecting and Display," *The Art Bulletin* vol. 77, no. 1 (March 1995), p. 21.

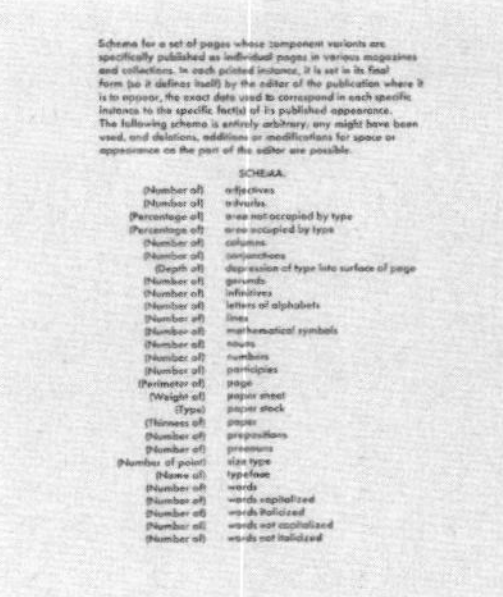

Schema for a set of pages whose component variants are specifically published as individual pages in various magazines and collections. In each printed instance, it is set in its final form (so it defines itself) by the editor of the publication where it is to appear, the exact data used to correspond in each specific instance to the specific fact(s) of its published appearance. The following schema is entirely arbitrary; any might have been used, and deletions, additions or modifications for space or appearance on the part of the editor are possible.

SCHEMA:

(Number of) adjectives
(Number of) adverbs
(Percentage of) area not occupied by type
(Percentage of) area occupied by type
(Number of) columns
(Number of) conjunctions
(Depth of) depression of type into surface of page
(Number of) gerunds
(Number of) infinitives
(Number of) letters of alphabets
(Number of) lines
(Number of) mathematical symbols
(Number of) nouns
(Number of) numbers
(Number of) participles
(Perimeter of) page
(Weight of) paper sheet
(Type) paper stock
(Thinness of) paper
(Number of) prepositions
(Number of) pronouns
(Number of point) size type
(Name of) typeface
(Number of) words
(Number of) words capitalized
(Number of) words italicized
(Number of) words not capitalized
(Number of) words not italicized

117 Dan Graham, *Schema*, March, 1966.

118 *Aspen* magazine can be considered a "multimedia magazine," which was published six times a year in various formats. Issue nos. 5 and 6 (1967), also called the "Minimalist issue," was edited by the Irish art critic Brian O'Doherty and included contributions by various artists and writers, such as Roland Barthes, John Cage, Merce Cunningham, Marcel Duchamp, Morty Feldman, Naum Gabo, Sol LeWitt, Robert Morris, and Susan Sontag, among others, in a two-piece cardboard box. It can be regarded an early example of a "magazine-exhibition," which deserves further study.

published as a photo-essay in *Arts Magazine*, titled *Homes for America: Early 20th-Century Possessable House to the Quasi-Discrete Cell of '66*. It was important to Graham that the photographs are regarded as part of an overall magazine article layout and not as a separate work: "They are illustrations of the text, or inversely, the text functions in relation to the photographs thereby modifying their meanings. The photographs and the texts are separate parts of a two-dimensional, schematic grid perspective system. The photographs correlate to the lists and columns of serial documentation and both 'represent' the serial logic of the housing developments which the article is about."[119] Graham emphasized that he did not consider himself to be an artist; consequently, he was not interested in how his projects would be received: "I think the fact that *Homes for America* was, in the end, only a magazine article, and made no claims for itself as a work of art is its most important feature."[120] In 1969, however, he ended his magazine/publication activities to further develop his work as an artist.

Elaborating on Graham's "photojournalism," Mel Bochner and Robert Smithson conceived "The Domain of the Great Bear,"[121] a fictional art project in the form of an article that was published in *Art Voices* (Fall 1966). The work/illustrated article reports on the American Museum of Natural History and Hayden Planetarium in New York, starting with the cosmic heights of planetary movements and gradually getting to the (disappointing) reality of institutional settings. The project, as Rorimer points out, while "eliminating the once firm division between the defining characteristics of an artwork versus those of a magazine article, it deliberately eludes typecasting as one or the other."[122] Set within the pages of an art magazine, this project was an obvious critical gesture directed at the authority of authorship, originality,

119 Dan Graham, in Gary Dufour, ed., *Dan Graham*, exh. cat. Perth (Art Gallery of Western Australia) 1985, pp. 8–13.

120 Ibid.

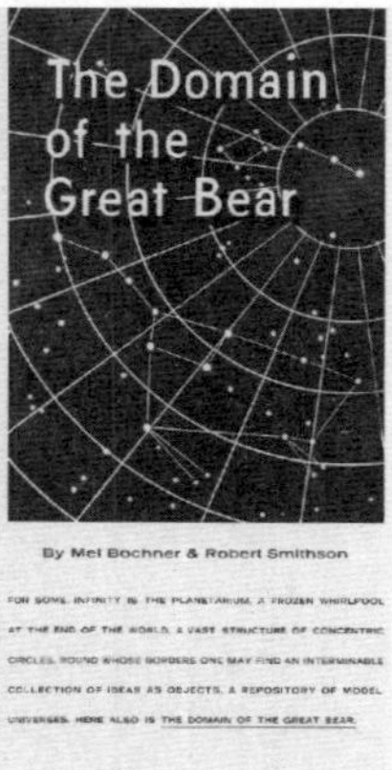

121 Mel Bochner and Robert Smithson, 'The Domain of the Great Bear,' published in *Art Voices*, Fall 1966.

122 Rorimer, in Newman and Bird 1999, p. 16. See also Michelle Grabner, "Mel Bochner at The Art Institute of Chicago," *Frieze* no. 105 (March 2007), <www.frieze.com/issue/print_back/mel_bochner/> (15-12-2011).

and truth (i.e., the parameters) of the (modernist) artwork.

A more playful or even provocative example of using the format of a magazine to subvert the position of the artwork is Stephen Kaltenbach's series of "ad-works"[123] in *Artforum*.[124] Like Kosuth, Kaltenbach was using the advertising pages of the magazine as an alternative exhibition space to counter expectations regarding the traditional forms and functions of art. The series consists of concise and suggestive phrases, such as "Expose Yourself," "Smoke," and "Tell a Lie," instructing or provoking viewers/readers and "offering an incursion into the weightiness of critical dogma found in art magazines."[125]

Another example of a magazine work that, contrary to Graham or Kosuth, deals with the page or format of the publication itself, is a dematerialized contribution by Robert Barry in *0 to 9* (July 1969).[126] Two works that are listed in the magazine's table of contents as "The space between pages 28 & 29" and "The space between pages 74 & 75" define the page in terms of its (non-)physicality; "as a two-dimensional entity that is one of a number of joined repeated elements forming a book or publication."[127] The "space" that Barry refers to is only imaginary: the first "space" is captured between the end of a project by Bernar Venet on page 28 and the start of an essay by Dan Graham on the reverse (page 29); the second refers to the space between pages 74 and 75 that can be entered by opening the magazine to these pages. Like other works by Barry from the late 1960s, such as the *Inert Gas* series or the *Carrier Wave* pieces, the work cannot be experienced in the manner of a traditional object, but exists in information that provokes the imagination of the reader.

Corresponding to these practices, Mel Bochner assembled *Working Drawings and Other Visible Things on Paper Not Necessarily Meant to Be Viewed as Art*[128] at the New

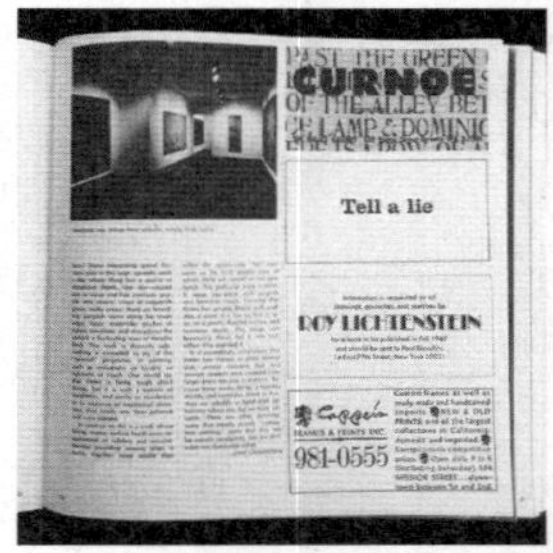

123 Stephen Kaltenbach, *Tell a Lie*, part of the series *Artforum Ads*, November 1968–December 1969.

124 Kaltenbach's ad-works appeared in the advertising section of *Artforum*'s issues starting in November 1968 and ending in December 1969.

125 Rorimer, in Newman and Bird 1999, p. 20.

126 Vito Acconci and Bernadette Mayer, eds., *0 to 9: The Complete Magazine, 1967–1969* (New York: Ugly Duckling Presse, 2006).

127 Rorimer, in Newman and Bird 1999, pp. 21–22.

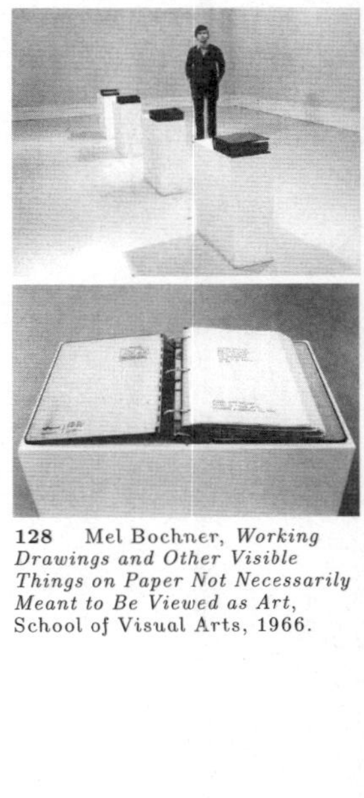

128 Mel Bochner, *Working Drawings and Other Visible Things on Paper Not Necessarily Meant to Be Viewed as Art*, School of Visual Arts, 1966.

School of Visual Arts in 1966, which can be considered the first exhibition in which the book was explicitly framed as an exibitionary format. In the school's gallery, Bochner exhibited four identical black, office-style box files with xeroxed working drawings and notes by a number of his artist friends (LeWitt, Judd, Flavin, and Darboven, among others) on four clean, white pedestals in the middle of the room.[129] The extreme mechanization of artistic production and distribution that Bochner had employed in this project must have been appealing to Siegelaub, since it was exactly this strategy that characterized his seminal "exhibition" the *Xerox Book*[130] (1968).[131] The *Xerox Book* could be regarded as the most explicit example in which Siegelaub's notion of primary and secondary information becomes manifest. The 175-page publication in a letter-size format consists of a collection of works/propositions by Andre, Barry, Huebler, Kosuth, LeWitt, Morris, and Weiner, each equally, or democratically, spread over the pages and distributed in an edition of 1,000.

It was Siegelaub's intention to "standardize the conditions of exhibition with the idea that the resulting differences in each artist's project or work would be precisely what the artist's work was about. It was an attempt to consciously standardize, in terms of an exhibition, book or project, the conditions of production underlying the exhibition process."[132] Siegelaub asked nine artists (De Maria and Smithson eventually withdrew) to make a twenty-five-page work on a standard letter-size page (21.59 × 27.94 cm), in which the new technique of the Xerox photocopier was intended to utilize its reproduction. As Alexander Alberro argued, Siegelaub's interest in the photocopy medium came out of the impersonal character of the xerography that depersonalized the production process and negated the skilled hand of the artist—essentially negating the aesthetic component.[133] In an inter-

129 See also James Meyer, "The Second Degree," in *Conceptual Art: Theory, Myth and Practice*, ed. Michael Corris (Cambridge: Cambridge University Press, 2004), pp. 108–122.

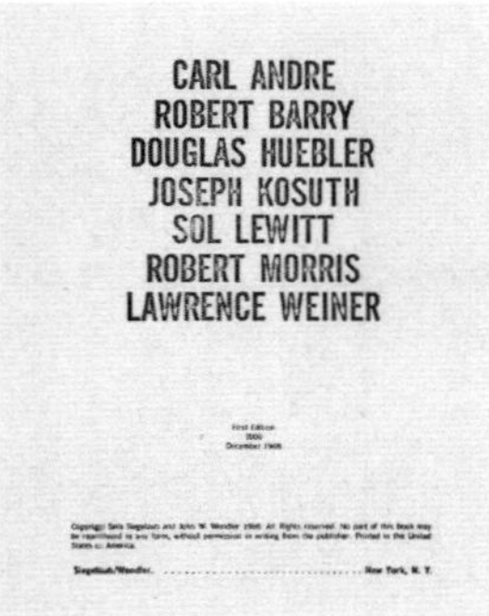
CARL ANDRE
ROBERT BARRY
DOUGLAS HUEBLER
JOSEPH KOSUTH
SOL LEWITT
ROBERT MORRIS
LAWRENCE WEINER

130 Seth Siegelaub, *Carl Andre, Robert Barry, Douglas Huebler, Joseph Kosuth, Sol LeWitt, Robert Morris, Lawrence Weiner* (the Xerox Book), John Wendler Gallery, New York, 1968.

131 Alexander Alberro linked the *Xerox Book* project by Siegelaub to Bochner's pivotal exhibition. Alberro 2003, p. 133.

132 Siegelaub, interviewed by Hans Ulrich Obrist in Obrist 2011, p. 122.

133 Alberro sees this attitude as being in line with the visionary writings of Marshall McLuhan and Quintin Fiore, in Alberro 2003, p. 135.

view about the project in 1969, he explained, "I chose Xerox as opposed to offset or any other process because it's such a bland, shitty reproduction, really just for the exchange of information. That's all a Xerox is about.... So Xerox just cuts down on the visual aspect of looking at the information."[134]

The deskilling practices that characterized the work of the artists represented by Siegelaub correlate with the idea of a plain distribution of information; above all, according to Alberro, "the electrostatic copying machine, with its leveling of all information to the zero degree, emphasized the new art's status as text, as *secondary* information."[135] At this point it is important to note that the partition of primary and secondary information in relation to the book is regarded as quite ambiguous here. Quite the opposite, Siegelaub has defined projects within the field of the catalogue/publication as primary information, which Rorimer explains in a broader perspective. "Works bound into a publication and/or bonded with the printed page... are not treated as a subsidiary or related illustration to a written text, as in earlier *livres d'artistes*, but are the very text *per se*—whether this so-called text be a visual or verbal or a linguistic and/or photographic manifestation on a page."[136] In this respect works bound in publications replace the formerly subsidiary or secondary information of the artists' works (bibliography, textual information, illustrations, or other documentation) and would accordingly become essentially primary information. However, in the case of conceptual art, the notions of primary and secondary information can be and have been interpreted alternately, since the essence of the works, in most cases, can merely be experienced by means of secondary information.

In fact, the notion of primary and secondary information can generate different models when applied to the works of the various artists involved. Whereas Kosuth "firmly adhered

134 Siegelaub, interview with Patricia Norvell, in Alberro and Norvell 2001, p. 39. In an interview I conducted with Siegelaub in 2010, he revealed that the *Xerox Book* in itself was a concept rather than an actual execution of the idea; he stated that the book was never xeroxed, but instead offset printed due to the high costs of the new technique. See Nathalie Zonnenberg, "The Context of Art (Continued): An Interview with Seth Siegelaub," *Manifesta Journal* 9 (2009–2010), pp. 41–51. See also Alberro 2003, p. 136.

135 Ibid. Emphasis mine.

136 Rorimer, in Newman and Bird 1999, pp. 25–26.

to a notion that only the primary information mattered (the secondary information is like a truck that carries the work to the gallery)," Huebler and Weiner "believed in the dominance of the secondary information since the primary was inaccessible and even undesirable."[137] Parallel to the *Xerox Book*, Siegelaub organized "solo exhibitions" of Huebler and Weiner, respectively in November and December of 1968, to which he referred as "the first exhibition in which the catalogue was the exhibition" and "the first exhibition in which the book is the exhibition."[138] Huebler's project was still "exhibited" within a traditional context as "work" in a private apartment, but the new practice introduced here functioned, as Poinsot has argued, "to operate a disconnection, a disassociation between, on the one hand, the idea of the work—understood generally as a proposition that contains reproducible image and language—and, on the other hand, its presentation, was primarily based on the decision in principle to privilege, in an almost exclusive manner, the effect of dematerialization of reproducibility, and to thereby cancel any interest in the documents reproduced."[139]

In accordance with Weiner's "Declaration of Intent" the "exhibition" *Statements* (1968) consisted of twenty-five general and specific statements; textual constructions referring to a possible material execution, published in a book format. After Weiner participated in Siegelaub's exhibition at Windham College in April/May 1968, with a work (a grid of "staples, stakes, twine, turf," 70 × 100 inches with a 10 × 20 inch notch removed, 6 inches off the ground, topologically variable)[140] that was soon to be destroyed by students, he realized that it did not need to be executed again; the description of the work would suffice. From this moment on, Weiner allows the description of the work (the secondary information) to become the work itself (the primary information); in

137 Alberro 2003, p. 122.

138 See Stichting Egress Foundation, Seth Siegelaub, Exhibitions, Catalogues, Books & Projects, Interviews, Articles and Reviews, <www.egressfoundation.net/egress/index.php?option=com_content&view=article&id=64&Itemid=371> (26-9-2016).

139 Poinsot 1999, p. 106 ("La pratique inaugurée par Huebler et Siegelaub qui consistait, dans une situation conventionnelle de production et de présentation de l'art, à opérer un décrochage, une dissociation entre d'une part, l'idée de l'œuvre,—entendue au sens de large d'une proposition pouvant comporter de l'image et du langage reproductibles –, et, d'autre part, sa présentation, reposait principalement sur la décision de principe de privilégier de manière quasiment exclusive l'effet de dématérialisation de la reproductibilité pour annuler par là même tout intérêt pour les documents reproduits.") My translation.

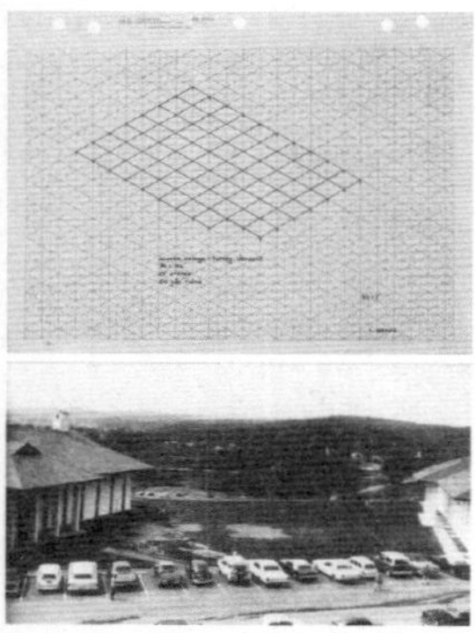

140 Lawrence Weiner, *Staples, Stakes, Twine and Turf*, design and installation view at Windham College, 1968.

his statements, the information that describes the work *equals* the existence of the work, and primary and secondary information become one and the same.[141]

In the case of the *Xerox Book*, the notion of primary and secondary information can eventually be interpreted either way, since each of the artists envisaged their own interpretation in its realization.[142] Nevertheless, Siegelaub's concept of primary and secondary information is applicable to the condition of the conceptual work itself, as Alberro emphasized. "It was now possible to split the artwork in what he [Siegelaub] referred to as 'primary information' ('the essence of the piece,' its ideational part), and 'secondary information' (the material information by which one becomes aware of the piece, the raw matter, the fabricated part, the form of presentation). This idealist conception of meaning as an *a priori* construct existing before its embodiment in form raised the issue of substitution and exchange in a social and economic sphere."[143] But this interpretation of primary and secondary information as a classical dichotomy of content and form is not sufficient to explain the complexities that are at stake within the exhibition of conceptual art. According to Poinsot, the "decoupling of the work and its presentation is a process that has contributed to endorse dematerialization, which was paralleled by the annexation of language and the real environment as concurring or interchangeable fields for the actualization of the work, as well as the utopian idea to substitute pure discursive activity in favor of some materialization that remains to be susceptible to alienation and fetishization."[144]

In the next exhibition that Siegelaub conceived, *January 5–31, 1969*,[145] the dilemma of these processes of exhibiting conceptual work became clear. The exhibition was installed in an empty office space at the McLendon Building in New York, although the physical presentation of the works,

141 For Weiner, the exhibitionary format of his statements was at first not important; a sheet of paper with the typed text was representative. Later he adhered to the spatial (re)-presentation of his text-based works.

142 Only Huebler, Kosuth, and Weiner made use of text as the primary material of their work for the *Xerox Book*; Andre used the technique of the Xerox machine to produce a work that he usually would not make in such a format; Barry made a piece with dots, and LeWitt included schematic drawings executed over the twenty-five pages. Morris showed photographs of planet Earth. Siegelaub stressed that his catalogue-exhibitions emerged from the several discussions he had with the artists with whom he worked. See Obrist 2011, p. 121.

143 Alberro 2003, p. 56. Alberro based his interpretation on an interview with Douglas Huebler in 1993, and on correspondence between Huebler and Siegelaub in 1966, from Siegelaub's archive.

144 Poinsot 1999, p. 105 ("D'une manière générale plusieurs processus ont contribué à avaliser cette dématérialisation: la dissociation de l'œuvre et de sa présentation, l'annexion du langage et du réel environnant comme champs concurrents ou interchangeables d'actualisation de l'œuvre, et enfin l'utopie d'une substitution d'une pure activité discursive à quelque matérialisation que ce soit toujours menacée d'aliénation et de fétichisation.")

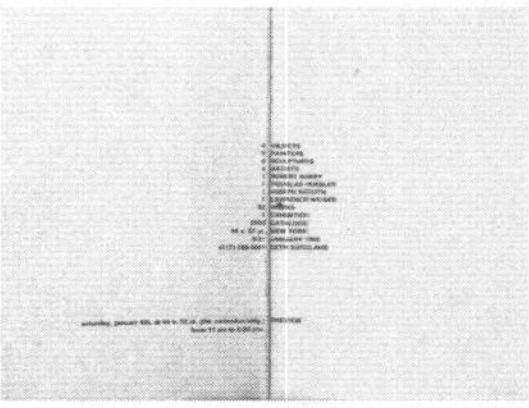

145 Invitation of Seth Siegelaub's *January 5–31, 1969* exhibition at 52nd Street, New York.

according to Siegelaub, was less important. "In my recollection the show exists entirely as a catalogue. After one and a half weeks we were not focusing our attention on the space anymore. It merely served as an office."[146] The project was referred to as "a group exhibition of the work of Robert Barry, Douglas Huebler, Joseph Kosuth and Lawrence Weiner in which the exhibition was the guide to the catalogue."[147] This implies that, for Siegelaub, the principles of the exhibition and its documentation in the catalogue had reversed. In this regard, as Poinsot has argued, the invitation of the *January 1969* show is illustrative: "the works have not disappeared [32 works], the objects count for nothing [0 objects] and the catalogue has an edition of 2000."[148]

Poinsot points out the contradictory character of the declarations of the artists in the catalogue, as well as the inconsistency in the making of an exhibition, to show something and at the same time deny the existence of that thing.[149] As he stated, "The denial of the exhibition, but not the renunciation of that practice, has been launched by the conceptual artists and their relative positions, especially the ones in the United States, in a particular polemic context. At the beginning of the 1960s, it appeared with utmost evidence that artistic activity is oriented towards the production of exhibitions, or events that take place, rather than towards the production of oeuvres that may eventually be exhibited."[150]

It was important to Siegelaub to refrain from the dominant strategies that the major museums and galleries applied, in order to change the methods of how art was received.[151] Although his projects might not have been as much a democratic endeavor as they were first proclaimed, as he later emphasized, they shared the intention to change the way in which art was presented and marketed by the big museums with the artists he worked with. "Isn't... one of the more important

146 Siegelaub, as cited in Honnef 1971, p. 27. My translation. Siegelaub nevertheless extensively documented the exhibition in the McLendon Building.

147 Egress Foundation website, <www.egressfoundation.net>.

148 Poinsot 1999, p. 106 ("L'arithmétique de l'invitation à l'exposition de janvier 1969 parle d'elle-même : les œuvres n'ont pas disparu, les objets ne comptent pour rien et les catalogues sont au nombre de deux mille. Pour lui [Siegelaub] les données sont inversées.")

149 Ibid., p. 104 ("Comment est-il possible de faire une exposition, de montrer quelque chose et simultanément d'en dénier l'existence en tant qu'œuvre ?")

150 Ibid. ("La dénégation de l'exposition, et non le renoncement à cette pratique, que vont entreprendre les artistes conceptuels et leurs proches prend place, et ceci plus particulièrement aux États-Unis, dans un contexte particulièrement polémique. Depuis le début des années soixante, il apparaît avec de plus d'évidence que l'activité artistique est orientée vers la production des expositions, ou des événements qui en tiennent lieu plus que vers la production d'œuvres susceptibles ultérieurement d'être exposées.")

151 Ibid.

functions of museums, to kill things, to finish them off, to give them the authority, and thus distance them from people by taking them out of their real everyday context? Even over and above the will of the actors involved with any given museum, I think the structure of museums tend toward this kind of activity: historicization. It is a sort of cemetery for art...."[152]

Interestingly enough, the museums rapidly adapted the new trend of catalogue-exhibitions that Siegelaub initiated. A number of important museums and institutions followed the model of the catalogue-exhibition, in which the exhibition's catalogue was used as an alternative space for projects that could not be exhibited in the traditional exhibition space. Examples are the catalogues of Wim Beeren's *Op losse schroeven* (Stedelijk Museum Amsterdam), Harald Szeemann's *When Attitudes Become Form* (Kunsthalle Bern), the Leverkusener *Konzeption-Conception* exhibition (Museum Schloss Morsbroich), Kynaston McShine's *Information* show (Museum of Modern Art, New York), Wim Beeren's *Sonsbeek buiten de perken* (Sonsbeek Park, Arnhem), and Harald Szeemann's Documenta 5 (Kassel).

The catalogue of Lucy Lippard's combined exhibitions *557,087*, at the Seattle Art Museum Pavilion (1969), and *955,000* at the Vancouver Art Gallery (1970), complemented Siegelaub's proposal to a large extent. It consisted of ninety-six and an additional forty-two unnumbered and unbounded index cards containing the works of the participating artists, as well as texts by Lippard, artists' quotes, and general information on the exhibition venues and project—all equally considered within the format of the 4 × 6 inch file card (10.2 × 15.3 cm).[153] The bulletins that were published by the Amsterdam *Art & Project* gallery applied their own format of exhibition parallel to these practices; art magazines such as *Studio International*[154] adopted the format and incidentally

152 In order to avoid the authority of museum spaces, as well as their cumbersome administrative structures (which galleries also have), Siegelaub developed a format that attempted to eliminate the overhead, such as rent, lighting, telephones, or secretary, "all the fixed expenses needed to maintain a permanent space." Obrist 2011, p. 120.

153 Lippard, but also Ursula Meyer, applied the same format in her early anthology on conceptual art; the same focus on the documentary materials of works that are collected in a publication can be distinguished here. For further information on the "Numbers Shows," see Butler 2012.

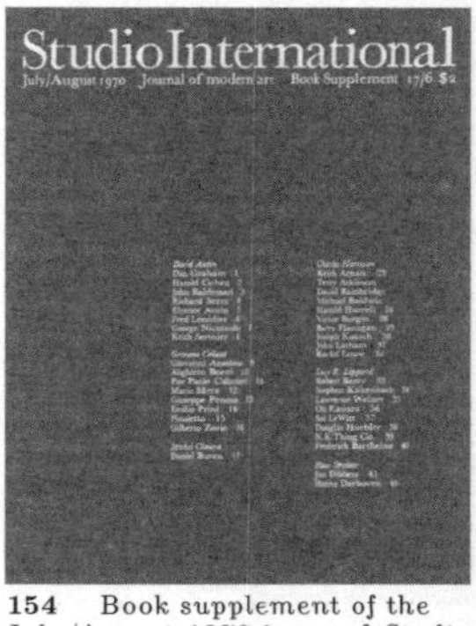

154 Book supplement of the July/August 1970 issue of *Studio International*, curated by Seth Siegelaub.

published "exhibitions," like the book supplement of the July/August 1970 issue with Siegelaub as guest editor, for which a number of curators were invited to "curate" a section of the journal.[155]

As Poinsot suggested, catalogues such as the abovementioned inverse the traditional model of the exhibition catalogue that merely consists of referential information next to the reproductions of autonomous works.[156] Instead, they provide "space" for every artist, open to either bio-bibliographic information or any photographic or textual information that involves or represents the work. The catalogue provided a stable model for the presentation of a type of art that, in a traditional exhibition setup, was very difficult to communicate.[157] According to Alberro, catalogues "as 'containers of information' that were 'unresponsive to the environment,' offered neutral sites in which to exhibit work."[158] He emphasized that Siegelaub restated on numerous occasions his intention to make the art he was promoting "known to the multitudes," and was well aware that catalogues could reach a much larger public than the more conventional material supports for art, "since the printed matter circulated in a myriad of different contexts and countries."[159]

The question is whether this was really the case, while it was not so much the catalogues that were circulating, but rather the artists themselves—traveling to different contexts and countries to install or present their works.[160] Significant to understand, however, is that the material realization of the idea, as in traditional object-based art, is deliberately left open; the secondary information, therefore, is not the materialization of the piece, but the presentation of an idea that may not always be an artwork. The role and meaning of documentation as a means to (re-)present the conceptual artwork should therefore be further examined.

155 Book Supplement of *Studio International* 17/6 (July/August 1970), with contributions by David Antin, Germano Celant, Michel Claura, Charles Harrison, Lucy R. Lippard, and Hans Strelow.

156 Poinsot 1999, p. 181 ("Cette invasion documentaire banalisée a conduit ceux qui, du fait même de la circulation rapide des œuvres et des informations, ne voulaient pas laisser une place indue à une information secondaire dont l'activation exigeait un travail encyclopédique du lecteur, à dénoncer à leur manière l'approximation et l'inintérêt de ces messages télégraphique." [In footnote:]"Il ne faut pas perdre de vue les difficultés soulevées par l'inflation du nombre de manifestations, le besoin de documentation énorme liée à un type de travail non réductible à une reproduction, les contrainte de place des publications et le désir légitime de leurs responsables à publier malgré tous ce qu'ils pouvaient considérer comme les informations les plus complète.")

157 A frequent comment made by visitors of early exhibitions of conceptual art was "Where's the exhibition?" because the spatial collection of words and papers was not accepted as an exhibition of works at the time.

158 Alberro 2003, p. 57.

159 Ibid.

160 As Konrad Fischer had stressed, instead of spending extensive budgets for the transport of big works, conceptual works of art could be sent by mail and the budget could be spent on accommodating the artists themselves, making the presence of the artist an important aspect of the work.

Newman's claim that "the necessity to make the [conceptual] work of art appear in one way or another meant that there were traces which remained (as notes and sketches or as documentation) that could consequently become marketable" proved contradictory to the concept of dematerialization and the rejection of the saleable object.[161] Although conceptual artists' rejection of the art object as a commodity and their preoccupations with the gallery system did not necessarily mean that they were against the selling of their work, the formats that they chose made that very difficult to achieve.[162] This is why Siegelaub's efforts as an organizer of catalogue/book-exhibitions were essential—surpassing the traditional function of the gallery as the place where art objects are being marketed and sold.

It was his intention to use the format of the book/catalogue as a possibility to distribute the artists' works to a specific, interested public, thus constructing a new market system for art that would generate income for the artists involved—an idea that was never fully realized.[163] In the same spirit, he developed, together with the New York lawyer Robert Projansky, his famous project "The Artist's Reserved Rights Transfer and Sale Agreement" (1971)—a contract that would give control to the artists over the financial aspects of their productions.[164] The "Artist's Contract," as it was also named, was distributed in four languages and served as an attempt to reform the dominant art market practices. It was sent to a number of museum curators and other art professionals but never became fully operative, although it did effect to some extent how art professionals dealt with (conceptual) works of art.[165]

Nevertheless, as conceptual art had separated art's "essence" from its presentation, and the exhibitionary format

161 Newman 1996, p. 105. My translation.

162 As Alexander Alberro suggested, "galleries survive only by selling products, and if the products cannot be displayed or have no material form, they are much more difficult, even impossible to market. But if some of the artists are antigallery, they are not necessarily antimarket," in Alberro and Norvell 2001, p. 11.

163 Siegelaub explained in an interview with Hans Ulrich Obrist that he thought artists should receive royalties when their works are reproduced, resold, exhibited, etc., just as applies to the work of composers, authors, and musicians. See Obrist 2011, p. 126.

164 For more information on this contract, see Alberro 2003, pp. 163–170.

165 Especially in Europe there was a great deal of interest in Siegelaub's contract; it was published in several art magazines (*Studio International* and *Museumjournaal*, among others) as well as in the catalogue of Documenta 5. As Siegelaub emphasized, "If it wasn't for the interest in the Contract by the people in Europe, like Harald Szeemann, or Germano Celant who worked on the Italian edition, it would have stayed as just an idea." See Maria Eichhorn, ed., *The Artist's Contract* (Cologne: Verlag der Buchhandlung Walther König, 2009), p. 41.

was by and large temporary or site-specific, documents or other (descriptive) documentation of these works were essential to transfer and conserve the work in one way or another.[166] To use documentation in their work was an aspect that most artists affiliated with conceptual art had accepted, to ensure evidence of what existed or occurred (as a historical validation), but it was also a problem for the artists, since the documentation of the works/events could be confused for the work itself. As Siegelaub explained, a "written statement about what was done.... Or two photographs... all this is a record of the work of art.... It's not the work of art."[167]

Ironically enough, the development of a new type of gallery at the end of the 1960s in Europe, the so-called "avant-garde gallery," generated a network that supported and distributed conceptual art at a large scale, already at a very early stage.[168] These new galleries, not unlike Siegelaub, worked in a personal and direct interaction with the artists and managed to mediate in making conceptual works accessible. Yet in doing so, the galleries also had to resolve the dilemma of conceptual art in some way, as illustrated by Siegelaub's statement, "In the case of Kosuth you have a newspaper. Even though it's not in fact the art, it's a record of the art—a public record of the art. Huebler has photographs.... But Barry is quite a bit different. There's absolutely nothing. Thus the challenge is how to make something out of nothing."[169] In this respect, as Barry himself has put it, "Certainly the galleries have had their influence on the way art looks."[170]

Indeed, as Alberro emphasized, it became retrospectively clear that "the artists... who have subsequently achieved the greatest commercial success are the ones who quickly figured out ways to provide the gallery with marketable documentation."[171] This fact, however, has given certain conceptual artists even more reason to be skeptical about the

166 As Ursula Meyer suggested in the early 1970s, "The aspect of documentation has become increasingly important for Conceptual Art. The camera as well as the Xerox machine can be used as dumb recording devices. Conceptual artists—among others On Kawara and Douglas Huebler—have used meaningless, everyday occurrences, maps, snapshots, diagrams as '*containers*' for their conceptions," Meyer 1972, pp. xi–xii. Emphasis mine.

167 Siegelaub, interviewed by Patricia Norvell in Alberro and Norvell 2001, p. 34.

168 For an extensive record on this, see Richard 2009.

169 Ibid., p. 7.

170 Alberro, in Alberro and Norvell 2001, p. 11.

171 Ibid., p. 12.

relation of the work to its documentation—sometimes changing their positions over the years.[172] Alberro states, "The very process that gives the photograph or other initially supplementary document (Siegelaub's 'secondary information') the value of art makes untenable the belief that art exists in an autonomous space or sphere, thus underscoring how completely art by the late 1960s had become a market-driven commodity. Perhaps this realization more than any other prompted so many of the artists... to remain ambivalent, if not apprehensive, about the relation of their work to its documentation."[173]

Consequently, to determine where the conceptual work of art ends and its documentation starts is not an easy task. The hesitation that various conceptual artists have expressed about the (confusion of) boundaries between artwork and document, between art and information about art, has proved still relevant today. Patricia Norvell's early interviews with the core group of conceptualists reveal some of the problems that these artists have with the documentation of their work. Robert Morris, for instance, stated, "Documentation is like a residue or sediment... but it's like one edge of the piece. And it has a sentimental value more than anything else. You can't locate the work in terms of its record. It's like a series of snapshots or something."[174] According to Norvell, Morris clearly predicates such comments on his worry that the public may unwittingly mistake the record for the art and thereby miss the artwork altogether. When examining many exhibitions with conceptual art today, one should admit that Morris's worry was not without reason, and many conceptual works have become what Boris Groys has termed "art documentation."[175] Art documentation, as Groys claims, "is by definition *not* art; it merely *refers* to art, and in precisely this way it makes clear that art, in this case, is no longer

172 Kosuth realized in the 1970s that the presentation of his work *One and Three Chairs* (1965?) had not been done properly at different venues. He then produced a certificate with very specific instructions for the installation of the work ("no other installation permittable"). See Poinsot 1999, pp. 42–43.

173 Alberro, in Alberro and Norvell 2001, p. 12.

174 Robert Morris, interviewed by Patricia Norvell in Alberro and Norvell 2001, p. 9.

175 Boris Groys, "Art in the Age of Biopolitics: From Artwork to Art Documentation," in Groys 2008, p. 53.

present and immediately visible but rather absent and hidden."[176]

Groys distinguished two different manners in which art documentation refers to art. First, art documentation may refer to art events that were present and visible at a particular time, like performances, temporary installations, or happenings that are documented, and the documentation is later exhibited as a means to recollect the original event. A second type of art documentation, which is increasingly being produced and exhibited, does not claim to make present any past art event: "Examples include complex and varied artistic interventions in daily life, lengthy and complicated processes of discussion and analysis, the creation of unusual living circumstances, artistic exploration into the reception of art in various cultures and milieus, and politically motivated artistic actions."[177] Since these artistic activities take place within the structures and processes of daily life and are therefore not a product or result of a "creative" activity, according to Groys, they cannot be presented except by means of art documentation. In such cases, "art documentation is neither the making present of a past event nor the promise of a coming artwork, but rather… the only possible form of reference to an artistic activity that cannot be represented in any other way."[178]

Whereas this first type of art documentation can be determined as the mere recording of an event, the second type is more paradoxical and diffuse in nature, both applicable to a variety of conceptual artworks. Correspondingly, Siegelaub's primary and secondary information could be similarly determined: if the art activity, or art practice cannot be (re-)presented in any other way than by means of documentation, it could be considered primary information; if the practice or activity has taken place within a specific time frame, and has been recorded as such, it could be considered secondary

176 Ibid.

177 Ibid., p. 54.

178 Ibid.

information. The second type of art documentation, which may comprise photographs, diagrams, written statements, sketches, books, catalogues, or other referential materials, principally allows a reproduction of the "original" event.[179]

As this may generally be relevant to conceptual artworks, different artists have different ideas about how to deal with the referential material adjoining their projects. In the work of various artists, documentation can either accompany or visualize the artwork, or end up somewhere in the middle, as in the work of Douglas Huebler. In Huebler's work it is difficult to separate the documentation from the artwork; they are interrelated. As he distinctively stated, "The world is full of objects, more or less interesting. I do not wish to add any more. I prefer, simply, to state the existence of things in terms of time and/or place. More specifically, the work concerns itself with things whose inter-relationship is beyond direct perceptual experience. Because the work is beyond direct perceptual experience, awareness of the work depends on a system of documentation. This documentation takes the form of photographs, maps, drawings, and descriptive language."[180] Considering the map as a documentary format, Huebler clearly illuminates his point when he writes, "The map is only a chart, you know. It isn't [a] real thing, and yet we begin to assume it is a real thing."[181]

As Alberro suggested, "the real thing" for Huebler is the ephemeral art event, but this elusive concept does not apply to every conceptual artist. Weiner, for instance, states that "an event can never be art."[182] Nevertheless, Huebler incorporated documentation into the initial process of production of his work, preferring to have an active hand in to determine which of its traces will remain. He proclaimed that "it's the documents that carry the idea. And documents have to exist."[183] Alberro emphasized that, for LeWitt, documen-

179 Roland Barthes, *La Chambre claire* (Paris: Cahiers du Cinéma; Gallimard; éd. Du Seuil, 1980), p. 126 and p. 16 ("La photo est littéralement une émanation du référent. [...] Telle photo, en effet, ne se distingue jamais de son référent [de ce qu'elle représente], ou du moins elle ne s'en distingue pas tout de suite ou pour tout le monde [ce que fait n'importe quelle image, encombrée dès l'abord et par statut de la façon dont l'objet est simulé]," as cited in Poinsot 1999, p. 98. "Barthes puise un grand plaisir... dans cette motivation du signe photographique, dans le fait que l'image présente sous ses yeux se donne pour l'enregistrement de l'avoir-été-là de l'objet ou de l'être représenté. Il renvoie du même coup tout ce qui sert à la représentation dans une rôle secondaire vis-à-vis de ce qui concourt à présenter encore. Les œuvres *in situ* donnent de même l'impression d'une révélation, d'une mise en prise directe de l'observateur avec la 'vérité' du réel qui l'entoure [e.g., the works of Sol LeWitt at the grande nef du Museé d'art contemporain Bordeaux (*Wall Drawing #2*, 1968/1990)]. Ce qui importe, c'est qu'effectivement le savoir-faire de l'artiste... est moins mobilisé pour représenter, figurer, former que pour établir une relation de contiguïté, voire de solidarité entre le réel et ce qui est donné à percevoir, où ce qui est figuré ou formé, l'est sous l'espèce de cette relation de motivation. [...] Ainsi, nombre d'œuvres 'site specific' ont été portées à la vue de leur public au moyen de cette émanation du référent qu'est la photographie.)

180 Douglas Huebler, in *January 5–31, 1969*, exh. cat. New York (Seth Siegelaub) 1969, as cited in Lippard 1973, p. 29.

181 Ibid.

182 See Alberro, in Alberro and Norvell 2001, p. 9.

183 Ibid., pp. 7–8.

tation not only functions as a record but also, "like a musical score, elaborates further on the work."[184] In his conceptual wall drawings,[185] however, LeWitt never shows the working drawings or the instructions or diagrams for their execution; these are explicitly declared not to be the work of art.[186]

In the case of Weiner's propositions, documentary material is never used by the artist himself, as he explains, "sharing my work would be done by publishing a book, just the statements *per se* of the work. It would be just as good as if the work was built."[187] Weiner considered the documentation to be distracting, "which is why I prefer for the work originally to be seen just in language.... I don't take photographs."[188] However, records of early text-based works that were executed by the artist, such as *The Residue of a Flare Ignited Upon a Boundary* (1969, for *Op losse schroeven*),[189] which is usually represented by a photograph of Weiner preparing the flare on the quay of an Amsterdam canal, do exist and can easily be confused for the work itself. An artist like Barry is for this reason explicitly rejecting documentation, believing that "documentation sort of gets in the way of art.... Some of the documentation has to be so involved that it just becomes like a little art object itself."[190]

Yet Barry has also produced documentation to "contain" his work that (eventually) became the artwork itself. Most well-known is the documentation of his invisible *Inert Gas* series,[191] a series of photographs of locations where he released various gases into the atmosphere, which have been exhibited at different venues worldwide and have never been questioned not to be the artwork, could even be defined some sort of "photo-conceptualism." Even the invitation card of his *Closed Gallery Piece* (1969), with the illustrious text "During the exhibition the gallery will be closed," has gained the status of an artwork. Because of the work's historicization, or

184 Ibid.

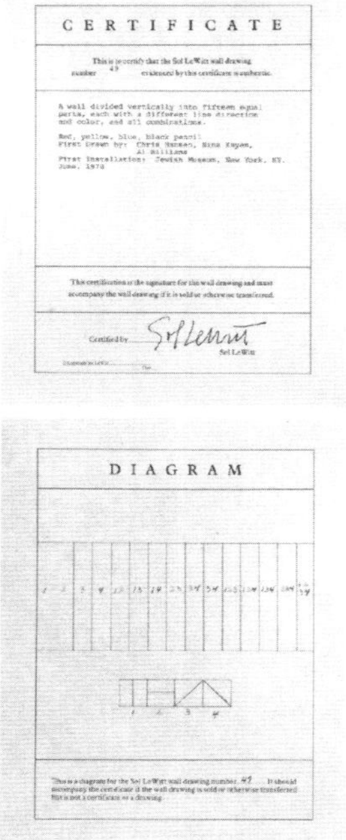

185 Sol LeWitt, certificate and diagram of *Wall Drawing #49*, 1970.

186 See Nathalie Zonnenberg, "Free Sol LeWitt & In-Between Minimalisms," *Manifesta Journal* no. 10 (2009–2010), pp. 98–103. In this article, I extensively analyze the character of Sol LeWitt's certificates.

187 Weiner, in "Art without Space" symposium, as cited in Lippard 1973, p. 128.

188 Lawrence Weiner, interviewed by Patricia Norvell in Alberro and Norvell 2001, p. 6. After his initial works, Weiner continued to produce text-based works that incorporate space; he defined them as "sculptures."

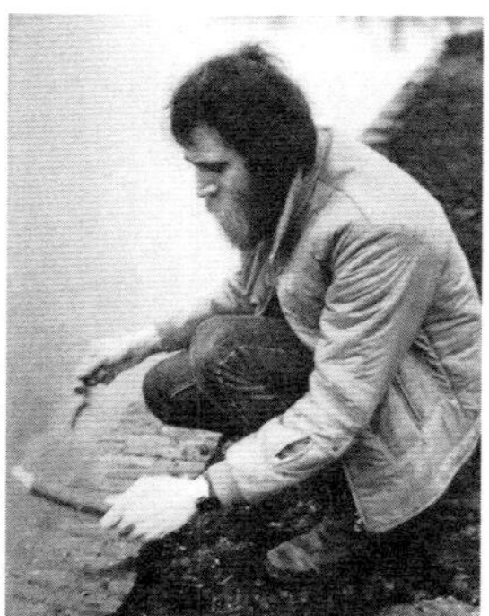

189 Lawrence Weiner, *The Residue of a Flare Ignited Upon a Boundary*, 1969.

190 Robert Barry, interviewed by Patricia Norvell in Alberro and Norvell 2001, p. 8.

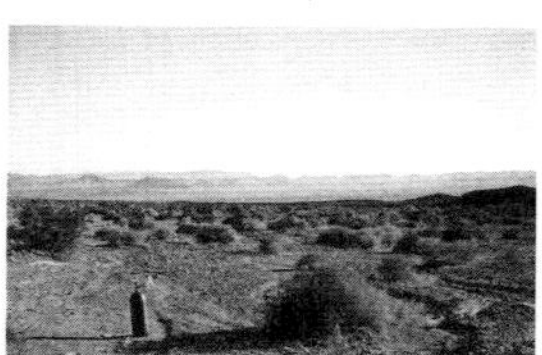

191 Robert Barry, *Inert Gas Series/Helium, Mojave Desert*, 1969.

canonization, by authors like McEvilley and others, collectors considered the document/invitation card as a desirable object to purchase.[192] The confusion between work and documentation made several conceptual artists very rigorous in their conceptual practices. The Dutch artist Stanley Brouwn, for example, persistently refused to allow documentary material (i.e., secondary information) to be included in catalogues or other representational formats. Alternatively, Daniel Buren determined all records of his *in situ* works "photo souvenirs" that are not supposed to be exhibited as such (although they were eventually).[193]

In order to determine to what extent the documentation of conceptual works is freestanding, and to what extent it is merely an archival record of something that did or did not take place, it is important to consider what Poinsot termed "les récits autorisés" (authorized records).[194] In examining the installations of the work *One and Three Chairs* by Kosuth,[195] he points out that the repetitive false exhibition of the work (in Centre Pompidou and MoMA) made the artist decide to produce specific certificates over the course of the 1970s that contain explicit instructions for installation (as in, "no other installation permittable").[196] In several of Kosuth's notations, Poinsot recognized "points where the artist doesn't support improvisation and usages where he has asserted them before."[197] But the difficulties encountered in the work of Kosuth do not stand on their own. Poinsot emphasizes that all works can be subject to misinterpretations, even the most conventional, if not preserved in authorized records. They can be found in different types of auctorial documents, such as comments, declarations, notes and illustrations, catalogues, projects, certificates, instructions, reviews, and descriptions for installation, and all other information that the artist has recognized at the time a work was conceived. These

192 See McEvilley's explanation of this work in "Anti-Art as Cognition: Themes and Strategies," in McEvilley 2005, p. 96.

193 Buren also established clauses on rights of reproduction, exhibition, attributing provenance, etc., in his *Avertissement*, a juridical contract he wrote together with his half-brother and lawyer Michel Claura in 1968–1969, and used for the sale of his work ever since. See Maria Eichhorn, "On the *Avertissement*: Interview with Daniel Buren (1998)," in *Institutional Critique and After*, ed. John C. Welchman (Zurich: JRP/Ringier, 2006), pp. 85–122.

194 Poinsot 1999, pp. 42–43: "Ces récits autorisés sont les commentaires, les déclarations, les notes qui flanquent les illustrations (reproductions) et éventuellement ces illustrations elles-mêmes dans les catalogues, les projets, certificats, notices de montage, recensions et descriptions a posteriori propres à l'art d'installation, mais aussi toutes les 'informations', tracts et autres documents que l'artiste diffuse dans le temps de sa prestation. Ces récits émanant directement de l'artiste s'imposent comme garants des véritables intentions de l'artiste. Ils portent à la fois le projet que l'artiste a de son œuvre et les interprétations légitimes qu'il lui reconnait. Ces récits sont proprement institutionnels, car systématiquement associés à la production des expositions ou conçus comme des moyens d'en assurer la 'possible répétition.' (...) Les récits autorisés permettent ainsi de préserver, ou du moins de faire savoir en quoi consiste l'intégrité des œuvres exposées et peuvent par les indications pratiques qu'ils donnent permettre de ne pas se tromper sur le statut sémiotique des composantes du signe esthétique."

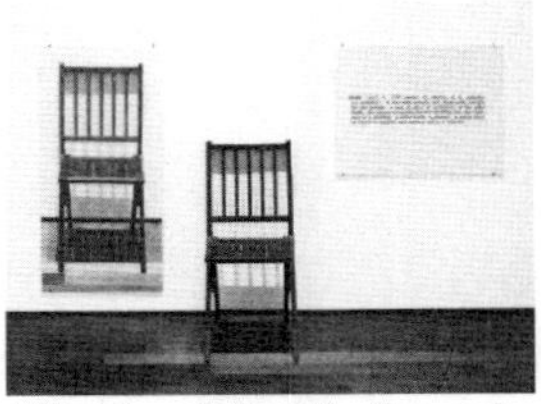

195 Joseph Kosuth, *One and Three Chairs*, 1965.

196 Poinsot 1999, pp. 42–43: "Tirant les lecons des installations fautives, certain certificats produits par Kosuth dans le cours des annees soixante-dix ont commencé à comporter des instructions d'installation circonstanciées et imperatives ('no other installation permittable')."

197 Ibid.

documents, according to Poinsot, can be regarded as veritable references of the initial intentions of the artist and provide legitimate information for the actualization or potential reappearance of his work.

The certificate of authenticity is the most explicit and legally verifiable form of such documents, which has been developed by and accompanied the works of several artists at the end of the 1960s. In some cases—LeWitt's, for instance—the distinction between the work and the documentary or accompanying materials that support the work are contained in the certificate and thus instructive for executing the work. As LeWitt has stated, "The people who buy the certificate usually also have the supplementary photograph or the diagram, and the certificate can also be used as a program for the realization of the piece as a musical partition. The wall drawings are temporary and could be redone. It's relatively simple…"[198] Yet even in these works, misinterpretations have been made and the certificates have been exhibited as if they are the artwork.[199]

The principle difficulty within such works, as Poinsot has asserted, "lies in the fact that they integrate a part of the world, a fragment of the real, and thus implicate the keeper/owner of the piece in a particular responsibility, who is then assigned to make concrete decisions in order to realize the work."[200] Although, generally speaking, the certificate should provide the modalities of realization that are consigned by the artist, essential specifications, practical as well as conceptual, are often lacking. In the case of LeWitt, to make sure that his certificates are realized in the correct manner the artist developed a method to carry out the wall drawings that has been explicated in several texts by his hand.[201] As he stated, the realization of the work should only be done by "the proper draftsmen," who can be found in assistants situated all

198 "Les gens qui achètent le certificat ont aussi habituellement la photographie ou le diagramme qui l'accompagne et le certificat peut aussi être utilisé comme un programme pour réaliser la pièce comme le partitions de musique. Les dessins muraux sont temporaires et peuvent être refaits. C'est relativement simple…" Unedited interview with Sol LeWitt on February 19, 1987, as cited in Poinsot 1999, p. 162.

199 For example, in the exhibition *In-Between Minimalisms* at the Van Abbemuseum in Eindhoven in 2010. See Zonnenberg 2009–2010, pp. 98–103.

200 Poinsot 1999, p. 162. My translation.

201 "The artist conceives and plans the wall drawing. It is realized by the draftsmen (the artist can operate as the proper draftsman); the plan (drawn, spoken, or designed) is interpreted by the draftsman. The artist has to authorize different interpretations of his plan. The artist and the draftsman become collaborators in the fabrication of the art." Sol LeWitt, in "Wall Drawings," *Arts Magazine* 44, no. 6 (April 1970), p. 45, and "Doing Wall Drawings," *Art Now* vol. 3, no. 2 (June 1971), n.p., reprinted in *Sol LeWitt*, exh. cat. New York (Museum of Modern Art) 1978, p. 169, as cited in Poinsot 1999 p. 164.

around the world and should be approved by the LeWitt Estate.[202] These specifications, however, have never been included in the certificate. The signed certificate, as Poinsot points out, thus merely functions as a testimony of an authentic work but it does not guarantee the correct handling of the auctorial responsibility. In this respect the certificate can even further complicate how the specific conceptual work of art should be determined within the shared auctorial responsibility that it involves, and again creates further misunderstanding about the status of these particular documents.

That many artists such as LeWitt, but also Dan Flavin, Joseph Kosuth, Gordon Matta-Clark, Richard Long, and others, make note on their certificates that these are not the artwork and cannot or should not be duplicated, is indicative of the fact that their potential use is subject to various assumptions. The causes of misuse or misinterpretation of the certificates are not difficult to understand, as Poinsot asserted, while the art market is still attached to objects and not to "deeds" (*prestations*).[203] As Barry emphasized, the conceptual work of art also adapted itself to be able to negotiate such "deeds," but in doing so might have surpassed its initial goal. However, museums and galleries do not support artists in order to interfere with the basic goals of their existence. Diverse attempts to change the principles of the art market, such as Siegelaub and Projanski's Artist's Contract, have not accommodated or certified the right of "demonstration." The reproductions or documents of artists' activities that are not provided with some sort of authentification or signature indication have not gained economic significance, and as such remain invisible in the system of art.[204]

In the rare cases where the certificate leaves little room for interpretation other than the artist's will, as in the case of Daniel Buren, a lifetime awareness regarding the work

202 LeWitt 1970.

203 Susan Hapgood and Cornelia Lauf use the term "deed" to describe the aspect of the artwork's manifestation that is often contained in a certificate in conceptual art. Susan Hapgood and Cornelia Lauf, "Doodles, Deeds and Claims," in Hapgood and Lauf 2011, p. 78.

204 Poinsot 1999, p. 165.

ceaselessly binds the collector to the artist. Together with his half-brother Michel Claura, a lawyer and curator, Buren produced certificates to the extent that the work cannot exist without it, and may not be sold at auction without the artist's approval. Also, the contract cannot be reproduced without the artist's permission.[205] Whereas Siegelaub and Projanski's Artist's Contract[206] was modeled after Buren's, it may come as no surprise that it also offers little foundation for the continued existence of conceptual artworks, but is merely based upon the sale of the work.[207]

According to Siegelaub, Buren "always used some kind of contract concerning the placement and the use of his work, because they are site-specific and he is very careful about his interests when the piece is sold. There have been a number of people, like Carl Andre, Sol LeWitt, and especially Hans Haacke, who have used The Artist's Reserved Rights Transfer and Sale Agreement.... In fact, most artists were not that interested at all, more against it than for it."[208] It was very difficult to implement contracts in the art business at the time because, according to Siegelaub, "During the late 1960s and early '70s, the art world was in a state of relative poverty and thus the Contract was seen as just another problem in selling work."[209] Lawrence Alloway suggested an interesting critique that the artists might have had in this respect, considering the contract would attach the artist to an eternal curation of his or her work—an activity to which many artists are not likely to submit, but emphasizes the impending role of the curator.[210]

At the time, however, Siegelaub was not so much concerned with the intervention of the curator, but instead emphasized the role of the collector. He mentioned that he presumed Herman Daled, Anton Herbert, or Panza had signed his contract, but for many collectors it was only complicating sales. "In the late 1960s when the issue of artists'

205 Hapgood and Lauf 2011, p. 81.

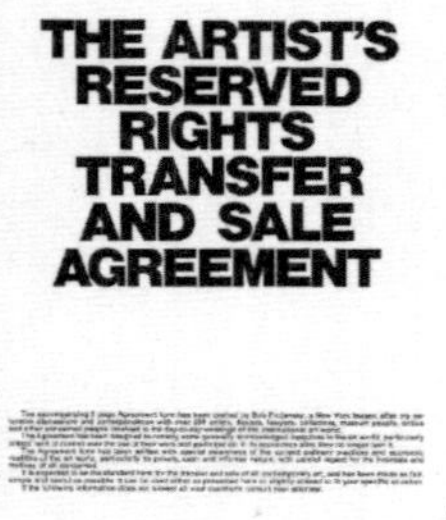
THE ARTIST'S RESERVED RIGHTS TRANSFER AND SALE AGREEMENT

206 Seth Siegelaub and Robert Projansky, *The Artist's Reserved Rights Transfer and Sale Agreement*, 1971.

207 Siegelaub mentioned that there were no artists involved in the drawing up of the contract, but a precedent for its form was Daniel Buren. See Eichhorn 2009, p. 41.

208 Ibid.

209 Eichhorn 2009, p. 41.

210 Lawrence Alloway, "'Reality': Ideology at D5," *Artforum* 11 (October 1972), p. 31, as cited in Hapgood and Lauf 2011, p. 81.

rights was becoming more important, some gallery owners were enthusiastic about the idea of a contract and said they would use it, while others were absolutely against it. I remember in particular André Emmerich in New York who said people wouldn't buy art anymore."[211] In this respect the responses of two curators to Siegelaub's distributed contract, included in Maria Eichhorn's book *The Artist's Contract* (2009), are quite revealing. Jean Leering, director of the Van Abbemuseum in Eindhoven, replied to Siegelaub as follows:

> My opinion is twofold: a. The agreement would mean a strengthening of the capitalistic point of view. To my opinion art has nothing to do with money: the aspect of the (art)-work (as object), which has to do with money, is its stamp-value; its rareness. To proof [*sic*] this we have only to look to objects of architecture: after having paid the architect's fee one does not pay the artistic value any more; any expectation regarding increase of value of a piece of architecture is in vain because of its immobility. b. I do not think you did study, as is said, every facet of this question, because a very important element is missing: the role of the public in the appreciation of art.... That is the reason I do not agree with your veto for the artists. By this I think you are making larger the existing gap between art and public.[212]

Harald Szeemann replied, "Your paper is a very good idea and a very useful thing if it is really applicated [*sic*]... we can of course distribute it during Documenta next year. The only critique I have about it: The Contract is finally only through its distribution and through its author a work for the so called avant-garde. This means that if it's not used by all the local artists all over the world it doesn't become what you think it should be."[213]

211 Eichhorn 2009.

212 Ibid., pp. 32–35.

213 Ibid.

214 Weiner, in conversation with Cornelia Lauf, as cited in Hapgood and Lauf 2011, p. 86.

215 See Alberro 2003, p. 147.

216 Hapgood and Lauf 2011, p. 80.

Especially Leering's reaction illuminates the contradictory aspect in the contract that tried to secure the position of the artist only in terms of capital. Weiner had similarly pointed out this deficit, and for this reason had never made use of the contract. According to Weiner, the contract is contradictory, as "it is geared to an artist's work being protected only if it gains in value. If it diminishes in value, the owner is under no obligation to compensate the artist and thus participate in the gamble that the artist intrinsically faces."[214] The other aspect Leering points out, the difficulty of adequately implementing the contract's consequences in museum practices to make it accessible to the public, also seems contradictory in regard to the work of conceptual artists such as Weiner, who reserved a number of his statements to function in the "collection public freehold." In principle these works could be "owned" or used by anyone who, for instance, purchased the catalogue or book in which they were published. Weiner also distinguishes "private freehold," which refers to the works that are principally owned by the person or organization that paid for them, "where the only people that can own the piece are the people who ask for it when it's freehold," in the artist's words.[215]

Regarding private freehold, however, Weiner has little concern to reassure his collectors, as Cornelia Lauf and Susan Hapgood have pointed out. "He takes the barest steps necessary in his documentary practice by recording ownership of his works through letters that he sent to an archive (formerly to its lawyer, Jerald Ordover) and to the owner, whom he often refers to as having 'accepted responsibility' for the work of art. Weiner's practice makes clear that there is a condition of trust involved, implying that no amount of coddling, documentation, or binding verbiage will accomplish much."[216] It is important to reconsider the implications of the involved responsibility, or the "proof of receivership" that Weiner provides. Whereas the private collector can have his personal engagement to this document, the museum of contemporary art has the task of somehow "disclosing" the works in its collection to the public—possibly applying methods of reconstruction or refabrication. Therefore, it is first and foremost relevant to not categorically define the documents as autonomous artworks, but rather as *signs* that contain information *representing* an artwork; they refer to a possible work of art, but are not by definition themselves works of art—or at least not in some final or definite form.[217]

As Hapgood claimed, "The artist's initial intention would be important to a reconsideration of refabrication, but it would not be the sole factor... due to inherent conflicts of interest, refabrication decisions should not rest in the hands of any single party—museum, gallery, collector, or artist."[218] Since the original context of artworks at the time of their first public exhibition, including the participation of the curator, has often determined the artwork in the case of conceptual art, it is crucial to take the curatorial histories and methodologies of conceptual art into account to define the current ontological condition of conceptual works of art. After briefly reevaluating the general literature on conceptual art and its shifting terminologies, and the analysis of three specific notions of conceptual art, the curatorial mission within conceptual art's dilemma of exhibition has become most apparent. This reevaluation of the discourse on conceptual art, from the early artists' texts to more theoretical assertions concerning the aesthetic strategies of conceptual art, will serve as a framework to assess the three case studies presented in the following chapters.

217 See also Groys 2008.

218 Susan Hapgood, "Remaking Art History," *Art in America* vol. 78, no. 7 (July 1990), p. 181.

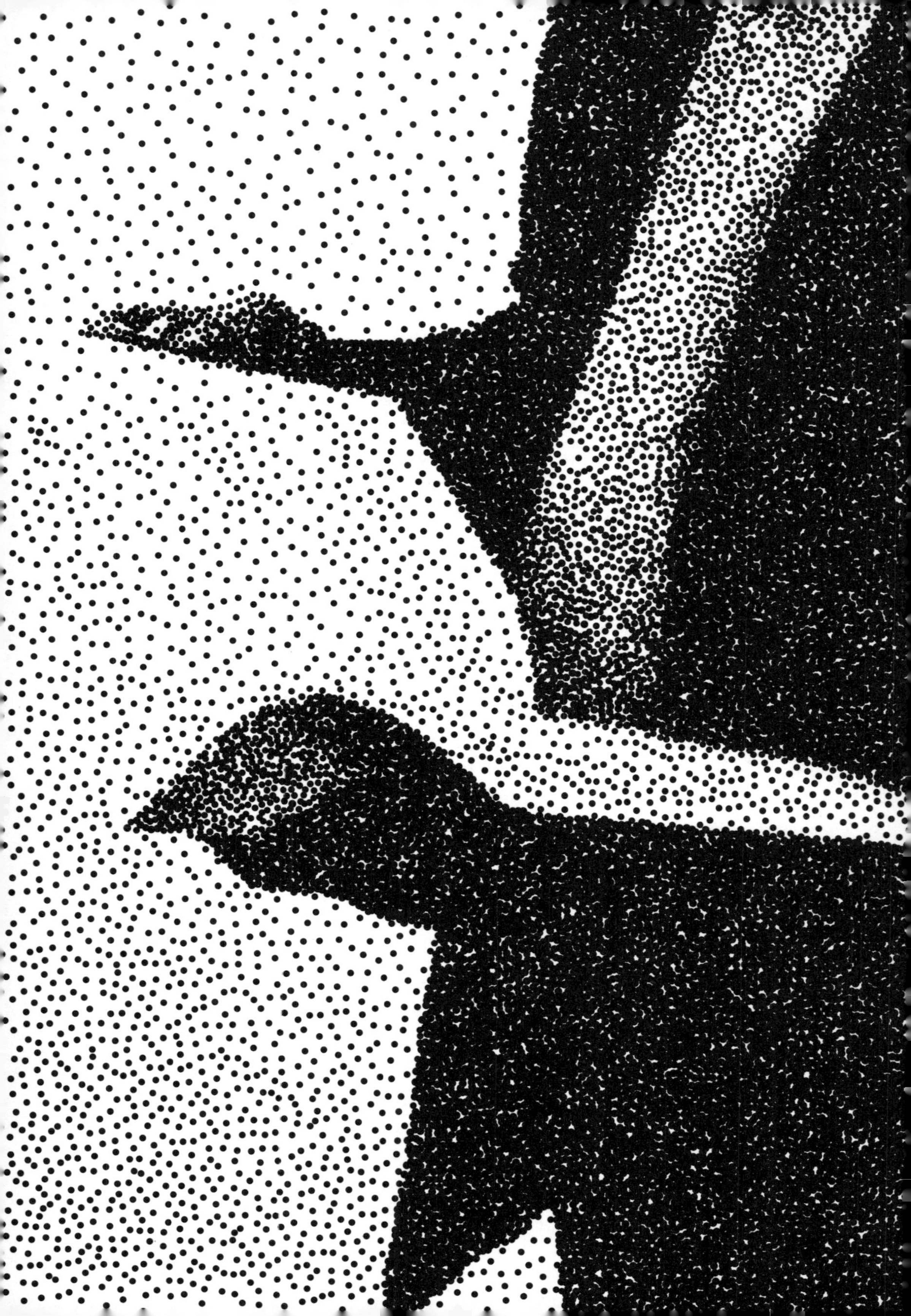

Chapter 2
Case Study
Konzeption–Conception: Documentation of a To-day's Art Tendency
at the Städtisches Museum Schloss Morsbroich Leverkusen (1969)

Museums are an archive of visual art. And when a museum puts on an exhibition of contemporary art it ought to do so in a museum-like way, that is, logically and coherently. Extending a tradition into the future: that's the way a museum ought to raise the value of tradition, through bringing in new tendencies, and not depreciate it as usually happens today.
— Konrad Fischer[1]

1 Georg Jappe, "Konrad Fischer interviewed by Georg Jappe," *Studio International* vol. 181, no. 930 (February 1971), p. 71.

A First Overview of Conceptual Art

Among the flood of conceptual art exhibitions that took place around the world in 1969, *Konzeption-Conception: Documentation of a To-day's Art Tendency* may not seem the most prominent.[2] Nonetheless, this exhibition, curated by Konrad Fischer and Rolf Wedewer and shown at the Städtisches Museum Schloss Morsbroich in Leverkusen from October 10 until November 30, 1969, can be considered the first overview show of conceptual art in Europe.[3] The

2 The year 1969 proved paramount to conceptual art, with Seth Siegelaub's *January* and *March 1969* exhibitions in New York, *Op losse schroeven* at the Stedelijk Museum in Amsterdam, *When Attitudes Become Form* at the Kunsthalle in Bern, and Lucy Lippard's *557,087* at the pavilion of the Seattle Art Museum, among others. Significant projects of conceptual art, however, preceded these exhibitions, such as Mel Bochner's *Working Drawings* show at the School of Visual Arts in New York (1966), Paul Maenz's *19:45–21:55, September 9th, 1967, Frankfurt, Germany* at the Dorothea Loehr Galerie in Frankfurt (1967), and Germano Celant's *Arte Povera + Azioni Povere* in Amalfi (1968). For a more complete record of events and activities in 1969, see Lucy Lippard's *Six Years*.

3 The exhibition included works by Keith Arnatt, John Baldessari, Robert Barry, Iain Baxter, Bernd & Hilla Becher, Mel Bochner, Alighiero Boetti, Marcel Broodthaers, Stanley Brouwn, Daniel Buren, Victor Burgin, Donald Burgy, Eugenia P. Butler, Pier Paolo Calzolari, Paul Cotton, Hanne Darboven, Jan Dibbets, Hamish Fulton, Gilbert & George, Dan Graham, Douglas Huebler, Richard Jackson, Stephen Kaltenbach, On Kawara, Michael Kirby, Joseph Kosuth, David Lamelas, Sol LeWitt, Bruce McLean, Bruce Nauman, Guiseppe Penone, Adrian Piper, Sigmar Polke, Emilio Prini, Markus Raetz, Allen Ruppersberg, Ed Ruscha, Fred Sandback, Richard Sladden, Robert Smithson, Timm Ulrichs, Bernar Venet, Lawrence Weiner, and Zaj (Walter Marchetti).

Image appropriated from Marcel Broodthaers looking into the catalogue *Konzeption–Conception*, 1969. Original photo Traudel Schmitz/Stadtarchiv Leverkusen. See also p. 97.

municipal museum Schloss Morsbroich, based in a former Baroque castle, was the first postwar museum in North Rhine-Westphalia dedicated to contemporary art, and held a relatively progressive course during the directorship of Wedewer (1965–1995). When he proposed his exhibition to the culture committee of the city of Leverkusen, conceptual art had already obtained some recognition in Germany, as Kunsthalle Düsseldorf director Jürgen Harten stated in an interview on *Prospect 69* earlier that year.[4] It thus seems appropriate that the proposal was unanimously accepted.[5] Being an art historian, Wedewer had frequently published on new tendencies in painting, and acquired many works of Art Informel, Zero, Op art, and analytic and monochrome painting for the museum's collection. In his catalogue introduction, he placed conceptual art within an art historical continuum more specifically aligned to Earth or Land art: "Out of this emerged Conceptual art that, for the first time, represents an art that only consists of planning sketches whose execution and transformation into the final work of art is considered of secondary importance and, therefore, can be dismissed."[6]

It seems ambiguous that Wedewer co-curated the exhibition with Fischer, who was the main dealer of many of the artists involved; about half of the artists in the show (twenty out of forty-four) were represented by him. Most likely, Fischer's particular expertise on conceptual art and contacts within the scene, which he had been establishing since 1967, was preferable to any possible objections.[7] His intermediary role at the time was outstanding, as Brigitte Kölle proclaims in her thesis "Die Kunst des Ausstellens. Untersuchungen zum Werk des Künstlers und Kunstvermittlers Konrad Lueg/Fischer (1939–1996)": "The way in which the traditional, limited distribution of tasks between cultural producer and cultural mediator was broken open [is] something for which

4 Harten stated that the phenomenon of conceptual art was known in Germany for about one and a half years. Broadcasting of *Das Feuilleton*, Deutschlandfunk, Wednesday October 1, 1969 (21:40–22:00). Stadtarchiv Düsseldorf (IV 29367).

5 A note dated July 14, 1969, reads that the exhibition "Konzeptkunst" was approved by the culture committee. Stadtarchiv Leverkusen (410.1302).

6 Rolf Wedewer, "Introduction," in *Konzeption—Conception: Documentation of a Today's Art Tendency*, eds. Konrad Fischer and Rolf Wedewer, in exh. cat. Leverkusen (Städtisches Museum Schloss Morsbroich), 1969, n.p. Transation by Nora Alter in Alberro and Stimson 1999, p. 142.

7 Fischer's leading role for the production, distribution, and reception of conceptual art, especially in Europe, is extensively described in Brigitte Kölle's study "Die Kunst des Ausstellens: Untersuchungen zum Werk des Künstlers und Kunstvermittlers Konrad Lueg/Fischer (1939–1996)," (dissertation University of Hildesheim, 2005). Also, Sophie Richard emphasized Fischer's position as the major dealer of conceptual art in Europe. See Richard 2009.

Konrad Fischer, like almost no other figure in the second half of the 20th century, exemplarily stands."[8] As mediator and advisor, as well as the lender of a great number of conceptual works, Fischer had already taken a significant role in *Op losse schroeven* in Amsterdam and *When Attitudes Become Form* in Bern and at the Haus Lange in Krefeld; in Leverkusen, he extended this role as the (co-)curator of the exhibition.[9]

The enterprise of making an institutional show that historically founded the type of art that Fischer was representing as a new art "movement" must surely have been beneficial to the emerging status of his gallery. It can therefore be questioned to what extent *Konzeption* fits into a commercial strategy that Fischer was developing at the time. Almost simultaneously with the exhibition in Leverkusen, together with Hans Strelow he organized the art fair/exhibition *Prospect 69* at the Kunsthalle Düsseldorf, which was more specifically conceived as a promotional event. Remarkably, the commercial *Prospect 69* was rather positively received by the press, whereas *Konzeption* was more disapprovingly received as "a show that showed nothing at all."[10] It is not unlikely that Fischer in his overloaded role as curator-dealer had to make decisions about where to put his focus, and the exhibition in Leverkusen was of lower priority than the art fair/exhibition that he was organizing in the prosperous milieu of Düsseldorf.[11] But it may also be that the latter exhibition, in its first attempt to categorize the new phenomenon of conceptual art, was more radical, and therefore more exemplary than the former.

Although the exhibition has been largely credited in the historiography of conceptual art, a thorough study of *Konzeption* has never been made, possibly due to a lack of visual documentation.[12] Lucy Lippard and Klaus Honnef refer to the exhibition in their early anthologies of conceptual

8 Kölle 2005, p. 6.

9 Fischer boldly stated, "There's hardly a single big exhibition that's not put on with my help. Think of *Attitudes* or the Conceptual Art show in Leverkusen, or the Haus Lange show, to mention only those near here." Jappe 1971, p. 71. Kölle writes, "Fischer, der viele der in Amsterdam und Bern eingeladenen Künstler wie Carl Andre, Hanne Darboven, Sol LeWitt, Reiner Ruthenbeck, Robert Ryman, Fred Sandback und andere vertritt, ist ein wichtiger Leihgeber dieser Ausstellungen und beim Aufbau und bei den Eröffnungen der Ausstellungen persönlich anwesend." Kölle 2005, pp. 51–52.

10 Fischer conceived and organized several editions of *Prospect* together with Hans Strelow at the Kunsthalle Düsseldorf between 1968 and 1976 as an alternative "art fair" that was meant to counter the Cologne art fair (founded in 1967), which concentrated on German galleries only. Fischer wanted to open up a more international and avant-garde type of art fair, and asked several galleries from both Europe and the United States to collaborate. This initiative, accurately compiled for the Kunsthalle, has been generally received as an exhibition. Around 1972, however, there was an increasing critique on his positioning and the conflict of business and autonomous artistic interests. This eventually led to the ending of the *Prospect* shows in 1976.

11 In the same month that *Prospect 69* and *Konzeption* opened, Fischer was also represented for the first time at the Cologne art fair. Besides this, he organized fourteen international exhibitions in his space at the Neubrückstraße, which included many artist debuts. See Kölle 2005, p. 52.

12 Noteworthy is that, in terms of visual documentation, progress reports, correspondence concerning the content of the exhibition, etc., *Prospect 69* is much better preserved than *Konzeption*, of which only few records have been kept. See also Stadtarchiv Leverkusen and Stadtarchiv Düsseldorf.

art, and Seth Siegelaub considered it a key exhibition of conceptual art—next to his own *March 1969* in New York, Wim Beeren's *Op losse schroeven* at the Stedelijk Museum in Amsterdam, Harald Szeemann's *When Attitudes Become Form* at the Kunsthalle in Bern, and Konrad Fischer's *Prospect 69* at the Kunsthalle in Düsseldorf.[13] In Alexander Alberro and Blake Stimson's *Conceptual Art: A Critical Anthology*, the exhibition gained recognition by the subsequent reference to its catalogue. The seminal text "Beware" by Daniel Buren, which is included in this anthology, was originally published (in French) in the *Konzeption* catalogue under the title "Mise-en-garde," preceded by Wedewer's introduction to the exhibition, originally written as the proposal to the culture committee of Leverkusen.[14] Furthermore, the design of the catalogue, radically breaking with the standard for catalogues of exhibitions of visual art—not unlike the publication practices of Siegelaub—has become an important document of conceptual art. It made use of publishing, as Catherine Moseley has pointed out, "to present primary, unmediated information, as far as possible, to let people think about art for themselves."[15] According to Moseley, this specific format of the catalogue, "in which a form of exhibition takes place," as well as the fact that Fischer, as a commercial art dealer, was organizing an exhibition on conceptual art within the institutional framework of a public museum, has contributed to the significance of the exhibition.[16]

Since proper visual documentation of the exhibition is not available, it might not seem opportune to analyze this exhibition in depth. Nonetheless, the extensive newspaper reviews published at the time and a small amount of documents related to the organization of the show, kept in the archives of the city of Leverkusen, provide sufficient information to sketch a reconstruction of the spatial exhibition.[17]

13 Siegelaub selected these exhibitions for his retrospective project on conceptual art, "The Context of Art/The Art of Context" (*Kunst & Museumjournaal* vol. 7, nos. 1–3, 1996).

14 Alberro and Stimson 1999 includes English translations of the contributions by Wedewer and Buren.

15 Catherine Moseley, "A History of an Infrastructure," in *Conception: Conceptual Documents 1968 to 1972* (Norwich: Norwich School of Art & Design/Birmingham: Article Press, 2001), p. 165.

16 Ibid., pp. 156–157. Moseley does not further elaborate these observations.

17 In the private archive of Konrad Fischer there is no further documentation of *Konzeption*. Communication with the artists may have been done over the phone, or via Fischer's gallery during the preparations of other exhibitions. A few correspondences in regard to *Konzeption* are described in Richard 2009, p. 97. Recently, some documents of correspondence showed up in the bequest of Thérèse Bonney at the University of California, Berkeley Art Museum and Pacific Film Archive, as published in *More Konzeption Conception Now*, ed. Stefanie Kreuzer, exh. cat. Leverkusen (Museum Morsbroich) 2015.

The dilemma of exhibition is explicitly problematized in *Konzeption*, both in the recognition of the catalogue as the "primary" exhibition space of the works and the rather paradoxical insistence on the "secondary" exhibition at the site of the museum.

It is essential to study and define how the spatial exhibition differed from the catalogue-exhibition in order to determine the initial exhibitionary status of conceptual art. In addition, the role of Fischer as the curator of the exhibition is analyzed with regard to the changing conditions of the work of art, as well as the position of the artist. In their attempt to frame conceptual art as an art historical movement, Fischer and Wedewer instigated a fierce debate—not only in the exhibition's reception but also with some of the artists involved—which reveals a critical undertone to the project that forced the curators to mediate respective artistic positions within the institutional space.[18] I would argue that this positioning in many respects already anticipated the future mediation of the curator within the re-exhibition of conceptual art.

18 See the harsh reception of the exhibition in the local and national German newspapers, as well as Daniel Buren's critique, expressed in his catalogue essay.

The Catalogue (as) Exhibition

In the application to the culture committee of the city of Leverkusen to support his exhibition—only slightly but in its last paragraph significantly differing from the catalogue's introduction—Wedewer formulated in clear phrasing the radical transformation of the visual arts that he presumed conceptual art to be. This transformation was not so much conceived in the formal or thematic appearance of art, but, as he wrote, "in its fundamental nature."[19] Going beyond the temporary exhibition, conceptual art's most important characteristic, according to Wedewer, was its openness; the possibility

19 Wedewer, proposal to the culture committee of the city of Leverkusen, June 20, 1969, Stadtarchiv Leverkusen (410.1302).

that this type of art holds to generate innumerous shapes or appearances within time and space—depending on its different "receivers." In this regard he refers to "utopian architecture," ascribing conceptual art a sociopolitical characteristic that could potentially change the perspective on our surroundings or life in general:

> This art exists merely as a draft and withdraws from a total realization or execution of its initial ideas as of secondary importance only. Consequently, this means that this art's tendency is no longer the presentation of something… but becomes as it were exemplary of its open form.… The individual draft is only a proposition that instigates an associative "to act through." The result is that the creational moment of these partly far-reaching de-visualizing drafts lies in a methodological showing of possibilities, that retrospectively relate to subjective positions, which, however, thereafter could also relate to issues of a different kind, like "utopian architecture."[20]

That the catalogue was assumed to better present the essence of this type of art than a traditional exhibition, or even to "surpass it as a document and communication format," fits within the spirit of the moment.[21] Siegelaub had already proclaimed the publication or catalogue an alternative "space" that would more appropriately "exhibit" an information-based art—revising the format of the artists' books that were in circulation since the early 1960s.[22] The curators of *Konzeption* had most certainly made use of these earlier experiments. Their exhibition catalogue was conceived following the same principle as Siegelaub's *Xerox Book* (1968); each of the forty-four participating artists was provided with five pages in the catalogue, in which their work could be presented or "exhibited."[23] Whereas in the *Xerox Book* the works of the artists

20 Ibid. "Es sich erstmals um eine Kunst handelt, die nur im Entwurf noch besteht und auf jegliche Verwirklichung oder Ausführung ihrer jeweiligen Ideen als nur von sekundärer Bedeutung verzichtet." My translation. This sociopolitical explanation by Wedewer, similar to Lippard and Chandler's coining of the term "dematerialization," can also be read as a legitimization of the project towards the municipal funders, since this paragraph is not included in the catalogue but replaced by another.

21 See, for example, Hanno Reuther, "Die Ashe in Urnen aufbewahren? Das Museum Leverkusen zeigt die 'Dokumentation einer heutigen Kunstrichtung,'" *Frankfurter Rundschau* November 8, 1969. My translation.

22 See, for example, Germano Celant, *Book as Artwork* (1972), in which a compilation of artists' book titles from Claes Oldenburg, Dieter Roth, John Cage, Piero Manzoni, Ed Ruscha, Yoko Ono, Alan Kaprow, Mel Bochner, Art & Language, Robert Filliou, Dan Graham, Sol LeWitt, Stanley Brouwn, Bruce Nauman, Lawrence Weiner, and many others is listed. Siegelaub was familiar with these practices, since he was in contact with Dan Graham as early as 1966. See Alberro 2001.

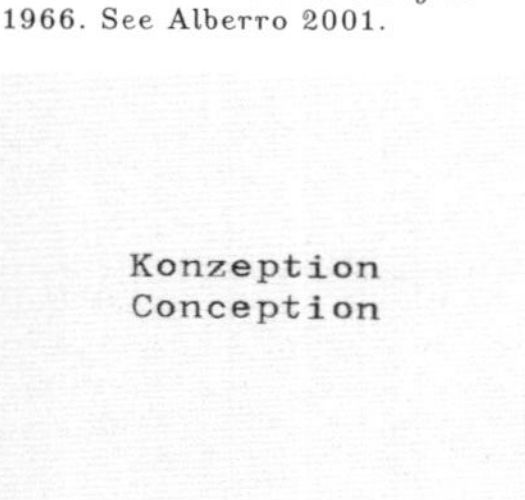

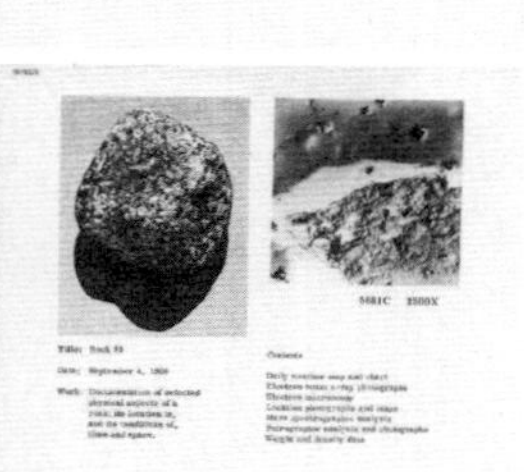

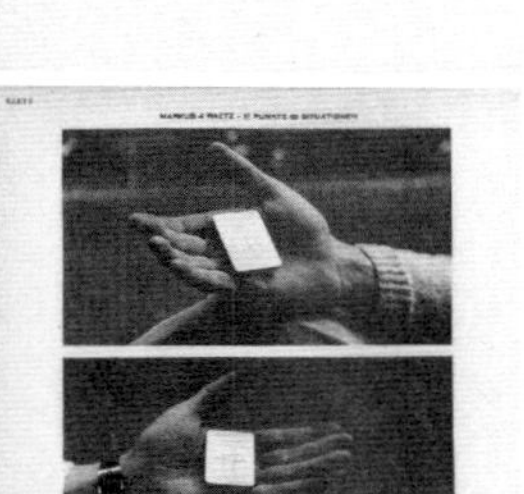

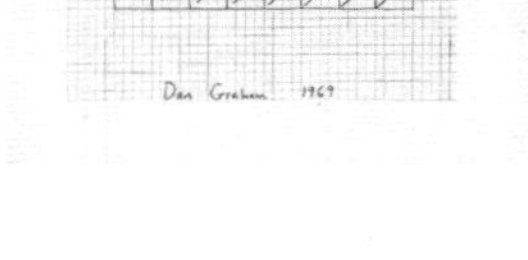

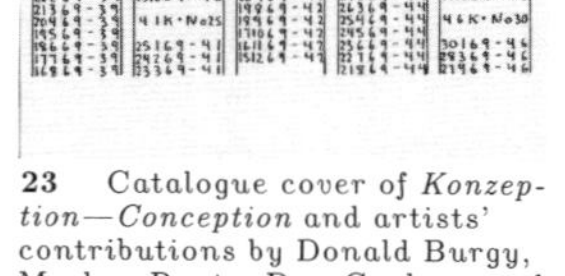

23 Catalogue cover of *Konzeption—Conception* and artists' contributions by Donald Burgy, Markus Raetz, Dan Graham and Hanne Darboven.

(Andre, Barry, Huebler, Kosuth, LeWitt, Morris, and Weiner, each covering twenty-five pages) were exhibited in alphabetical order, the contributions to the Leverkusen catalogue were randomly spread over the pages. The principle of "primary information" was largely adapted, leaving all finalizing implications/interpretations to the reader/receiver ("consumer") of the book, but in contrast to Siegelaub's publication the primary information was accompanied by secondary information in the form of artists' biographies that were published at the end of the catalogue.

Furthermore, the *Xerox Book* had no physical presentation next to the publication; *Konzeption* presented the primary information of the participating artists in both the catalogue and in a spatial configuration in the museum. In a memo that was probably sent to all the collaborating artists, a reference is made to "the materials" to be exhibited; the plans, concepts, photos, etc., that the invited artists would provide were confirmed to be installed at the site by the museum personnel.[24] Added in the same memo is that every artist would have about five pages (20 × 22 cm) in the book, which suggests that the provided "materials" would be adapted for both the exhibition and catalogue.[25] This is affirmed by an indication in the financial report of the exhibition, which notes that the publication, the "catalogue-book," should be similar to the "space-catalogue."[26] Remarkably, the definition "(space)-catalogue" is used here to refer to the spatial display of the collection of primary information, which is similarly used for the catalogue. The traditional curatorial assignment of compiling works for an exhibition is herewith eliminated; instead the focus is merely on the transmission of "information." That in this respect more importance is given to the catalogue (-book) than the exhibition is also illustrated by the estimated costs for the project: the budget for the catalogue exceeded

24 "The material for be exhibited: plans, concepts, fotos a.s.o. could be copied in large sizes and could be framed in the museum. For the eventually execution of ideas we have here some specialists [*sic*]." Memo "Concerning exhibition CONCEPT ART", Stadtarchiv Leverkusen (410.1302), n.d.

25 A last phrase in the memo reads that in case of any additional questions they should write to the museum, which none of the artists did, or at least no record of this correspondence was kept.

26 "Ausstellung 'Konzeptkunst,'" financial report, Stadtarchiv Leverkusen (410.1302), n.d., June 10, 1969.

the combined budget for the physical show.[27] In general, the costs for the project were limited and the production of the exhibition and catalogue relatively simple: all the necessary information for the realization was principally covered with the transport of a medium-sized box containing all the artists' projects. This method of work resembled the format used by Lucy Lippard in her Numbers Shows, which she herself referred to as "suitcase exhibitions."[28]

There are some interesting analogies between *Konzeption* and Lippard's *557,087* show that took place in Seattle from September 5 until October 5, 1969.[29] Lippard also sent a standard letter/questionnaire to the artists she wanted to collaborate with, a bit more specific than the memo by Fischer and Wedewer, in which she asked for their plans for both catalogue and exhibition.[30] These plans were printed on index cards, one for each artist in the show, and were to be used as the exhibition's catalogue.[31] Not bound together in a book, but just assembled as a set of cards in an envelope, the idea was that the person who bought them could arrange the catalogue according to their own taste, "democratically" avoiding a prescribed hierarchy of one artist above the other.[32] Furthermore, Lippard's own textual contribution to the catalogue does not read as an explanation for either the works or the catalogue-exhibition, but stands on its own, similar to the artists' contributions. In the *Konzeption* catalogue, the different artists' contributions, generally plans that could be subsequently executed, are also randomly, not alphabetically, included. Contrary to the "democratic design" that Siegelaub and Lippard were propagating, however, is Wedewer's introduction to the catalogue that explained the works in their relative context; an art historical labeling.
It is followed by LeWitt's "Sentences on Conceptual Art," which are translated into German. Also, the short biographies

27 Ibid. The costs for the execution of the catalogue (14,000 DM) exceed the estimated costs for the execution of the exhibition, consisting of the transport of a box sized 1.2 × 1.5 × 0.5 meters, with works coming from and returning to New York (3,000 DM); reproductions of photographs and drawings (1,000 DM); the rental of slide projectors, etc. (4,000 DM); and insurance (500 DM).

28 Lucy Lippard, "Curating by Numbers," *Tate Papers* no. 12 ("Landmark Exhibitions" issue, Autumn 2009), <www.tate.org.uk/download/file/fid/7268> (18-7-2013).

29 Fischer, who was responsible for the production of the catalogue of *Konzeption*, should have been familiar with the format of this show by Lippard; some of the artists involved were also in his gallery (Andre, Dibbets, Buren, Kawara, Weiner), and it could very well be that he had adopted the format in some way, although he claimed to be the first to have used installation sketches and plans for his invitation cards. Jappe 1971. In her book *Unconcealed*, Sophie Richard mentions that Fischer sent a letter to Lippard and Siegelaub to ask for their advice on how to put together a document-oriented exhibition. There is no record of their response. Richard 2009, p. 97.

30 See Butler 2012, pp. 31 and 38. Originally from the Lucy R. Lippard papers, Archives of American Art, Smithsonian Institution.

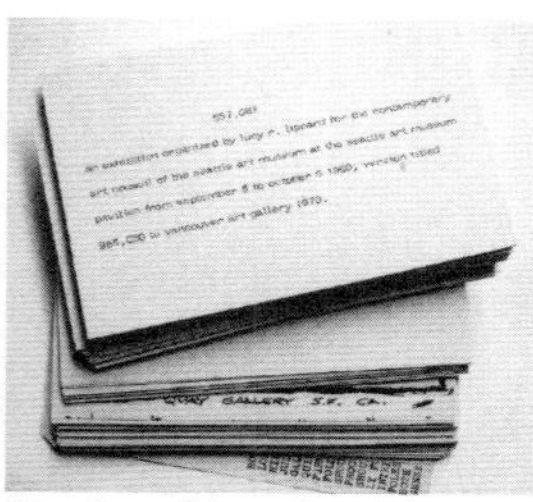

31 Lucy Lippard, catalogue *557,087* Seattle, 1969.

32 In an interview with Jo Melvin, Siegelaub, who was responsible for the production of the Seattle catalogue, explains that this was the most important motive for the random selection system of the catalogue for both him and Lippard, in Butler 2012, pp. 257–259.

of the artists that are alphabetically listed in the back of the catalogue are contrasting the idea of primary communication.[33]

Nevertheless, within the artists' contributions in the catalogue no distinction is made between the discursive component of (some of) the texts and the visual of the sketches/plans. Especially Daniel Buren's contribution to the catalogue is significant in this respect. Instead of handing in a plan/concept of a work (either in sketch or text) like the other artists did, Buren contributed with his critical essay "Mise-en-garde," which is randomly placed, although a bit towards the end of the catalogue, between the other contributions. According to Georg Jappe, Buren provided an *in situ* work for the exhibition, one of his *affichages sauvages,*[34] which was not executed in Leverkusen but placed on billboards at the Grabbeplatz in Düsseldorf, in front of the Kunsthalle where *Prospect 69* took place.[35] In *Konzeption* an annotation on the wall pointed visitors towards this fact. Although Buren documents his works *in situ,* he wants to emphasize the different type of information that these photos hold (secondary), not to confuse them with the work of art represented, and therefore defines them as "*photo-souvenirs.*" That Buren did not use his five pages in the catalogue for the documentation of his work underlines the importance of the momentary experience for him, even in its publication, and the applied opportunity to make a point about the framing of conceptual art within the specific context of this exhibition.

Buren wrote his text for *Konzeption* prior to the exhibition and thus did not see the other works selected. After the exhibition's opening, however, he decided to rewrite certain aspects of the text that was subsequently translated into English and published in *Studio International.*[36] As he stated, "My skepticism in certain respects was proved justified."[37]

33 According to Siegelaub's logic, this additional information for the artists' contributions can be regarded as secondary information.

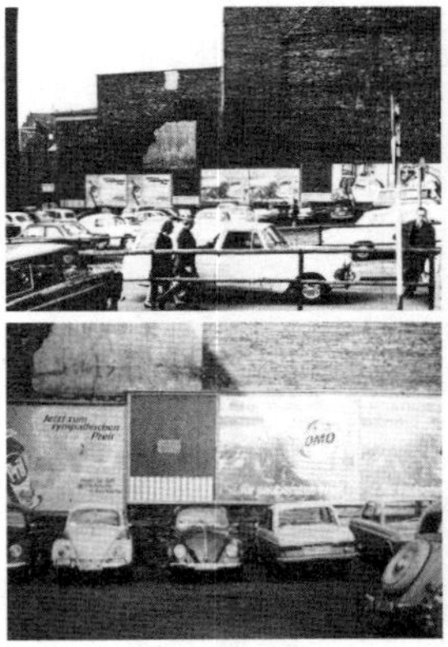

34 Daniel Buren, *Photo-souvenir: Affichage sauvage,* site-specific work, Grabbeplatz, Düsseldorf, 1969.

35 Georg Jappe, "Revision in Sachen Konzept-Kunst? Eine Ausstellung im Schloss Morsbroich," *Frankfurter Allgemeine Zeitung* no. 268 (November 18, 1969).

36 Daniel Buren, "Beware!," *Studio International* vol. 179, no. 920 (March 1970), pp. 100–104. The additional/revised fragments are italicized and placed in between brackets in the text.

37 Ibid., p. 100.

Most of the considerations that he expressed already in his first text were left unchanged; only a few parts are emphasized with additional fragments. In the reprinted text, Buren criticizes the exhibition and different contributions to the exhibition as not consistent with the initial motives for a conceptual art—a denominator with which he himself did not feel allied. He distinguished four (previously three) different meanings/usages of the term conceptual art: 1. concept = project; 2. concept = mannerism (concept = verbiage); and 3. concept = idea = art. Buren used these to criticize and indicate "considerations which will serve as a warning," saying, "We can affirm that at least nine-tenths of the works gathered together for [*the exhibition at Leverkusen*] (or its counterparts) [*relied on one of the four points*] raised above or even, for some people, [*partook subtly of all four at once*]. They rely on the traditional and 'evergreen' in art or, if you like, rely on idealism or utopianism, the original defects which art has not yet succeeded in eradicating."[38]

Within the specific context in which it was conceived, Buren's essay provided an interesting insight into the selection process of *Konzeption* (i.e., what was considered "conceptual art" at the time within a European perspective). Examining the contributions in the catalogue, Buren's classification seems applicable in many respects. Because the majority of "works" in the catalogue can be placed within the category "concept = project," proposals to be realized at some point may be the result of the open question posed to the invited artists to send in their "plans, concepts and photos" as a starting point for the show—although it remains ambiguous whether the plans and concepts that are assembled in the catalogue were equally (re-)presented in the physical exhibition.[39] That, as Buren suggests, many of the artists "in their striving after reality become anecdotal [art = mannerism]" and

38 Ibid.

39 See the letter regarding the organization of the exhibition (Stadtarchiv Leverkusen, [410.1302]); in his review of the show, Georg Jappe states that many of the works in the show differ from those in the catalogue. Jappe 1969.

take the pose of a "gardener, scientist, sociologist, philosopher, storyteller, chemist, sportsman" may not be the most severe defect of the artist's changing attitude—although Bernar Venet's weather calculations[40] or Donald Burgy's body measurements and birth photographs[41] may be a bit confusing in this sense.[42] But the addition to this category that Buren described in the English version of his text, namely that conceptual art that has become "verbiage art," an excessive and meaningless use of words, is a more explicit critique. In their "attempt to explain to us what a conceptual art would be, could be, or should be," Buren stated, "[they are] making a conceptual work."[43] Indeed, artists like Weiner or Kosuth are not explicitly drawing a distinction between their discursive and artistic work, as LeWitt is doing, for example, interchanging the categories of primary and secondary information as defined by Siegelaub.[44] Further elaborating on this type of conceptual art, Buren defines "the most dangerous category… concept = idea = art," in which he recognized a tendency "to take any sort of an 'idea,' to make art of it and call it 'concept'…. To exhibit a 'concept,' or to use the word concept to signify art, comes to the same thing as putting the concept itself on a level with the object. This would be to suggest that we must think in terms of a 'concept-object'—which would be an aberration."[45] With his summary, Buren emphasized that at the time of this exhibition the "category" of conceptual art was already roughly delineated, as well as highly problematized.[46]

Following his "warning," Buren positions and reflects on his own work—although the use of the *pluralis maiestatis* suggests that he is representing a generation of artists. Avoiding the trap of thinking of a concept, which he defines an "*ideal-object*," as essentially different than an object, Buren presents a method or framework that at the same time

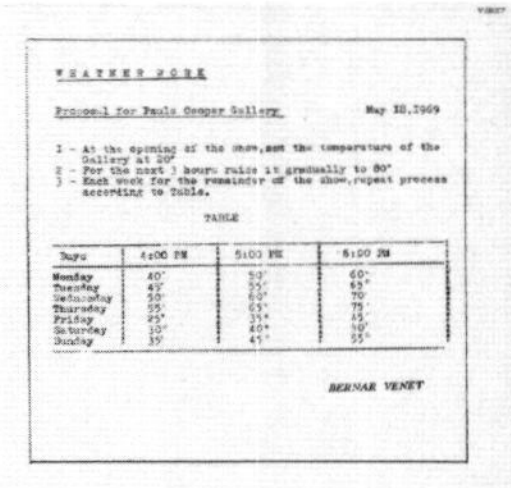

WEATHER WORK

Proposal for Paula Cooper Gallery May 10,1969

1 - At the opening of the show, set the temperature of the Gallery at 20°
2 - For the next 3 hours raise it gradually to 80°
3 - Each week for the remainder of the show, repeat process according to Table.

TABLE

Days	4:00 PM	5:00 PM	6:00 PM
Monday	40°	50°	60°
Tuesday	45°	55°	65°
Wednesday	50°	60°	70°
Thursday	55°	65°	75°
Friday	25°	35°	45°
Saturday	30°	40°	50°
Sunday	35°	45°	55°

BERNAR VENET

40 Bernar Venet, *Weather Work*, 1969.

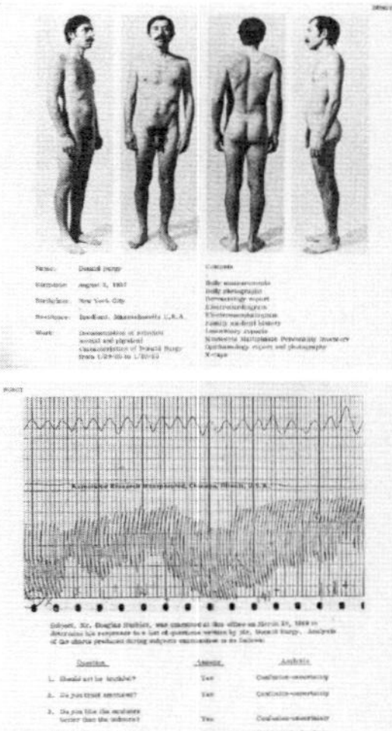

41 Donald Burgy, *Check-up*, 1969.

42 Buren 1970, p. 100.

43 Ibid.

44 Around the time of the Leverkusen exhibition Kosuth published his famous text "Art after Philosophy," in which he explicitly emphasizes the fact that the writing on art can be regarded a practice of art. See Kosuth 1969.

45 Ibid.

46 Jappe prescribed Buren a "prophetic reading." Jappe 1969.

questions its own existence. In doing so, the site in which it is presented becomes a key element. The critic Michel Claura, Buren's half-brother, further emphasizes the distinguished position that Buren prescribes himself in a comment published after the *Studio International* article:

> When the first version of the text upon which we are here commenting was published at Leverkusen, it was included in an exhibition entitled "Conception." This exhibition/catalogue relates to a requirement of art in its conceptual form. Buren's text is a "clinical study" of this proposition. In the context of the exhibition/catalogue the critical aspect of the text was emphasized. In other respects, having already faulted the perfect ordering of the book through the "surprising" content of the text, Buren, in presenting his own proposition, turns the tables on the exhibition, providing "something to see." In this way the conceptual contiguity is broken.[47]

Whether Buren succeeded in overcoming the pitfalls described in his catalogue contribution *via* this specific catalogue contribution, as Claura suggests, is questionable. The essay was not translated into German or English, like most of the contributions in the catalogue, and the number of readers, or receivers, either of German or other European origin, that would have been able to understand the essence of the text was surely limited. Buren's contribution nonetheless complicated an unambiguous understanding of the new type of art, as can be concluded from a critic's comment: "Buren and Sol LeWitt formulate tracts and sentences about 'Conceptual Art,' whereas LeWitt restrictively indicates: 'These sentences comment on art, but are not art.' In the unnumbered catalogue, however, they stand indistinguishably next to the art, sketches, fragments of ideas, photographs."[48] Through his

47 Michel Claura, "Comment (on Buren's text)," *Studio International* vol. 179, no. 920 (March 1970), p. 105.

48 Christian Zepter, "Signatur um Mitternacht. Nicht-Mitteilbares soll mitgeteilt werden," *Leverkusener* Anzeiger, November 5, 1969. My translation.

"intervention" Buren points at the insufficiency in the distinction between primary and secondary information, not only by his colleague-artists but also by the curators of the exhibition, and is thereby urging further debate on conceptualism.

Buren's idea of the problematic nature of photographic documentation in regard to "conceptual" art, however, is in some respect similar to Fischer's. In her review of Fischer's exhibitions, Barbara Hess pointed out his attitude towards documentation of exhibitions or works presented in exhibitions in comparison to Buren's idea of the "photo-souvenir."[49] In an interview with Georg Jappe for *Studio International* in 1970, Fischer abstained from illustrating his statements with documentation of the exhibitions and projects that he organized (as well as his portrait), because he held these to be "random installation photos, things of the past."[50] Instead, he provided the reproductions of the invitation cards of his gallery, on which the "primary information" of his exhibitions, installation drawings, sketches, descriptions, etc., were printed.[51] With this point of view, Fischer strictly distinguished between the concept and the spatial (temporal) execution of the work—something he nevertheless valued highly.[52]

This principle that Fischer adopted in the invitation cards of his gallery openings was incorporated in the catalogue of *Konzeption*, and in a way it could be read as an announcement or advertisement of the works in the show that did not necessarily provide the same information. In favor of Buren's critique on the danger of concepts becoming objects without further consequences, Fischer may not have regarded the exhibition secondary to the catalogue that contains the "original" plans and ideas, as was suggested in the reviews of the exhibition: "As it is presented in Leverkusen, the exhibition is only the highly unnecessary addition to the much more

49 Barbara Hess, "30 Jahre Ausstellungen bei Konrad Fischer 1967–1997," Sediment *Mitteilungen zur Geschichte des Kunsthandels* (Heft 2) (Bonn: Zentralarchiv des Deutschen und Internationalen Kunsthandels e.V., 1997), p. 22.

50 Jappe 1971.

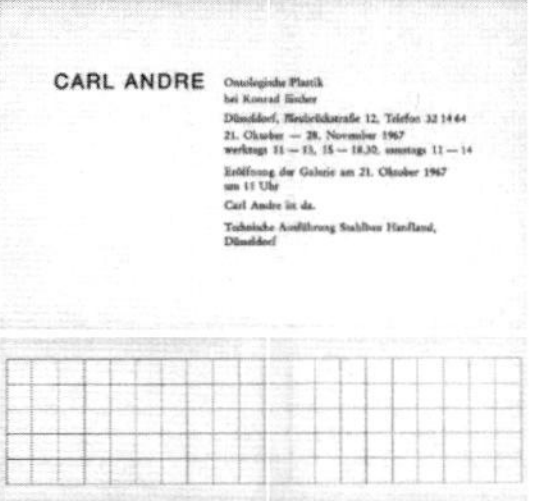

51 First invitation card of Konrad Fischer in Düsseldorf (1967) enclosing the floor plan of Carl Andre's sculpture *5 × 20 Altstadt Rectangle*, which covered the whole floor of the gallery space.

52 Brigitte Kölle claimed that Fischer was very much concerned with the mounting of the exhibition, something that she ascribes him doing in the various shows in which he collaborated. Kölle 2005, pp. 51–52. Fischer stressed that, for him, the exhibition is the most important test—contrary to the position that artists take through their writings. In this respect he is explicitly criticizing (the texts of) Kosuth: "When he puffs himself up in *Studio International*, that's the sort of thing I can't take." Jappe 1971, p. 70.

adequate information in the extensive catalogue; besides that the exhibition doesn't communicate any additional vision."[53] Or, as another commenter put it even more bluntly, "It is better not to go to Leverkusen, but instead to order the catalogue: it is much more interesting and also more 'visual.'"[54]

Although the observation that the catalogue was more illustrative than the exhibition may seem correct, the curators still mounted a physical show and they must have had a reason for it.[55] Fischer and Wedewer were more than generally informed about the implications of the type of art they were promoting and it is legitimate to regard the exhibition as a fully complementary part of the enterprise. This can be concluded from the fact that the blueprints of the catalogue were also exhibited in the exhibition, to illustrate that the "concepts" or "plans" were prior to the exhibition.[56] Like in Lippard's Seattle and subsequent Numbers Shows, these documents, which were sent by mail, could provide all the necessary information to mount the physical show. It is therefore inadequate to evaluate the importance of *Konzeption* merely through the catalogue as exhibition, and essential to analyze how the physical exhibition was installed in correspondence with the catalogue. In the following section of this chapter, a reconstruction as well as an analysis of the exhibition is made in regard to the published newspaper reviews.

53 Jürgen Morschel, "Aus dem Zettelkasten, Conceptual Art im Leverkusener Museum," *Süddeutsche Zeitung*, November 18, 1969.

54 John Anthony Thwaites, "Katalog genügt: Ideenspuk im Schloss," *Christ und Welt*, November 11, 1969. My translation.

55 Helga Meister stated, "But even these minimal written or printed little somethings are too much. While concept art is theoretical, not practical. The catalogue, which is more illustrative than the exhibition..." See Helga Meister, "Das Ende vom Lied," *Westdeutsche Zeitung*, November 20, 1969.

56 As can be read in one of the reviews, "The galley proofs of the catalogue are mounted on a wall next to the staircase." See Thomas Nehls, "Vor allem wurde viel gelächelt: Zur Ausstellungseröffnung gab's einen Film," *Leverkusener Anzeiger*, no. 250 (October 28, 1969).

Where's the Exhibition?

That conceptual art, according to Wedewer's notion, would discharge the final execution of the planning sketch to the final work of art—while this last step was considered less important—may be a bit oversimplified. The fact that the conceptual artists conceived a type of art that was not intended to be realized into a final product but consisted in a mental process that could be affected by different "receivers" in different ways, however, frustrated the traditional presentation of art. For the physical presentation of *Konzeption* within the museum spaces at the Schloss Morsbroich, Wedewer and Fischer had to find ways to do justice to the type of work selected, and consequently experiment with formats of exhibition that were yet unknown. In doing so, the exhibition encountered quite some misunderstanding, cleverly described in a local newspaper: "The question was without irony; the somewhat helplessly wandering man was eager to let himself into the adventure of the youngest art: If they could please tell him where's the exhibition. That he was in the midst of the exhibition he hadn't noticed."[57]

Regarding the standard conditions or formats of visual art exhibitions at the time, *Konzeption* was rejected by the press, not only "because there wasn't a single object to be shown," but moreover because it "renounced the fundamental of an exhibition, that is, to exhibit."[58] In spite of the skeptical tone that reverberated, the reception of *Konzeption* provided a critical understanding of conceptual art, which, possibly as a result of this skepticism, acknowledged conceptual art's problem of exhibition already at this point. The fact that Wedewer, in his interpretation of conceptual art, was specifically pointing at its significance as a theoretical art complicated the proper validation of the exhibition in this respect.[59] One of the more interesting observations at the time stressed that "this first 'Conception' exhibition has concurrently also illustrated the limits of this tendency. That, too, is an important result.... In his preface to the catalogue [Wedewer] characterized conceptual art as a theoretical art, with which he seized upon the dilemma: concepts are not exposable."[60]

57 Morschel 1969.

58 Heiner Stachelhaus, "Entwurf ist kein tragfähiger Wurf," *NRZ Neue Ruhr-Zeitung*, November 21, 1969; F. H., "Worte ohne Bilder. 'Conception-art in Leverkusen,'" *Mündensche Nachrichten*, January 30, 1959. My translation.

59 "Its significance lies in being something like a theoretical art," Wedewer, in exh. cat. Leverkusen 1969. As translated in Alberro and Stimson 1999, p. 143.

60 Stachelhaus 1969. My translation.

In addition, Daniel Buren's critical contribution to the catalogue prompted critics of the exhibition to regard conceptual art as a problematic category *per se*. Georg Jappe, in a more sophisticated review on the exhibition, saw his criticism of the exhibition reflected in Buren's text. He emphasized the confusion of terminology taking place in the exhibition catalogue, and remarks that "under the slogan 'Live in your head'… a lot has been thrown in the same box."[61] Referring to Szeemann's exhibition, which in its full title already represented the intellectual aspect of the new type of art, Jappe particularly appreciated the theoretical potential brought together in *Konzeption*. Although he considered the art itself to remain underdeveloped, he claimed that the first signs of a new role for art had become apparent and a new theory had developed: "A concept is not something that one shows, it is not a sketch, but a proposition. In other words: a concept is something that one has and demonstrates through examples. The examples are not objectified commodities but the exemplary of a method. The method is not to innovate the laws of art (like form, color, surface), so not to find a new style, but a new understanding of art, a new self-understanding outside the realm of form—aesthetic responsiveness—sale and use."[62]

Jappe is the only critic approaching a deeper understanding of the conceptual project, regarding the new artistic "method" as being a progression in the context of art rather than the autonomous artwork. He nevertheless evaluated the outcome of the theory in a traditional art historical manner or aesthetics, stressing that many of the works merely exemplify a new method of artistic practice instead of actually putting it into practice, and questioning whether the artists will succeed in this. According to Michael Newman, it was exactly the "failure" of conceptual art that, in hindsight, made it possible to write its history, which emphasized that within the

61 Jappe 1969. Jappe here refers to Szeemann's exhibition *Live in Your Head: When Attitudes Become Form*, which took place at the Kunsthalle Bern earlier that year. My translation.

62 Ibid.

institutional framework of the museum the broader mission of conceptual art was difficult to realize in any case.[63]

Although in the preparations for *When Attitudes Become Form* Szeemann had already proclaimed that the gestures of the new type of art he had encountered could not be exhibited, *Konzeption* nevertheless further scrutinized the boundaries of the exhibitionary format.[64] The reference to the exhibition as a "space-catalogue" that was supposed to be comparable to the "catalogue-book" already emphasized the textual arrangement of the exhibition, and indeed *Konzeption* was described as "sober, office-like, un-museum-like."[65] On the walls of the museum spaces (as well as on tables and floor), indexes, plans and photographs were fixed, "as analysis as well as stories, as questionnaire and diary note, as snapshots and as draft," or, as a more cynical comment puts it, "loads of letters written in English and 'nonsense photos.'"[66] The general characterization of the exhibition seems effectively summarized in the following description: "The total negation of the object, the withdrawal in the head of the artist, the totally subjective, even narcissistic behavior and the expressive romantic gesture of the conceptualists, all this is in Schloss Morsbroich in the form of small notes, letters, instructions, graphic representations and photographs signaled from the walls."[67]

In comparison to the reception of the exhibitions *Op losse schroeven* and *When Attitudes Become Form*, which also received severe criticism, the reception of *Konzeption* developed a different historical reputation. The criticism of these earlier exhibitions was against an art that was regarded as "nothing but upgraded rubbish," but at least the art that was shown was still object-based and could be defined as "anti-art."[68] *Konzeption* clearly had a different setup; that the exhibition lacked any regular objects was confusing and

63 See Newman 1996, p. 102. "Het succes van het werk kan worden afgemeten aan de mate waarin het zich verzet tegen opname in een historicistisch continuüm, aangezien het de doelstelling van de beste van deze kunst was om een dergelijk continuüm te beëindigen of op te blazen; we zouden dus kunnen stellen dat het alleen te danken is aan die gedeeltelijke mislukking van de 'beweging' dat de geschiedenis ervan geschreven kan worden."

64 "In the beginning was Dibbets's gesture to water a lawn on a table. But you cannot exhibit gestures." See Harald Szeemann, "How Does an Exhibition Come into Being?," in Rattemeyer et al. 2010, p. 173.

65 Meister 1969. My translation.

66 Nehls 1969. My translation.

67 Stachelhaus 1969.

68 Lambert Tegenbosch, "Op losse schroeven," *de Volkskrant*, March 14, 1969. For a closer examination of the reception of these exhibitions, see Steven ten Thije, "'Op losse schroeven' and 'When Attitudes Become Form': Public Reception in the Netherlands and Switzerland," in Rattemeyer et al. 2010, pp. 212–219. Because of the different types of art that were brought together in these exhibitions, I would not define them as conceptual art exhibitions, as is generally the case.

created the impression at the time that there was "nothing to see."[69] Also illuminating in this regard is that almost none of the reviews of the exhibition were accompanied by photographic material.[70] Interestingly enough, the curators also did not make an effort to document the exhibition—in contrast to the huge amount of photographs that Szeemann had generated—and likely, in regard to Fischer's attitude, the catalogue was considered the "container" of the primary information, more appropriately representing the artists' projects than any photographic registration of the spatial configuration would achieve.[71]

That the curators would have dealt with all the contributions correspondingly, principally not distinguishing between the type of conceptual work and directly implementing the contributions as such in the exhibition, like they did in the catalogue, would be in line with LeWitt's dictum "Ideas alone can be works of art."[72] According to some of the critics, this became the leitmotif for the exhibition, possibly as a result of the rather dogmatic application of LeWitt's "Sentences" as an overture for the artists' contributions in the catalogue.[73] That the critics generally interpreted conceptual art as the one part of the classical dichotomy of idea and form that is now proclaimed as the "end product" underlined once more the inadequacy of Siegelaub's notions of primary and secondary information.

Critic Anna Klapheck acknowledged this confusion. Referring to Leonardo da Vinci, she commented, "There have always been concepts, sketches, and utopian architecture, though these were generally intended to eventually be put into practice. For the conceptual artists of today, design is the final form, the end product. Designs can be reproduced, photos copied. In this regard the catalogue produced as a guide to the exhibition is close to the exhibition itself."[74]

69 Hajo Schroeder, "Es gibt nichts zu sehen: Konzeption—Conception im Schloss eröffnet," *Kölnerische Rundschau*, no. 250, October 28, 1969.

70 The poor pictorial representation centers around the work of Keith Arnatt (probably the most pictorial) and two pictures that show a glimpse of the exhibition; a photograph of Marcel Broodthaers reading the catalogue in front of the work of Bochner, and another one (in *Der Spiegel*) in which a couple of visitors wander around the exhibition (one also seems to be looking in the catalogue, or at least reading instead of looking at the works) with a work by an unidentifiable artist in the foreground (the work is not represented in the catalogue).

71 The remake of the exhibition *When Attitudes Become Form* at the Fondazione Prada in Venice in 2013 included hundreds of photographs of the original exhibition, the exhibition process, and the artists involved in the catalogue.

72 LeWitt, "Sentences on Conceptual Art," in exh. cat. Leverkusen 1969.

73 Mentioned in the catalogue's contents is "Einführung: Sol LeWitt" ("Introduction: Sol LeWitt").

74 Anna Klapheck, "Ideen als Kunstwerke: Die Ausstellung 'Konzeption' in Leverkusen/Sol LeWitt in Krefeld," *Rheinische Post*, November 15, 1969. My translation.

LeWitt himself, however, would never have defined the concept as the end product, or even considered exhibiting it as such (whereas other artists thought the presentation of the idea would suffice). According to his dictum "Once the idea of the piece is established in the artist's mind and the final form is decided, the process is carried out blindly," the proposal would have been executed without further discussion. This is exactly what LeWitt's contribution to the exhibition included: his proposal or concept that was printed in the catalogue, "Project for Leverkusen"—four squares of 1 × 1 m with a specific number of lines that were to be drawn on the wall—was realized according to this description.[75]

The consequent realization of the concept-proposition was also applicable to Mel Bochner's measurement pieces, which were executed in the Leverkusen exhibition spaces, as can be concluded from an obscure installation view of the exhibition represented in a single photograph[76] in a local newspaper.[77] Yet other contributions, such as Adrian Piper's *Relocated Planes, Indoor Series/Outdoor Series,*[78] Victor Burgin's "Leverkusen proposal,"[79] or Bruce Nauman's concept for a performance piece in two parts (one for the exhibition and one for the catalogue), seem to have had no other manifestation than the proposition in the catalogue. However, there is a significant difference between contributions by artists like Marcel Broodthaers and Alighiero Boetti, who insisted on the exact publication/exhibition of their letters/proposals and Nauman's proposed performance, for example, for which "the five pages of the book will be publicity photographs of the dancer hired to do my piece with his name affixed."[80] These precise instructions were obviously ignored, since his proposal is printed in the catalogue without the photographic reference and only accompanied by the German translation. Whether Nauman's proposal for the exhibition, a

75 Although there are no photographs of this piece at the Leverkusen show, it is included in the catalogue of the exhibition *L'art conceptuel* show in Paris, where it was reexecuted. Exh. cat. Paris 1989, p. 209. In this catalogue a reference is made to *Sol LeWitt: Wall Drawings 1968–1984*, in which the work is also mentioned, although not in exactly the same phrasing and without date. See R. H. Fuchs et al., eds., *Sol LeWitt: Wall Drawings 1968–1984*, exh. cat. Amsterdam (Stedelijk Museum Amsterdam); Eindhoven (Van Abbemuseum); Hartford (Wadsworth Atheneum) 1984, p. 33.

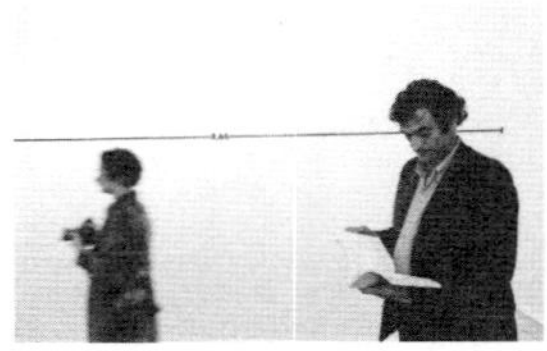

76 Installation view of *Konzeption* with Marcel Broodthaers looking into the catalogue in front of a work by Mel Bochner. Photo Traudel Schmitz/Stadarchiv Leverkusen.

77 W. Künze, "Die neueste Kunst gibt's nur als Entwurf," *Leverkusener Rundschau*, October 24, 1969.

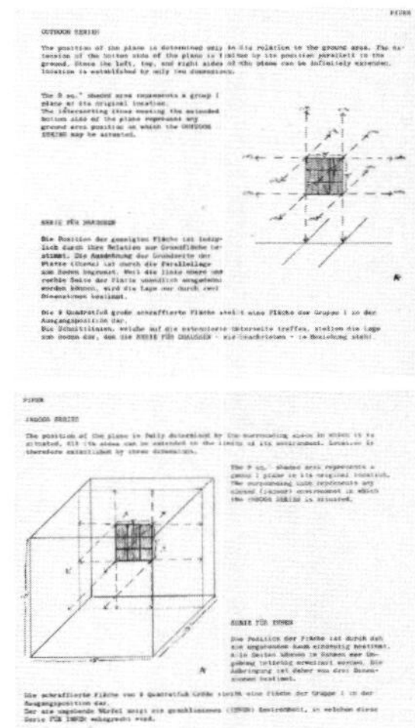

78 Adrian Piper, *Relocated Planes, Indoor Series/Outdoor Series*, 1969.

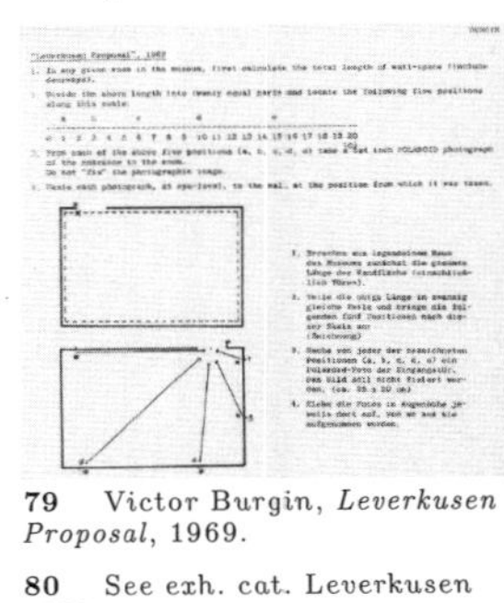

79 Victor Burgin, *Leverkusen Proposal*, 1969.

80 See exh. cat. Leverkusen 1969, n.p.

dancer that was supposed to perform several exercises within a thirty-minute time frame in a room that would be cleared out by museum guards, was actually executed is not clear; in any case, it has not been described in any of the reviews.

As Jappe had already pointed out, several of the contributions in the catalogue did not correspond with those in the exhibition. Although it seems only natural that in the eventual installation of the exhibition at some points interpretations of the contributions had to be implemented, this demonstrates that double standards were applied in the spatial exhibition. However, the spatial surroundings were still important to effectively show the work, as is illustrated by Fred Sandback's *Eight-part Sculpture for Der Grosse Saal*. The room in which it was presented, the south room of the museum (the "Spiegelsaal," or mirror room[81]), was described as "squeamishly empty" and a typescript on the wall read that the variable proportions of eight gasses (nitrogen, oxygen, hydrogen, krypton, helium, neon, xenon, and argon) were present: "The following eight proposals exist simultaneously in the same general space. Their content varies, and one or all of them may cease to exist for a time, depending on deviations from normal atmospheric conditions."[82] Obviously, reading this information printed in the catalogue could not provide the same experience of the work as reading the same information on the captions within the architecture of the mirror room in Schloss Morsbroich would.

Sandback's piece may have been an exception within the exhibition. Closer to artist's projects like Yves Klein's *The Void* (1958) or Art & Language's *Air Conditioning Show* (1972), *Eight-part Sculpture for Der Grosse Saal* can be regarded as a prelude to the "empty" or "non-" exhibition, in which "dematerialization" was established through the transition of language to architecture.[83] Although the occupancy of

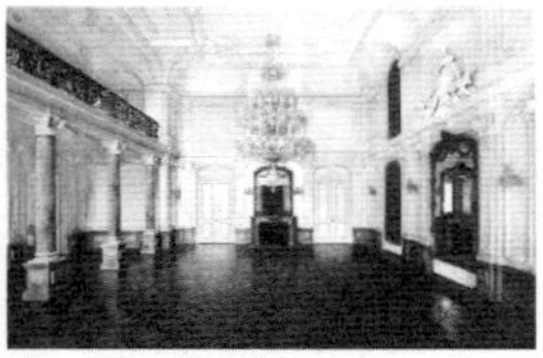

81 Candida Höfer, *Spiegelsaal des Museum Morsbroich Leverkusen 1*, 2002.

82 Fred Sandback, in exh. cat. Leverkusen 1969, n.p.

83 For further reading on these exhibitions, see John Armleder, Matthieu Copeland et al., eds., *Voids: A Retrospective*, exh. cat. Paris (Centre Pompidou) 2009; (Zurich: JRP/Ringier). Michael Newman claimed that the materialized present and assumed autonomous art object is avoided by the conceptualists through social systems in real time and real space, with the risk that the materialization is shifted from the object to the conditions. Newman 1996.

space was not explicitly an aspect that the curators of *Konzeption* intended to implement, it is nevertheless an important aspect of conceptual art.[84] Several works in *Konzeption* that were described to have "nothing to do with the theme of the exhibition," because they were not literally transmitting information (that was understood by some critics to be the intention of the curators), but were in fact anticipating the theory so precisely described by Wedewer in a spatial configuration, like the series of photographs of industrial architecture[85] by Bernd and Hilla Becher.[86] In that sense the exhibition was giving way to different "lineages" of conceptual art that have only been defined in a historical development of the movement.[87]

It is noteworthy that *Konzeption* in its historical framing ignored influences stemming from minimal art. Apart from LeWitt's seminal text and his contribution to the exhibition, a wall drawing that was included in the catalogue as an instruction, (post-)minimal practices were lacking in the exhibition.[88] Works from artists like Carl Andre and Robert Morris, frequently associated with early conceptual art and included in earlier conceptual projects and shows (by Siegelaub, for example), were not included. Instead, many of the works in *Konzeption* were close to Land art and thereby represented the stage that precedes a strict conceptualism, following Wedewer's interpretation: "Because most of the Land art objects are based in distant places, photographs and descriptions must take the place of the object itself."[89]

The new usage of photography as a registration or documentation of events and constellations that took place outside the exhibition space was correspondingly overly represented. The series of photographs of Keith Arnatt registering the artist in all phases of being buried in the sand can be considered most revealing in this sense, since it was used as a recurring

84 From the modest photographic documentation, as well as the descriptions in the papers, it is clear that the curators had no intention to work on the theme of emptiness.

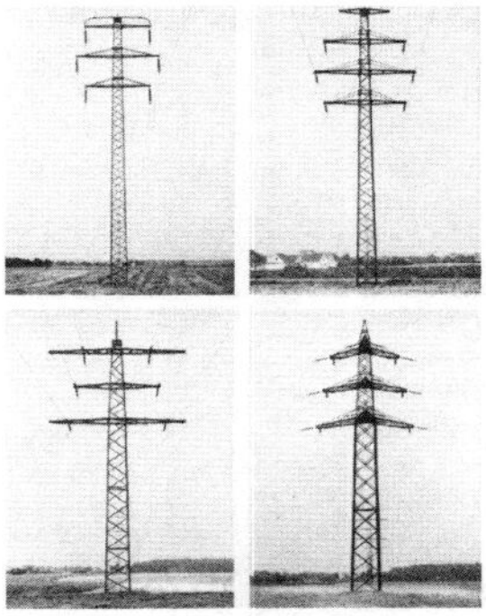

85 Bernd and Hilla Becher, *Four Electrical Towers*, 1969.

86 See, for example, Künze 1969. "The museum this time, with the help of the German gallery Konrad Fischer, only specifically wants to inform. But about what really?" My translation.

87 See, for example, Newman and Bird 1999; Alberro and Stimson 1999; and Osborne 2002.

88 Following the descriptions, there were a few pieces in the exhibition, defined as "curiosa," that were still object-based and could refer to minimal art, though it seems that these works were selected at a later moment, since they were not included in the catalogue: "On the floor is a white rectangle with a spirit level placed on it and on another spot there is a triangle with a compass affixed to it. In one corner there are black angles whose area decreases towards the top." Anna Klapheck, "Leverkusen Exhibition of Conceptual Art: Is It a Swindle or Not a Swindle?," *The German Tribune*, December 9, 1969 (originally published in German in *Hannoversche Allgemeine*, November 14, 1969).

89 Ibid.

(although sparse) illustration to the reviews.[90] Other works that can be placed within the category of Land art are Robert Smithson's *Sites Photographed for Ruhr-District Non-Sites,*[91] Bruce McLean's *Five Part Landscape Painting*, and Hamish Fulton's landscape photographs. Donald Burgy's walk in Massachusetts, where he found a stone that was then analyzed for its optical, geological, and mathematical characteristics, the results of which were captured in a spreadsheet, analysis, and photographs, already takes a step beyond Land art and introduces conceptualist motives.[92] Iain Baxter's *You Are Now in the Middle of an N.E. Thing Co. Landscape* (1968–1969),[93] in which a board with text is "erected on a site which meets the V.S.I. (Visual Sensitivity Information) qualifications of an N.E. THING CO. Landscape," can be regarded a decisive link towards conceptual art that "does away with the concrete point of departure, and… does not aim at an available, but possible object. It describes processes and events and is therefore close to the happening."[94]

Retrospectively, according to Rosalind Krauss's definition of "Sculpture in the Expanded Field," Land art's relation to (post-)minimal art has been outlined, but at the time this relationship was not yet clearly described.[95] The German art historian Klaus Honnef considers conceptual art, similar to his American contemporaries Lucy Lippard and Ursula Meyer, an outcome of minimal art in his influential anthology of conceptual art from 1971.[96] Fischer in fact regarded conceptual art "a byproduct of minimal art," and was also greatly in favor of the American artists.[97] Wedewer's framing of conceptual art as a consequence of Land art could have been prompted by Gerry Schum's Fernsehgalerie, which broadcasted works from conceptual and Land art artists under the title *Land Art*[98] in May 1969.[99] But, more importantly, in his embrace of Land art, Wedewer could place conceptual art

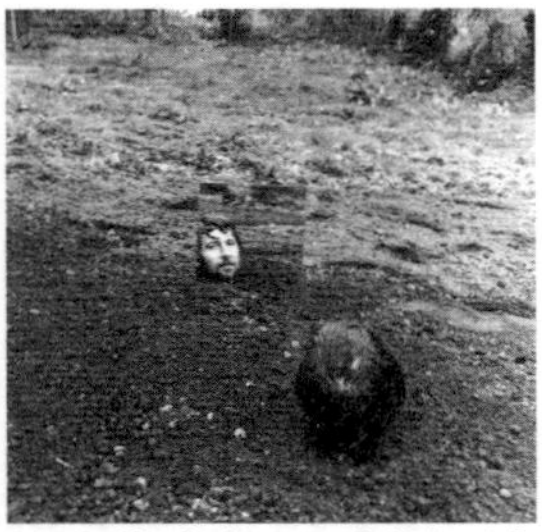

90a Keith Arnatt, *Self-Burial with Mirror*, 1969.

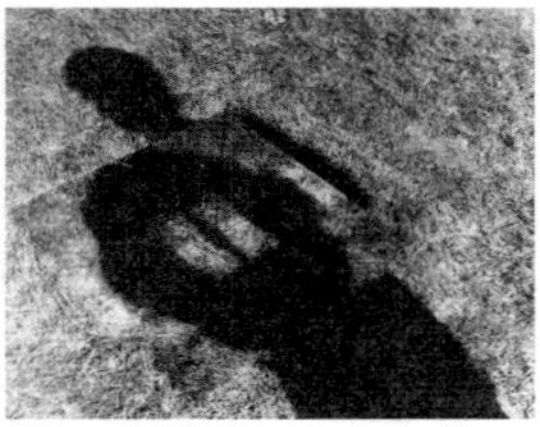

90b Keith Arnatt, *Invisible Hole Revealed by the Shadow of the Artist*, 1968.

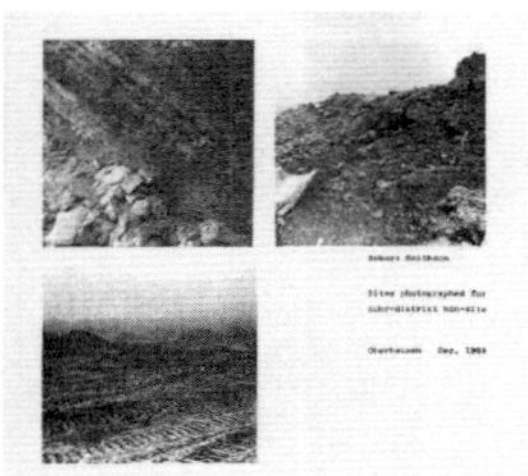

91 Robert Smithson, *Sites Photographed for Ruhr-District Non-Sites*, 1969.

92 Meister 1969.

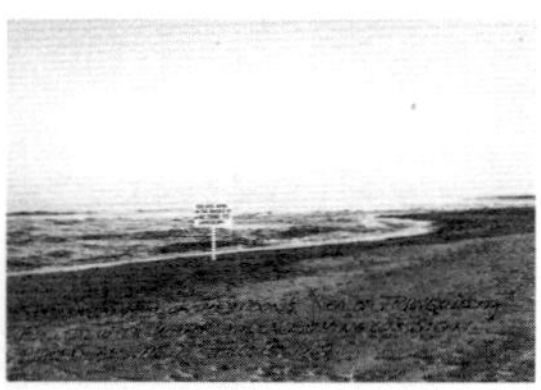

93 Iain and Ingrid Baxter, *You Are Now in the Middle of an N.E. Thing Co. Landscape*, 1968–1969.

94 Certificate printed in exh. cat. Leverkusen 1969, n.p.; Klapheck 1969.

95 Rosalind Krauss, "Sculpture in the Expanded Field," *October* vol. 8 (Spring 1979), pp. 30–44.

96 Klaus Honnef, *Concept Art* (Cologne: Phaidon, 1971). This book has been very influential in the reception of conceptual art, both in Germany and the Netherlands. Remarkably, according to Lynda Morris, Honnef has credited Fischer for his collaboration on the "book." See Morris, "Unconcealment," in Richard 2009. p. 20. Clearly, however, Honnef is referring to the catalogue of Documenta 5, for which he wrote the introductory text to the section he organized together with Fischer. His book *Concept Art* had been published the year before, and was probably the reason that Szeemann invited Honnef to collaborate on Documenta 5.

97 Heinz-Norbert Jocks, "You Have to Be One-Sided so that Something Will Progress," in *Okey, Dokey Konrad Fischer*, ed. Brigitte Kölle (Cologne: Verlag der Buchhandlung Walther König, 2007), p. 298. Originally published in *Kunstforum* no. 127 (September/ October, 1994). Translation by Karl Hoffmann.

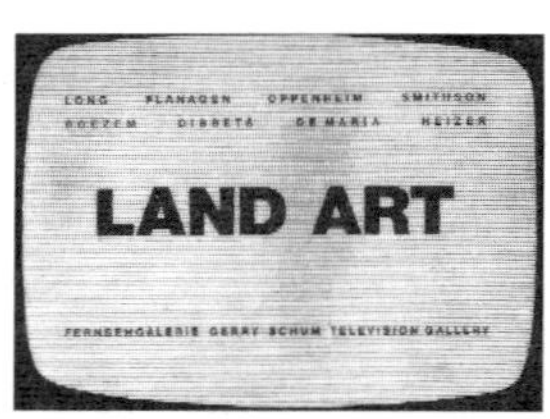

98 Gerry Schum, Fernsehgalerie still from *Land Art*, 1969.

99 At 9 p.m. on March 28, 1969, Schum's Fernsehgalerie, with works by Marinus Boezem, Jan Dibbets, Barry Flanagan, Mike Heizer, Richard Long, Walter de Maria, Dennis Oppenheim, and Robert Smithson, was "opened" on the Sender Freies Berlin (Studio C, Kaiserdamm 77, Berlin) with an inaugural speech by Jean Leering.

within a European tradition of avant-garde art that, in comparison to the American tradition, was less concerned with the denunciation of the object/commodification.

The European embedding of conceptual art could have been an important motivation for this first survey in Germany. Art practices developing in the United States had been growing stronger since the late 1950s, and it was only few years prior that the most prestigious exhibition in the world, the Venice Biennale, proclaimed an American to be the most promising artist of the exhibition by awarding Robert Rauschenberg the Grand Prize for Painting in 1964. The turmoil that this award generated in a way affirmed that the leading position of European culture and art worldwide was in decline.[100] Especially in Germany the anxiety about the American recuperation was strong. When Fischer was preparing *Prospect 69* in Düsseldorf with a large selection of American galleries, he was asked, "If an exhibition like 'Prospect' does not strongly reinforce the supremacy of American art—of which we can certainly speak—will this not be to the chagrin of the German art dealers and the German artists represented by them?"[101] In his disapproving response, Fischer emphasized the aspect that he wanted to offer information about a young generation of avant-garde artists for whom prices were relatively low:

> Of course, this can also be very beneficial, when suddenly the collectors see that there are perhaps more interesting things to be had somewhere else, or something. But that can only be of use to the German art dealers in order to stock up with better quality. The fact that Europeans travel to the United States and buy there is illusory, since the cost of the trip would automatically double, because travel, transport, insurance, etc. are

100 See Willi Bongard, "When Rauschenberg Won the Biennale," *Studio International* 175 (June 1968), pp. 288–289.

101 Wird eine solche Ausstellung wie "Prospect" nicht die Vorherrschaft der amerikanischen Kunst—davon kann man ja doch wohl reden—sehr bestärken und wird das nicht zum Leidwesen der deutschen Kunsthändler und der von ihnen vertretenen deutschen Künstler passieren? Anon., Radio interview with Fischer and Kunsthalle director Jürgen Harten in "Das Feuilleton," *Deutschlandfunk*, October 1, 1969 (21.40–22.00). Transcription in Stadtarchiv Düsseldorf (IV 29367). My translation.

included. Otherwise the task of the art dealer would be to buy not just one piece in the United States, but a whole stock, or a few exhibitions, procured in just one trip.[102]

If Fischer was committed to bringing American and European influences and artists together, Wedewer insisted on the European prehistory of the new art first ascribed to the United States.[103] Interestingly, Jappe, in his critical review of the exhibition, also contributed to the differentiation of the European and American artists.[104] When he described the works in the exhibition, despite the intentions of the artists, as "pre-artistic snooping and stammering," he adds that "especially the American artists seem in their newborn personal meditation to have trouble distinguishing between subjective and private."[105] Nonetheless, in its physical installation, Fischer and Wedewer's European overview of conceptual art shows quite a few similarities with Lippard's exhibition *557,087*, and could even be considered its European counterpart. It is therefore useful to analyze to what extent the exhibition in Leverkusen drew from American influences, and if so, whether Fischer's method of work was defining for the execution of *Konzeption*.

102 "Das kann natürlich auch sehr vorteilhaft sein, wenn plötzlich die Sammler sehen, dass woanders doch vielleicht noch interessantere Sachen zu haben sind oder so. Aber das würde ja nur dem deutschen Kunsthändler nützen, sich mit besserer Qualität einzudecken. Dass Europäer nach Amerika gehen und da einkaufen, ist ja doch recht illusorisch, da der Reise sich ja automatisch verdoppeln würde, da darin Fahrten, Transporte, Versicherungen usw. sind, was ja sonst Aufgabe des Kunsthändlers ist, in Amerika einzukaufen, nicht nur eins, einen ganzen Schock [sic] oder einige Ausstellungen mit einer Fahrt besorgen usw." Ibid. My translation.

103 Richard mentions that the collaboration between Fischer and Wedewer did not go well, and that at the end of the show Fischer decided not to work with the museum director again. Although she refers to the letters sent by artists not receiving catalogues or their promised fees from the museum, there is no reference of Fischer's position in this matter. Richard 2009, p. 97.

104 Jappe and Wedewer had possibly been in contact about the theoretical framework of the exhibition, while Wedewer mentions following a "formula" by Jappe in his introduction.

105 Jappe 1969. My translation.

The Exhibition as (Free) Publicity

The ironic comment from one of the reviewers that "museum directors can look forward to see themselves enabled to mount an exhibition without paying for the costs of transport, insurance and security" in fact positively corresponded with the new practices in exhibition-making.[106] Operating on the idea of dematerialization, Lippard was particularly concerned

106 "Museumdirektoren dürfen sich freuen, weil sie in die Lage versetzt werden, eine Ausstellung zu veranstalten, ohne für Transportkosten, Versicherungspolicen und Wachpersonal aufkommen zu müssen," Wolf Schön, "Etwas, das es nicht gibt: 'Konzeption'—eine Ausstellung im Leverkusener Museum," *Rheinische Merkur*, November 7, 1969. In fact, this comment also corresponds with the exhibition's financial report.

with "doing more with less" in her so-called suitcase exhibitions—and applied a socioeconomic principle within the production processes of public exhibitions. This was prompted by the different, more intellectual, position that the artists had taken, which stipulated the detachment of the production process and the role of the public to be more participatory or democraticized. In comparison, Siegelaub's efforts were more specifically focused on the broad distribution of the work of his artists to the "multitudes," encouraging a new system of compensation, not so much in the financial appreciation of the end product, but in the intellectual work that the artist had done.

Theoretically, these ideological aspects were also recognized in the show in Leverkusen, but within the traditional context of the museum they could hardly be realized. Museum director Wedewer was certainly not drawing conclusions from his intellectual framing of the new art, and Fischer, although personally affiliated with many of the artists, was less politically engaged than his American colleagues.[107] Nonetheless, it was probably Fischer who could be held responsible for the final installation of the show in Leverkusen, while his commitment to the artists and the installation of their work has been frequently described.[108] Also, he declared himself in favor of making museum shows, stating, "Perhaps I'm not an ordinary art dealer. I'm not interested in this whole gallery business. I want to convey information, to show an artist's work; I couldn't care less where I do it. I have never put a notice in a paper. I'd rather do museum exhibitions which are linked with my name."[109]

Fischer never deliberately presented himself as a curator, and neither did he consciously develop a curatorial method, but he had very specific ideas about how to position his artists within the art scene of the time. The nonchalant attitude

107 Various letters were sent by the artists to the museum in Leverkusen long after the exhibition had closed, requesting to receive catalogues or the fees for the participation in the show. The director seemed to have no knowledge of fees. Stadtarchiv Leverkusen.

108 See, for example, Lynda Morris, who described how Fischer was the only one present during the installation of *When Attitudes Become Form* at the ICA in London. Szeemann was not able to come, and Charles Harrison, who was the co-curator of the London show, was also not there. Richard 2009.

109 Jappe 1971, p. 71.

that he demonstrates in the above statement suggests that his success as an art dealer is a fortuitous consequence rather than a predetermined strategy, but this precise behavior should not be underestimated.[110] With his sophisticated working method, Fischer was actually as effective in the promotion of his artists as Siegelaub was considered to have been.[111] Once he started to represent the work of artists like Carl Andre, Jan Dibbets, Richard Long, and Bruce Nauman in 1967, he developed a precise strategy that would secure these artists' positions within the professional art circuit.

Fischer came across the work of the minimal artists while still working as an artist himself, and was intrigued by the clear, objective, or even ascetic characteristics that were so contrary to the Pop-like work he and his Düsseldorf colleagues Sigmar Polke and Gerhard Richter[112] were making in the early to mid-1960s.[113] His basic idea was to bring international artists to Düsseldorf—essentially, those who were not yet known in Germany, or more generally in Europe. He "came upon what was brand-new and currently on view in America and had connections to Europe as well. That was at first an external criterion, but I was convinced of the quality of what I saw there. I was lucky that nobody had done this before."[114]

Being very keen to select and work with artists who were not yet represented by other galleries ("that wouldn't have brought us any further"), Fischer made clever use of the limited means he had at the time and, instead of transporting their artworks, invited artists to produce these at the site of his gallery.[115] This method was closer to the process-based, *in situ* work of the minimal and conceptual artists, and cheaper than transporting and insuring the works. It was also important for Fischer to meet the artists in person before working with them; to have a good understanding between them—

110 Kaspar König, in a conversation with Brigitte Kölle, says about Fischer, "He always conveyed the impression that he had nothing to do. As if everything was running on its own. He always did so with great efficiency and intelligence, while acting as if it had appeared from nowhere." Kölle 2007, p. 91.

111 See Alberro 2003.

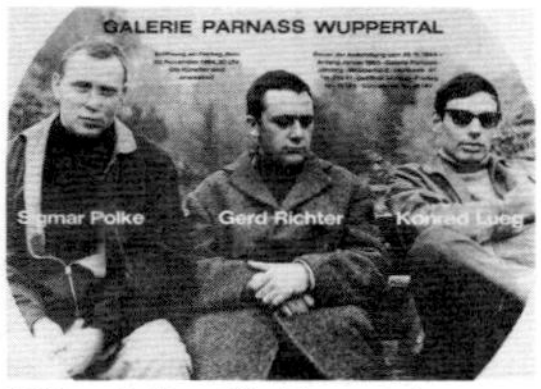

112 Polke, Richter, and Fischer as presented on the invitation card of Galerie Parnass in Wuppertal, 1964.

113 Fischer started his gallery by focusing on (post-)minimal art in 1967, soon after Paul Maenz's exhibition-event *19:45–21:55, September 9th, 1967, Frankfurt, Germany* in which he participated as an artist under his mother's maiden name, Lueg. The title of the exhibition-event, held at the Dorothea Loehr gallery in Frankfurt, in both the interior and exterior spaces of what were formerly stables, underlined the temporality of the project, which included ephemeral works by Jan Dibbets, Barry Flanagan, Bernard Höke, John Johnson, Richard Long, and Charlotte Posenenske.

114 Jocks, as cited in Kölle 2007, p. 295.

115 Kaspar König stated that if "an artist had already exhibited elsewhere, Konrad was no longer interested. He wanted to be the first one and to have direct contact with the artists." See Richard 2009, p. 62. This quote, supposedly taken from an interview that Kölle conducted with König, is surprisingly lacking in the referenced interview. The gallery space at the Neubrückstrasse, where Fischer started, was actually an archway between two houses that was closed up with doors on both sides. The space was only 11 × 3 meters and, according to several artists, a challenge to use as a starting point for their work. See, for example, the interview with Bruce Nauman, Kölle 2007, p. 18.

to talk with them and drink beer in Düsseldorf—was a more decisive factor in the partnership than the quality of the work, as he once stated:

> If I haven't met the artist and I don't like him, I do not exhibit him. Occasionally, I do exhibitions with artists to see whether I like their work over a longer period of time. Only after a month do I know whether their work appeals to me, and sometimes the relationship peters out. Sometimes, the reason that some artists only exhibit once is that we didn't get along too well. It doesn't always have to do with their art. If you don't get along well, you don't have to keep on trying.[116]

Once Fischer decided to affiliate with the artists of his choice, however, he strongly committed to them. The close relationship with his artists is illustrated by the fact that all of them stayed in Fischer's private apartment when visiting Düsseldorf. Besides saving money on expensive hotels, he thus had the chance to get to know them on a personal level.[117] In his very particular manner of associating with them, generally as an artist among artists, he was constantly on the lookout for opportunities that would provide them with the highest visibility. In an interview from 1989 he recalls his motivations, stating, "It is very important for me to look after my artists, especially so that they can exhibit in other galleries. Of course not in Cologne, that's too near, I wouldn't like that, but in Milan, London, Munich. And then it's important that they get into museums!"[118]

In order to promote his artists abroad, Fischer established a network of like-minded galleries, both in Europe and the United States, such as Heiner Friedrich in Munich, Gian Enzo Sperone in Turin, and Dwan Gallery in New York, with which he shared the expenses for the tours, and in some

116 Jocks, as cited in Kölle 2007, p. 297.

117 See Kölle 2005, p. 124. "Da in den sechziger und siebziger Jahren das billigste transatlantische Flugticket an einen dreiwöchigen Mindestaufenthalt gebunden war, hatten Konrad Fischer und seine Künstler Gelegenheit, sich in Ruhe kennen zu lernen und (was Fischer immer gerne tat) gemeinsam durch Düsseldorfs Altstadtkneipen zu ziehen. Alle Künstler wohnten gleichsam als artists in residence in Konrad und Dorothee Fischers Wohnung; zunächst in einem ausgebauten Dachgeschoss über ihrer Wohnung in der Poststraße, ab 1969 in der sehr geräumigen Altbauwohnung in der Prinz Georg Straße."

118 Stella Baum, "I Enjoy Looking Back on the Years: Record of a Conversation with Konrad Fischer," in Kölle 2007, p. 281. Originally published in *Kunstforum International* no. 104 (November/December, 1989). Translation by Karl Hoffmann.

119 Kölle writes that Fischer made his first three-week trip to New York from March 27 to April 19, 1968. The expensive costs for the flight at the time were shared with gallerist Heiner Friedrich, who could also benefit from Fischer's research and studio visits to the artists represented by him. Kölle 2005, p. 49.

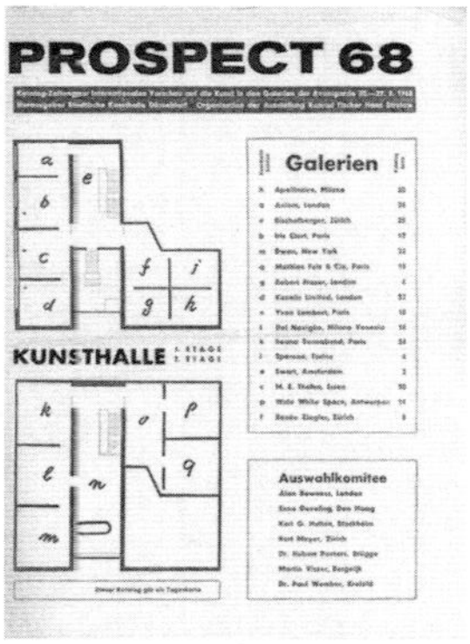

120 Hand-out/catalogue of *Prospect 68*, Kunsthalle, Düsseldorf.

121 The "exhibition catalogue" of *Prospect 68*, more like a publicity handout, had the subtitle, *Katalog-Zeitung zur internationalen Vorschau auf die Kunst in den Galerien der Avantgarde*. Archive Städtische Kunsthalle, Düsseldorf. It was not only to Fischer's benefit that an alternative art fair was organized in Düsseldorf; the director of the Kunsthalle, Karl Ruhrberg, proposed to the head of the Organization of Progressive German Art Dealers (VPDK) shortly after the opening of the first Cologne art fair to host the next art fair in Düsseldorf. When this proposal was rejected and *Prospect 68* launched, a commercial rivalry between the two cities was created. See Richard 2010, pp. 79–80.

122 The participating galleries were Apollinaire (Milan), Axiom (London), Bischofberger (Zurich), Iris Clert (Paris), Dwan (New York), Mathias Fels & Cie (Paris), Robert Fraser (London), Kasmin Limited (London), Yvon Lambert (Paris), Del Naviglio (Milan and Venice), Ileana Sonnabend (Paris), Sperone (Turin), Riekje Swart (Amsterdam), M.E. Thelen (Essen), Wide White Space (Antwerp), and René Ziegler (Zurich). Other members of the selection committee were museum director Paul Wember, art critics Alan Bowness and Kurt Meyer, and private collector Hubert Peeters.

cases also the commission on sales.[119] In developing this network of galleries devoted to conceptualism, the launch of *Prospect 68*, held from September 20 to 29, 1968, at the Kunsthalle Düsseldorf, contributed significantly.[120] As a reaction to the Cologne Kunstmarkt, which opened in 1967, and in which he was not invited to participate, Fischer organized an alternative art fair/exhibition together with the art critic Hans Strelow, more subtly announced as an "international preview of art from the avant-garde galleries."[121] A jury or committee, including important art professionals like Enno Develing, Pontus Hultén, and Martin Visser, selected sixteen, mainly European, galleries to participate.[122] Remarkably, Fischer himself was not selected, possibly because he was also the organizer of the event. Yet it was a great success, drawing 15,000 visitors, among them important figures in the conceptual art scene like Johannes Cladders and Harald Szeemann. The opportunity for the new galleries to extend their commercial interest must have been substantial.

Prospect 69,[123] which took place from September 30 to October 12, 1969, could be regarded even more successful because of the participation of many "international" galleries—about half of the sixteen participating galleries were American.[124] Like the year before, the selection of the galleries was made by a jury/committee of important art professionals, with the difference that this time the artists were selected prior to the galleries.[125] Because of this focus the art fair was more exclusively positioned as an exhibition.[126] At the opening of *Prospect 69*, Harald Szeemann, seated in the selection committee, gave an inimitable speech in which he critically reflected on the milieu of contemporary art, which he described as "the triangle studio—gallery—collection + museum."[127] He emphasized the role of the museum in crediting the actions of conceptualist artists, saying, "It is

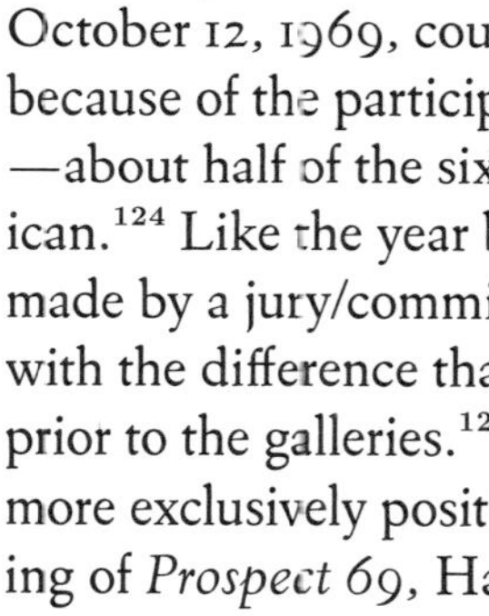

123 Hand-out/catalogue of *Prospect 69*, Kunsthalle, Düsseldorf.

124 The participating galleries were ACE (Los Angeles), Art & Project (Amsterdam), l'Attico (Rome), Eugenia Butler (Los Angeles), Bykert (New York), Dwan (New York), Fischbach (New York), Toni Gerber (Bern), Yvon Lambert (Paris and Milan), Mickery (Loenersloot), Seiquer (Madrid), Ileana Sonnabend (Paris), Sperone (Turin), Wide White Space (Antwerp), Howard Wise (New York), and Seth Siegelaub (New York).

125 The jury included José Luis de Castillejo, Martin Visser, Michel Claura, Enno Develing, Jasia Reichardt, Paul Wember, and Harald Szeemann. The participating artists were Robert Barry, Bernd and Hilla Becher, Lynda Benglis, Joseph Beuys, Alighiero Boetti, Stanley Brouwn, Daniel Buren, Pier Paolo Calzolari, Cooper, Darboven, Dibbets, Griffa, Groner, Michael Heizer, Hidalgo, Huebler, Kosuth, Kounellis, Lamelas, LeWitt, Long, Mattiacci, Marchetti, Marden, Ohlson, Oppenheim, Penone, Prentice, Prini, Raetz, Ross, Ruthenbeck, Ryman, Schnyder, Smithson, Toroni, Weiner, and Wheeler.

foremost important that they are realized, that they take place in a museum, either financed by taxpayers or private persons. This will give them the character of publicness and at the same time the irrationality of artistic events."[128] According to Szeemann, the museums could bring artists something that the galleries could not, which he defined as "consecration."[129]

If he did not already, Fischer would certainly have understood at this moment the importance of the show he was organizing in Leverkusen, and the question is how he proceeded with this information. From March 25 to April 9, 1969, Fischer made a trip to New York where he met several gallerists, artists, and other contacts cooperative in the furthering of *Prospect 69*, as well as his own gallery practice. Presumably, this trip would also have been of use for *Konzeption*, but there are no records that confirm this. What is more, although Fischer met Siegelaub in New York, he only wrote to him and Lippard on July 11, 1969, to ask for advice on how to set up a "documentary-oriented exhibition."[130] It therefore seems that he was not yet involved in or engaged with the Leverkusen exhibition at the time of his New York visit. It could be that Fischer, like in earlier projects, was first consulted for his expertise and only later extended this role, but the lack of reference to *Konzeption* in his personal records nevertheless suggests that this exhibition was not his priority at the time.

After his collective endeavor with Wedewer in Leverkusen, Fischer had in any case managed to establish a position as (co-)curator and was increasingly involved in museum projects and exhibitions on conceptual art (in Germany). The highlight, no doubt, was his participation in Documenta 5 in 1972, where he organized a section of the exhibition devoted to conceptual art, titled *Idee + Idee/Licht*,[131] together with Klaus Honnef.[132] Fischer's expertise on conceptual art was,

126 Deputy director Jürgen Harten noted in a radio interview that the selection committee first made a selection of artist names, and after this the corresponding galleries were approached to participate. This procedure was followed to avoid that the galleries would have too much exposure/authority and the exhibition could also be experienced as a real exhibition. Deutschlandfunk 1969.

127 Harald Szeemann, opening speech *Prospect 69*, Stadtarchiv Düsseldorf (IV 29367). Szeemann was invited by Jürgen Harten to host a "more serious" opening event instead of the free jazz and beat opening of the previous edition "to avoid massive overcrowding." He was asked for a critical comment to "the situation of contemporary art in museums and galleries." Harten, in a letter to Szeemann, September 5, 1969, Stadtarchiv Düsseldorf (IV 29367).

128 Ibid. Szeemann speaks more specifically about a "Kunsthaus." My translation.

129 Ibid.

130 Richard 2009, p. 97. There is no record of Siegelaub and Lippard's response.

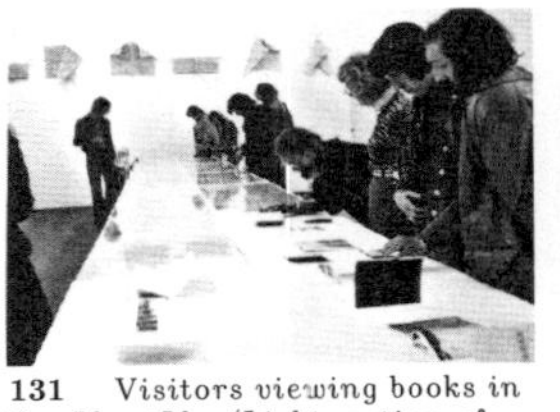

131 Visitors viewing books in the *Idee+Idee/Licht* section of Documenta 5, 1972. Photo Erhard Wehrmann, Courtesy Kunststiftung Poll, Berlin.

132 Harald Szeemann wanted to include a conceptual art section in his Documenta 5 (1972), but was not particularly interested in this type of art and invited Honnef to do it, who in turn asked Fischer to collaborate, since he considered him to be the expert on conceptual art. Honnef himself says that Szeemann invited him to do the section with Fischer.

again, the reason he was asked to collaborate, as Honnef recalls, "[M]y feeling was that I could still learn a few things and I opted to work with Fischer."[133] At the time there were apparently no objections to the ambiguous position that Fischer had maneuvered himself into, but by then he had just about consummated his strategy. According to Honnef, Documenta 5 has been was fundamental for the individual careers of the conceptual artists that who started working shortly thereafter.[134]

In his analysis of the strategies that Siegelaub implemented when developing new formats for the exhibition of conceptual art, Alberro already suggested that it was exactly the distribution of information that eventually "sold" the work.[135] Also, Fischer was well aware of this principle when he stated, "The capital, as far as the artist and I are concerned, is the publicity. What's important for me is not how to sell things but how to get information across to those who are interested, so that in due course the artists I represent get somewhere, and people say, 'Fischer got the right man.'"[136] Fischer's comment on "the capital is the publicity" corresponds with Alberro's notion that it became irrelevant to distinguish between positive or negative criticism within the emergent art marketplace of the 1960s, because they both add to the same result: "The passage directs attention to the shift during this decade from serious intellectual critique and analysis to the crucial importance of publicity."[137]

Thus, the general opinion of misunderstanding and the critical press review about his conceptual art show were of little importance to Fischer. The publicity generated by the negative reception of *Konzeption* would nevertheless contribute to its subsequent success.[138] Moreover, supplement to the production of publicity, Fischer understood that, for the broad distribution of his artists, it was important to get them

133 Sophie Richard, "Interview with Klaus Honnef," in Richard 2009, p. 447.

134 Ibid., p. 448.

135 Alexander Alberro, "Art, Advertising, Sign Value," in Alberro 2003, p. 10. Alberro describes Siegelaub's publicity strategies in detail, but ignores the evaluation of these actions in terms of commercial success.

136 Jappe 1971, p. 71.

137 Alberro 2003. Alberro adds that a new type of dealer emerged within this atmosphere, one who had to appeal to collectors but maintain a distance from them at the same time.

138 Szeemann pointed out in his diary of the preparations for *When Attitudes Become Form* that "at least the exhibition will provide with lots of material for discussion (in the papers)." Szeemann, in *Op losse schroeven: Situaties en cryptostructuren*, ed. Ank Marcar, exh. cat. Amsterdam (Stedelijk Museum) 1969, n.p.

into the official canons of art.[139] With the mounting of a large historical show in an important museum for contemporary art, he had brought the type of art he was representing to the attention of an international network of avant-garde art professionals and collectors, and favorably placed himself in the midst of the discourse.[140]

139 This notion might have been stipulated by the German economist Willi Bongard, who first published his "Kunstkompass," a ranking system for artists, in 1971 in the German magazine *Art Aktuell*. In his "objective" calculations of a "top 100" Bongard was specifically focused on the network surrounding the artists (exhibitions in important international galleries and museums, as well as publications and reviews in important art magazines and journals), and the system of art in general. It might also be that Bongard had drawn from Fischer's practice as a curator/dealer for his ranking system.

140 This might actually been a much more important drive for him than commercial transactions, which were nevertheless a lucrative outcome of his efforts. Sophie Richard's study on the European network of conceptual art shows the role Fischer has had in the distribution of conceptual art throughout Europe and the financial benefits that he earned, having about a quarter of the market of public institutions. See Richard 2009.

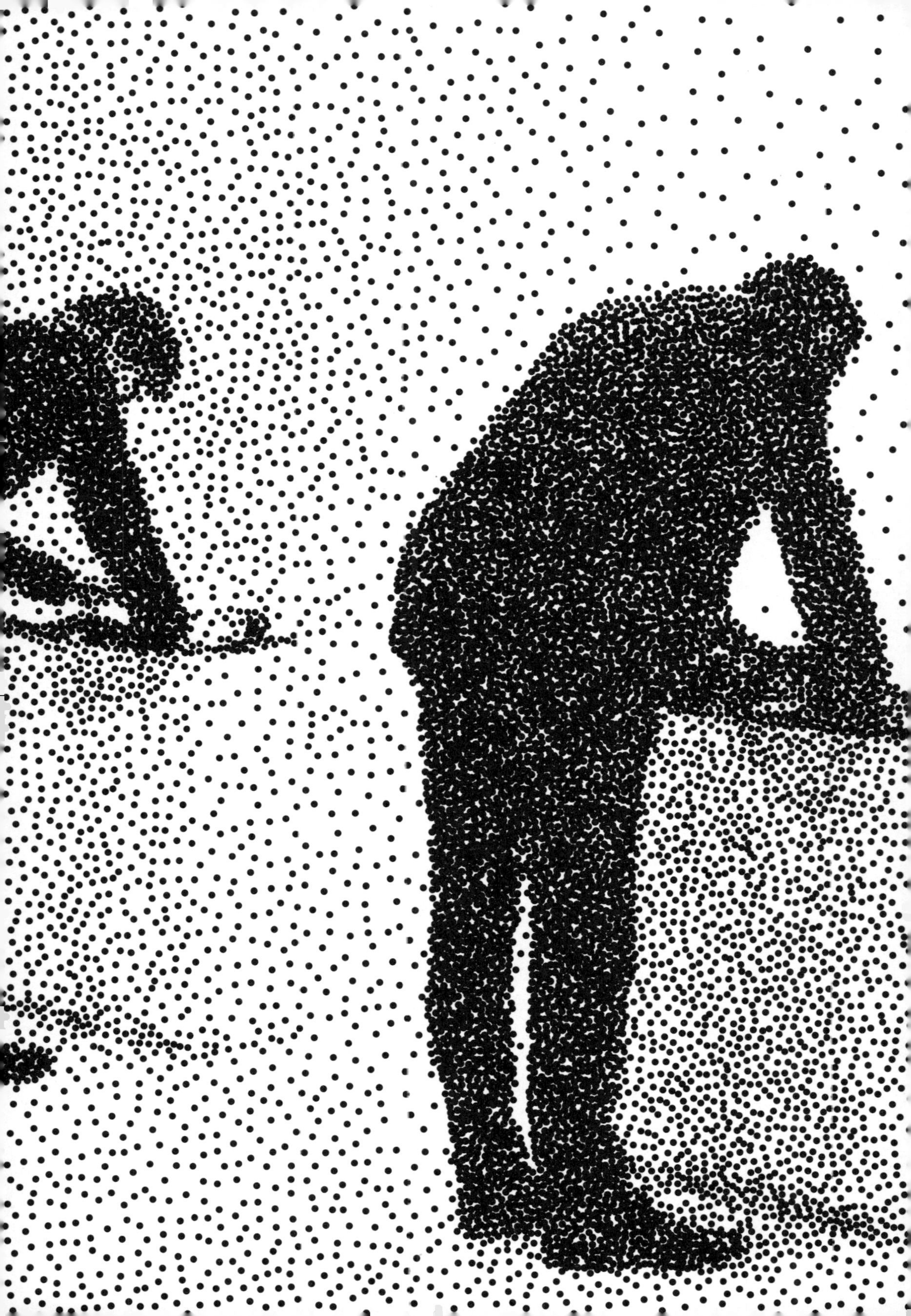

Chapter 3
Case Study
L'art conceptuel, une perspective
at the Musée d'art moderne de la ville de Paris (1989)

Historical objectification ought to be sped up while there is still a collective experience and memory which can assist in the clarity of an analysis while, simultaneously, opening up a space to ask fundamental questions regarding history-making.
— Michael Asher[1]

1 Michael Asher, as cited in Claude Gintz, "L'art conceptuel, une perspective: Notes on an Exhibition Project," in exh. cat. Paris 1989, p. 20.

A First Retrospective on Conceptual Art

In the same year in which the renowned exhibition *Magiciens de la terre* was shown at the Centre Pompidou in Paris, a retrospective exhibition on conceptual art opened at the Musée d'art moderne de la ville de Paris (MAMVP) on November 22, 1989.[2] In a cultural climate that centered on the topic of postcolonialism, and twenty years after conceptual art had reached its peak, the exhibition *L'art conceptuel, une perspective* seemed out of place.[3] As the French critic Ghislain Mollet-Viéville commented, "A retrospective on a movement that flourished in the late '60s and early '70s might

2 The exhibition ran in Paris until February 18, 1990, and was subsequently shown at Caja de Pensiones Madrid (March–April 1990), the Deichtorhallen in Hamburg (May–July 1990), and the Musée d'art contemporain de Montréal (August 5–October 21, 1990).

3 *Magiciens de la terre*, curated by Jean-Hubert Martin, opened at the Centre Georges Pompidou and the Grand halle de la Villette in Paris on May 18, 1989, creating a vibrant debate on ethnocentric practices within contemporary art at the time, and a much wider reception within exhibition history. See Lucy Steeds, ed., *Making Art Global: Volume 2: Magiciens de la Terre 1989* (Cologne: Walther König, 2013).

Image appropriated from Mel Bochner, *Working Drawings and Other Visible Things on Paper Not Necessarily Meant to Be Viewed as Art*, 1966, at the School of Visual Arts, New York. See also p. 135.

seem a bit premature, if not downright presumptuous, and some are sure to object that it is too early to grasp the import of such recent history."[4] It was not without a reason, however, that the MAMVP mounted a large retrospective at this specific moment: most of conceptual art's protagonists were still alive at the time the exhibition was conceived, and the organizers were of the opinion that the complex movement of conceptual art would shed light on issues that contemporary artists continued to explore.[5] Director Suzanne Pagé invited art historian and critic Claude Gintz to elaborate a project "concerning the coalescence, at a particular moment, of a trend (initiated by Duchamp) toward the conceptualization of the visual arts."[6] Gintz in turn chose Benjamin Buchloh to be his "partner in crime" in the conception of the project, which potentially stirred discussions. Buchloh's seminal essay, "Conceptual Art 1962–1969: From the Aesthetic of Administration to the Critique of Institutions," first published in the catalogue of the Paris exhibition, generated considerable controversy among the protagonists of conceptual art.[7]

Michael Newman has argued that the history of conceptual art was built up in the period between *L'art conceptuel, une perspective* (1989–1990)[8] and another important exhibition on conceptual art, *Reconsidering the Object of Art: 1965–1975*, curated by Anne Rorimer and Ann Goldstein at the Museum of Contemporary Art in Los Angeles (1995–1996).[9] Moreover, I would argue that Gintz's exhibition in Paris has largely instigated the historicization of conceptual art, particularly through the discourse that was produced in the catalogue and prolonged in *October* journal by Buchloh, Joseph Kosuth, and Seth Siegelaub. In this respect the catalogue has become more significant than the exhibition, which is consistent with the setup of the project. Gintz mainly concentrated on the theoretization of the project and the selection

4 Ghislain Mollet-Viéville, in "L'art Conceptuel, une perspective," *Galeries Magazine* (October/November, 1989), p. 100. The year before, however, an exhibition titled *Art Conceptuel 1*, with works by Art & Language, Robert Barry, Hanne Darboven, On Kawara, Joseph Kosuth, Robert Morris, and Lawrence Weiner had been organized at the Centre of Contemporary Visual Arts (CAPC) in Bordeaux. *L'art conceptuel, une perspective* included works by Giovanni Anselmo, Art & Language, Michael Asher, John Baldessari, Robert Barry, Mel Bochner, Alighiero e Boetti, Marcel Broodthaers, Stanley Brouwn, Daniel Buren, Victor Burgin, André Cadere, Hanne Darboven, Jan Dibbets, Marcel Duchamp, Dan Flavin, Dan Graham, Hans Haacke, Eva Hesse, Douglas Huebler, Jasper Johns, On Kawara, Yves Klein, Joseph Kosuth, Sol LeWitt, Piero Manzoni, Robert Morris, Bruce Nauman, Claes Oldenburg, Roman Opalka, Adrian Piper, Emilio Prini, Robert Rauschenberg, Ed Ruscha, Robert Smithson, Bernar Venet, Lawrence Weiner, and Ian Wilson.

5 Mollet-Viéville 1989, p. 100.

6 Suzanne Pagé, "Preface," in exh. cat. Paris 1989, p. 11.

7 Buchloh 1990, pp. 105–143. Gintz had discussed the theoretical framework for both the catalogue and exhibition with Buchloh. He emphasized that he had been close to Buchloh because he translated several of Buchloh's texts into French in the early 1980s. Conversation with Claude Gintz, Paris, December 3, 2011. Both Kosuth and Siegelaub had fiercely objected to Buchloh's "textbook history of conceptual art." See, for example, Erik Verhagen, "Histoires de l'art conceptuel une rétrospective," *Perspective* no. 3 (December 2007), p. 509.

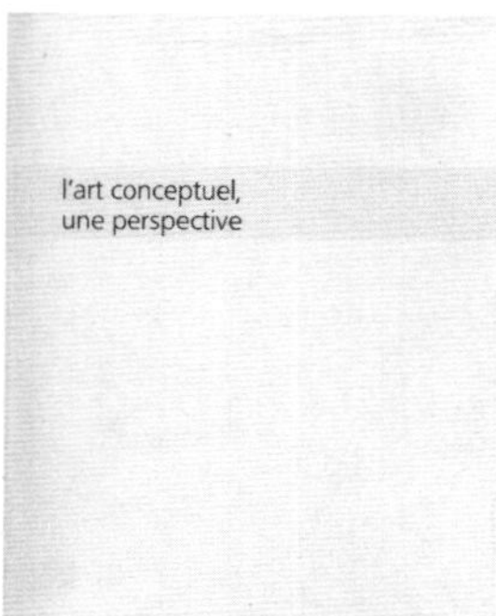

8 Catalogue cover of *L'art conceptuel, une perspective*, Paris 1989.

9 Newman 1996, p. 102. Newman credits Benjamin Buchloh, Birgit Pelzer, Anne Rorimer, Thomas Crow, Alexander Alberro, and William Wood in this respect.

of the artists and works, which is reflected in the catalogue, whereas ARC curator Juliette Laffon arranged the organization and installation in the museum spaces.[10] Although the focus on the catalogue fits the conceptual format of presentation, it is significant to explicate to what extent the curation of *L'art conceptuel* differs from the exhibition practices of the late 1960s and early 1970s.

Newman underlined the fundamental paradox that is faced when approaching works of conceptual art in a contemporary perspective: "The success of conceptual art can be measured according the amount of resistance against its adoption in the historical continuum, given the fact that the intention of the greatest of these works was to end or demolish this continuum, and it is thus partly thanks to the failure of the 'movement' that its history can be written."[11] Referring to the typical remains of the conceptual endeavor that are captured in authentic typewritten documents, Newman's statement emphasizes the curatorial approach of *L'art conceptuel*.[12] Conceived as a historical undertaking, the exhibition focused on the discourse of conceptual art rather than the problems this provoked for the making of an exhibition and ignored the dilemma of how to exhibit conceptual artworks that have become art documentation. The fact that the exhibition was executed as a traditional, rather modernist museum presentation brings about an interesting dialectic in *L'art conceptuel*: while historicizing the period of conceptual art by means of a selection of "autonomous" artworks, the ephemeral projects that lay at the root of this period were in a way transformed into commodified objects.

This aspect of the exhibition has been noted in the sparse reviews, but did not lead to further conclusions regarding the contemporary condition of works of conceptual art.[13] In contrast to the initial publishing practices of conceptual

10 Conversation with Gintz, Paris, December 3, 2011. In a letter that was sent to the artists selected for the show, Pagé wrote, "[the exhibition] will show the works of about thirty artists which have been selected by Claude Gintz; the realisation will be implemented by Juliette LAFFON, curator at the Museum." Archives MAMVP (Box 524/9).

11 Newman 1996. My translation.

12 Ibid. As Newman stated, "The historical distance of conceptual art to the present becomes visible in a manner that could not have been foreseen at the time; by the peculiar sight of the frames, instructions and documents made on old-fashioned typewriters, on which the typed errors were corrected with typex or simply disregarded." My translation.

13 The exhibition, after its first presentation in Paris, had only been sparsely reviewed. By the time the exhibition was opened in Montreal it had met much more response in the papers. Especially Thomas Wulffen in *Kunstforum International* and John Bentley Mays in *The Globe and Mail* addressed the "object-status" of many works in the exhibition. Siegelaub criticized the inert presentation of *L'art conceptuel*, remarkably more than ten years after the exhibition took place. In Hans Ulrich Obrist, "Interview with Seth Siegelaub," in *24th International Biennale of Graphic Arts*, exh. cat. Ljubljana (International Centre of Graphic Arts) 2001, p. 220.

artists concerned with the exhibition of "primary information" in a catalogue format, the exhibition and catalogue of *L'art conceptuel* were compiled in a traditionally art historical manner, without the direct participation of the artists. A selection of representative work was made by the curator, after which the "original" works were loaned from different private and museum collections, and in a few cases directly from the artists.[14] It was in the organization and installation of the exhibition, however, that the direct interaction with the artists elucidated the complexities of an endeavor to re-exhibit "primary" works of conceptual art within a different spatial-temporal configuration. This can be determined through the correspondence with the artists about the execution of their works in the exhibition; for example, the project proposed by Michael Asher. The efforts made by both Asher and museum staff to find a proper format to fit Asher's critique on a conceptual art retrospective into the exhibition are more significant than the final result, and illustrate that the institutional framework was the preferred place for conceptual discourse.

As the first prominent and extensive retrospective on conceptual art after its historical momentum in the 1960s and 1970s, *L'art conceptuel* was explicitly confronted with the problem of re-exhibiting conceptual works of art. In this respect the exhibition presents several indicative curatorial decisions relating to the problematic I presented in the first chapter, which requests a precise analysis of how this project has dealt with the specific paradox of historicizing conceptual art.

In the reevaluation of the catalogue and exhibition, respectively, I will explain how the discussions surrounding *L'art conceptuel* focused on the historical and theoretical aspects of conceptual art, whereas the curatorial aspects have been largely neglected. Notwithstanding the affirmation of a

14 I base these assumptions on the extensive examination of the exhibition's archive in the Musée d'art moderne de la ville de Paris and my conversation with Gintz.

"discursive turn" in both artistic and curatorial practice, this turning point is also—or primarily—defined by the questions that conceptual artists posed regarding the format or framework of the exhibition (i.e., institution). The traditional art historical, object-based approach, however, still prevailed in the historical definition of conceptual art, while the discursive aspects that are captured in the residue "materials" of its projects remained unrecognized.[15] That the exhibition problematized the historical validation of conceptual artworks is illustrated in the discussions surrounding the installation of *L'art conceptuel*. It is in these discussions that the crux of my thesis becomes most visible, along with the necessity to include these exhibition histories into the broader field of art history and thereby continue to expand the field of curatorial studies.

15 Residue materials, apart from actual work, can contain anything from artist's instructions, notes, (published) texts, correspondence about works in exhibitions, interviews, and photographic/documentary material of previous installations of works.

The Exhibition as Historicizing Venture

Although *L'art conceptuel* has been received as a perspective on conceptual art from the specific viewpoint of curator Gintz, defining conceptual art's place as a continuing object of discussion, there were a few principles that had been determined *a priori*.[16] The intention of director Pagé focused on questioning the contemporary implications of reactivating an artistic practice based on "ideas" which were criticizing or even rejecting traditional museum structures. As she wrote in the preface of the catalogue, "What might be indicated by showing works which, through 'dematerialization,' have been constructed explicitly to escape the grasp of institutions and the conditions of 'objects'?" Pagé also emphasized the fact that it was Europe that first recognized conceptual art, and that it is now once again in Europe that a reevaluation of conceptual art, the principal protagonists of which are

16 For a reflection on the exhibition, see Verhagen 2007, pp. 508–511.

American, has been initiated. These grandiloquent proclamations underline that it was of great importance for the museum to position itself within the international discourse of conceptual art and to claim a first historicization of the "movement."[17]

That this historicization was primarily done by means of the catalogue seemed to be prescribed by Pagé as well: "Given the importance of language in the works, the catalogue is particularly important in the case of conceptual art. Juliette Laffon and Angeline Scherf worked closely with Claude Gintz to analyze the works as rigorously as possible. They were very aware that they were contributing to the history of the movement. The goal was to present different viewpoints, and to confront them with the artists' explanations of their work."[18] Hence, the framework for the conceptualization and production of the exhibition, as well as Gintz's role in it, were clearly delineated. Gintz nevertheless stressed that he had not felt limited by the director's guidelines; his engagement had been an open question, and he was given a free hand in his approach and the selection of artists and works. It was his conviction to show that conceptualism influenced many artists, a positioning that Pagé appreciated: "That's why we did not limit the exhibit to the movement's most famous exponents."[19]

In accordance with Pagé, Gintz stressed that the catalogue was particularly important to him. Conventionally, the format of a catalogue book fits a historicizing endeavor better than a museum show; in the case of conceptual art the focus on the catalogue was even more obvious, because of the fact that these artists used the format of the catalogue as a site of exhibition. The transmission of "primary information," paramount to the conceptual period, however, was not adapted as a format for the catalogue of *L'art conceptuel*. Rather, the

17 This is confirmed through an interview with Pierre Landry in which Laffon declared, "In the past few years, there have been major retrospective exhibitions devoted to some of the artists present in this exhibition.... There was also the exhibition *Art Conceptuel 1* organized by CAPC in Bordeaux in 1988, but the intention there was different than ours.... As far as I know, there have been no other attempts in Europe or the U.S." Pierre Landry, "L'art conceptuel, une perspective: An Interview with Claude Gintz and Juliette Laffon," *Le journal du Musee d'art contemporain de Montréal* vol. 1, no. 2 (July/August 1990), n.p.

18 Mollet-Viéville 1989, p. 103.

19 Ibid., pp. 101–102.

format was based on a traditional exhibition catalogue: all the selected works in the exhibition were included, alphabetically listed by artist's name, and accompanied by short descriptions, ample photographic documentation, and individual exhibition histories.[20] Moreover, the thorough art historical essays that were included—besides those by Gintz and Buchloh were texts by Charles Harrison, Gabriele Guercio, Seth Siegelaub, and Robert C. Morgan—emphasize that the historical framing of conceptual art surpassed the intention to make a public exhibition.

In his catalogue text, Gintz takes the categorization of conceptual art as the outline for his exhibition: "The very title of this exhibition—'Conceptual Art: A Perspective'—raises the question of those limits within which such an exhibition should be contained. By which criteria may we determine what actually comprises Conceptual Art?"[21] In his theoretization on this question, Gintz discussed the positions of a number of artists that he considered "proto-conceptual," like Dan Graham and Robert Morris, but even earlier European progenitors as well, like Piero Manzoni and Yves Klein.[22] He also discussed several exhibitions that he considered to be conceptual, such as Siegelaub's *January 31, 1969* and *Summer Show (July, August, September 1969)*, Szeemann's *When Attitudes Become Form*, Konrad Fischer and Rolf Wedewer's *Konzeption-Conception*, and, with regard to the French context in which *L'art conceptuel* was conceived, the *Paris 18 IV 70* exhibition by Michel Claura, held at a temporary space on Rue Mouffetard in Paris and accompanied by a trilingual publication (in English, French, and German).[23] Gintz does not further elaborate on the conceptual characteristics of these exhibitions; rather, through a selection of artists who participated in these exhibitions, he problematizes the strict demarcation of conceptual art.

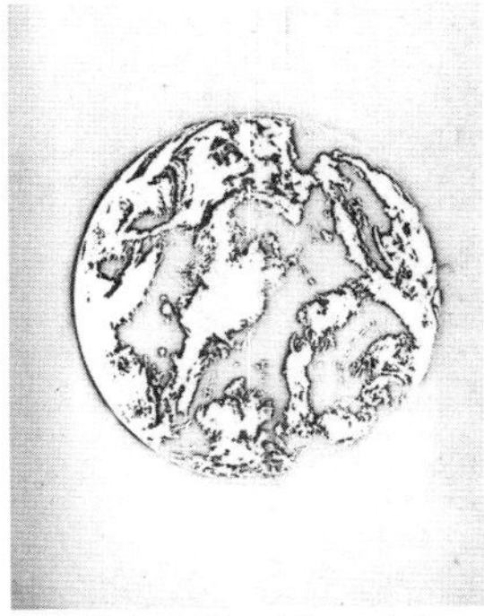

20 Robert Morris's contribution to Siegelaub's *Xerox Book*, 1968.

21 Gintz, in exh. cat. Paris 1989, p. 18.

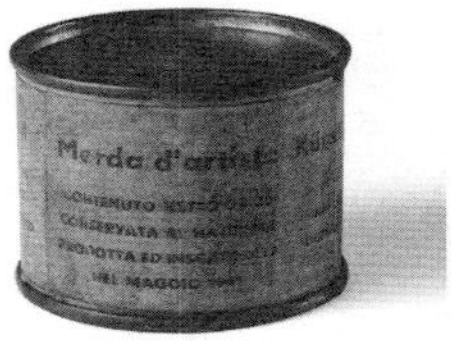

22a Piero Manzoni, *Merda d'artista* (Artist's Shit), 1961.

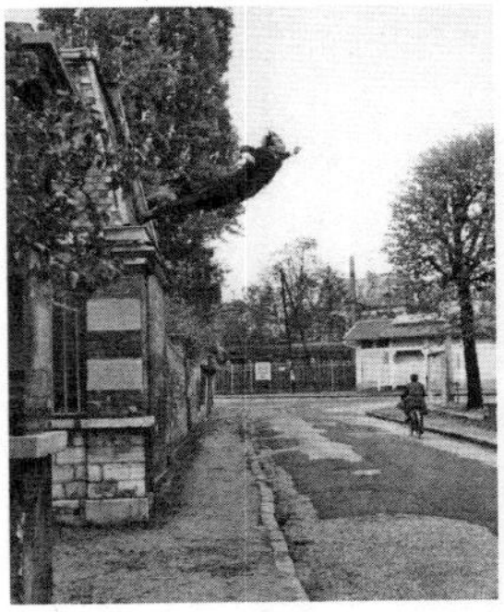

22b Yves Klein, *Leap into the Void*, 1960.

23 Michel Claura, ed., *Paris 18 IV 70* (New York: Seth Siegelaub, 1970). The participating artists in the exhibition were Ian Wilson, Lawrence Weiner, Niele Toroni, Robert Ryman, Edward Ruscha, Richard Long, Sol LeWitt, David Lamelas, On Kawara, Douglas Huebler, François Guinochet, Gilbert & George, Jean-Pierre Djian, Jan Dibbets, Daniel Buren, Stanley Brouwn, Marcel Broodthaers, and Robert Barry. See also <www.primaryinformation.org/product/siegelaub-18-paris-iv-70/> (19-10-2016).

In his intention to provide a broader perspective on conceptual art, Gintz emphasized the influence of European artists, such as Stanley Brouwn's early conceptualist practices in the city of Amsterdam,[24] as well as the interventions of Daniel Buren[25]—although he eventually considered the latter outside the realm of purely conceptualist art.[26] The work of Hans Haacke,[27] according to Gintz, echoes the discourse generated by Buren but, unlike Buren, his visual language is more related to that of "pure" conceptualist artists. Since Gintz generally focused in his essay on the positions/strategies of specific artists, the wide-ranging network of conceptual art is not further explored. The role that European galleries, such as Konrad Fischer in Düsseldorf, Gian Enzo Sperone in Turin, and Art & Project in Amsterdam, had in the exhibition, distribution, and subsequent reception of conceptual art in Europe, as well as the influence of earlier exhibitions and events in Europe with conceptual artists, such as Paul Maenz's *19:45–21:55, September 9th, 1967, Frankfurt, Germany* at the Dorothea Loehr Gallery in Frankfurt (the title represents the exact information of the event), are not mentioned.[28] Apparently, the relations between artists, galleries, and curators and the importance of their correlated interests was not yet a point of reference in 1989.

In his selection of conceptual works for the exhibition, Gintz invited several artists that fall outside the categorization of conceptual art as defined in his catalogue text. When asked about this in a conversation I had with him, he declared that he invited these artists to complement the European picture, saying, "I wouldn't have asked Bernar Venet or Opalka, if I had to decide purely by myself. They were invited because they were European artists and considered active in conceptual practices."[29] Whereas Gintz clearly delimitates conceptual art in his catalogue essay, in the compilation of his

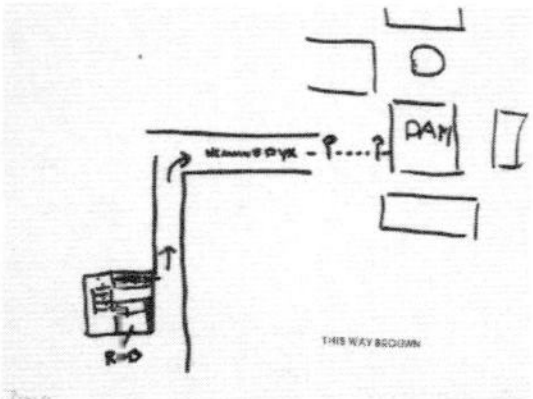

24 Stanley Brouwn, *This Way Brouwn*, 1964.

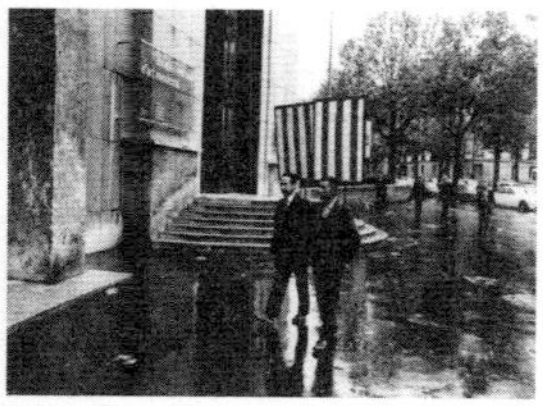

25 Daniel Buren, *Photo-souvenir: Hommes-Sandwichs*, site-specific work in front of the Musée national d'art moderne, Paris. Photo Bernard Boyer.

26 In my conversation with Gintz, he ultimately considered only a very few artists to be "pure conceptualists," besides Stanley Brouwn, Ian Wilson, and Michael Asher. Conversation with Gintz, 2011.

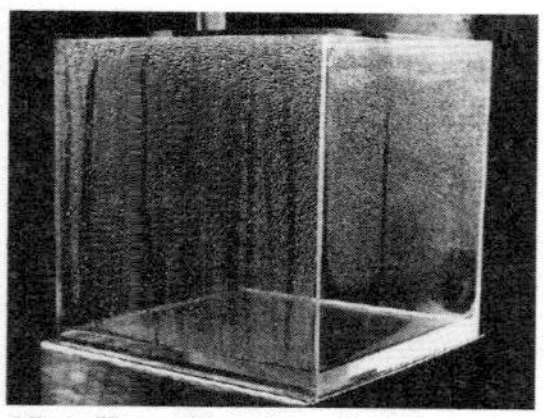

27 Hans Haacke, *Condensation Cube*, 1963–1965.

28 The exhibition is better known under its subtitle, *Dies alles Herzchen wird einmal Dir gehören* (Someday sweetheart this will all be yours). The participating artists were Jan Dibbets, Konrad (Fischer) Lueg, Charlotte Posenenske, Peter Roehr, Barry Flanagan, Bernhard Höke, John Johnson, and Richard Long. See Richard 2009, pp. 53–68.

29 Conversation with Gintz, 2011.

exhibition he was inclined to classify more in terms of a general conceptualism represented by different groups of artists, emphasizing that the particular moment in which conceptual art dominated artistic discourse was more important than the actual results of this in terms of artistic production.

This historical momentum is extensively analyzed in Buchloh's essay, "From the Aesthetic of Administration to Institutional Critique," which can be considered the first effort to frame conceptual art in an art historical sense. Like Gintz, Buchloh regards conceptual art as a reductionist structuralism that transpositions the object into an empty (linguistic) signifier, a process that was prefigured by Duchamp.[30] Buchloh sketched a lineage from Duchamp towards conceptual art, emphasizing the work of Cage, Rauschenberg, LeWitt, Morris, and others. Remarkably, Buchloh completely ignored the European context in his canonization of the conceptual movement—though as a former editor of *Interfunktionen* he should have been well-informed about European initiatives in the realm of conceptual art. Instead, he focused on the revision and theoretization of the written and accepted history of conceptual art until then, stating, "To historicize *Concept Art* (to use the term as it was coined by Henry Flint in 1961) at this moment requires more than merely a reconstruction of the movement's self-declared primary actors, or a scholarly obedience to their proclaimed purity of intentions and operations."[31] In a footnote added to this statement, Buchloh scarcely conceals that he aimed at the rash adoption of the writings by Joseph Kosuth, as cited in Gudrun Inboden's text "Joseph Kosuth: Artist and Critic of Modernism."[32] Moreover, one could argue that Kosuth's writings have served as a core theory in the early anthologies on conceptual art; for example, Ursula Meyer's book *Conceptual Art* from 1972.

30 Buchloh, *in exh. cat.* Paris 1989, p. 41.

31 Ibid., p. 42.

32 In Joseph Kosuth and Gudrun Inboden, *Joseph Kosuth: The Making of Meaning*, exh. cat. Stuttgart (Staatsgalerie) 1981, pp. 11–27.

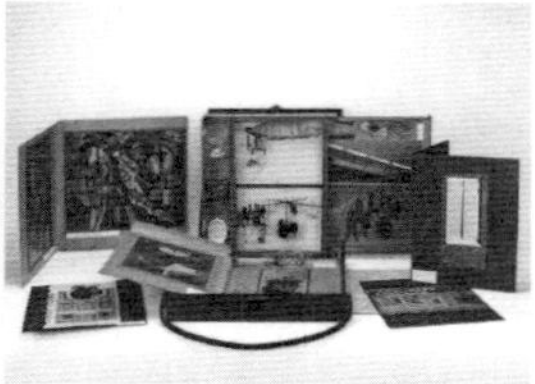

33 Marcel Duchamp, *La Boîte-en-valise*, 1935–1941.

34 Gintz, in exh. cat. Paris 1989, p. 21. Duchamp's *Boîte-en-valise* can be considered a sort of "portable museum," a suitcase with miniature replicas and reproductions of his work.

35 Mollet-Viéville 1989, p. 101. Mollet-Viéville was also one of the lenders to the exhibition.

In the determination of Duchamp as a progenitor of conceptual art—something Kosuth also claimed in his writings—Gintz drew a relation between the artist's *La Boîte-en-valise* (Box in a Suitcase) (1936–1941)[33] and the documentary exhibitions by Siegelaub: "If Duchamp seems to mimetically point to two characteristic features of contemporary 'high' culture... he also insists, in this age of mechanical reproduction, on the potentially unlimited accessibility of the artwork. This concern will turn up later at the center of the Conceptual problematic, to which the 'documentary' exhibitions of Seth Siegelaub well testified."[34] In an interview with Ghislain Mollet-Viéville, who stated that it was Duchamp who first equated art with mental choice, Gintz further elaborated on this:

> When Duchamp put a ready-made in a museum, he turned art into a question of choosing what to call art. Later, interest shifted from the objects that artists chose toward the institutional space in which they were displayed. The conceptualists went a step farther, and eliminated the object from art.... The exhibit is a retrospective. We wanted to show how the conceptualization of art that began after World War II culminated in the late '60s and early '70s. That was a period of crisis in art and society. Opposed ideologies were at war and it was impossible to predict the outcome.[35]

Although Gintz emphasizes the exhibitionary format of conceptual art that has been so important for the democratization of art in general, he does not further analyze this format. The so-called suitcase exhibitions that Lucy Lippard organized in the late 1960s, for example, are not described here but could be considered closer to Duchamp's *La Boîte-en-valise* in terms of distributing information through the format of the catalogue-exhibition.[36] Neither did Gintz use this specific model as an orientation for his own exhibition and catalogue. On the contrary, he stressed that he "made no pretence of trying to reconstruct the conceptual art catalogues produced at the time. They took place, they exist and are now part of history. The role of a retrospective exhibition is to begin to historicize.... To start, and carry out, the process. There is consequently a kind of alchemy or transformation that occurs and that would be pointless to try to resist."[37] Clearly, the act of historicizing was not regarded in a broader sociopolitical context, as instigated by conceptual art in the 1960s, in which the exhibition as such was subject to revision.

It was exactly this narrow art historical perspective on conceptual art that was highly criticized by Siegelaub—who was obviously strongly involved in the Paris endeavor.[38] In his intermediary activities for the artists he represented, Siegelaub had always tried to avoid overly strict art historical categorizations, and he was especially irritated by what he called the "Duchamp fixation" in Buchloh's text. In a letter to Juliette Laffon on December 12, 1989, he wrote:

> I have had the time to read the catalogue, and particularly the text of Buchloh, which is a very poor and incomplete "reading" of the period, especially in its Duchamp fixation and its omission of important actors and events of the period. If the exhibition travels and a catalogue is published in other languages, I would like to reply to the general ideas of his text as a postscript to my interview. I am now preparing this. What has been the reaction to the exhibition? Please, advise of plans, so I can get the text to you before a catalogue is prepared...[39]

On December 26 Laffon sent Siegelaub a positive reply about both the reactions of the public ("numerous and very inter-

36 According to Lippard, she began developing the ideas for these shows in the winter of 1968, while staying in Latin America. When she got back to New York and met Siegelaub, she learned that they had similar ideas. The Numbers Shows *557,087* and its follow-up *955,000*, in the Seattle Art Museum in 1969 and the Vancouver Art Gallery in January and February 1970, respectively, "could be transported from country to country by artists," bypassing the institutions and allowing more international networking and face-to-face interaction between artists, according to Lippard. See Lippard 2009.

37 Landry 1990, n.p.

38 Gintz had been in contact with Siegelaub about the exhibition, and the latter loaned several works from his collection to the ARC.

39 Archives MAMVP (Box 524/9). While the review of the exhibition by the (international) art press left a lot to be desired, the sale of the catalogue was going so well that a second edition was soon printed.

ested") and his idea to publish a postscript to his interview in a new edition of the catalogue.[40] In this "Addendum," which was published in the back of the second edition of the catalogue, Siegelaub criticized Buchloh in his "standard, conservative, hermeneutically sealed, textbook-type history of his idea of 'who-influenced-who'; 'who-did-what-first,' etc."[41] More specifically, Siegelaub emphasized the refusal to regard conceptual art within a broader sociopolitical context in which Europe—as he thought this exhibition proved—was the leader: "[Buchloh's] 'conceptual art' history is reductive for still another reason: for him, 'conceptual art is basically a history of what he thinks happened in Manhattan between 23rd Street and Canal Street, just like artists living in Paris or Berlin in the early part of the century."[42]

Siegelaub considered the fixation on Duchamp's legacy emblematic for this approach:

> Buchloh's history has been reduced almost exclusively to artists and ideas which can be situated—whether *pro* or *con*—within the Duchamp perspective, thus very carefully avoiding any other ideas, such as those of Andre, Weiner, Buren, and Barry, who have little, if anything to do with Duchamp, and often open directly onto social, moral and political issues, both art-related and more general. The obvious exclusion of Carl Andre from the beginnings of this history is especially revealing; it is nothing less than the exclusion of the "political."[43]

Ironically enough, Andre[44] did not consider himself to be a conceptual artist at all; quite the opposite, he strongly distanced himself from any possible references to conceptual art and therefore declined to participate in the show.[45] Furthermore, Siegelaub saw Buchloh's critique of Kosuth in the same light as his "Duchamp fixation," "as a disguised

40 Siegelaub's proposal is not discussed with Buchloh before January 29, 1990, when Laffon informs him about Siegelaub's request. Archives MAMVP (Box 524/1).

41 Siegelaub, in exh. cat. Paris 1989, p. 257.

42 Ibid.

43 Ibid., p. 258.

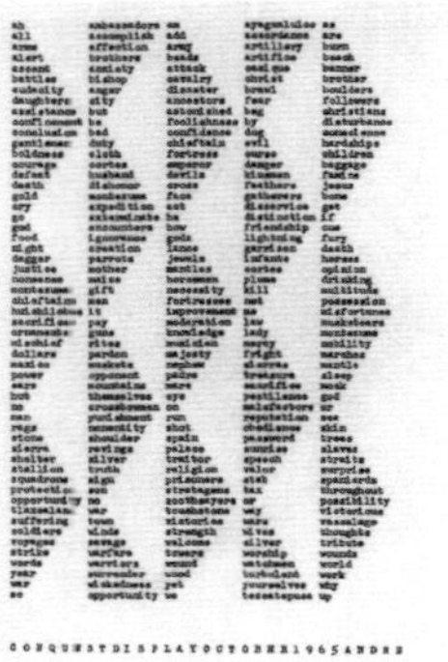

44 Carl Andre, *Conquest Display* 1965.

45 Andre, in response to Pagé's invitation to participate in the show, replied, "Dear Suzanne: How wonderful it was to see you at my show at Daniel Templon! My exhibition with you is one of my best times as an artist. Thank you for the courtesy of writing to me about Claude Gintz and his conceptual art project. Please understand that when I ask not to be part of the exhibition I do it out of friendship and solidarity with you. My poetry and sculpture have nothing to do with ideas or conceptual art. My work is very clear: no one wins if it is confused with something else. Much love carl andre." Archives MAMVP (Box 524/9).

dispute over the 'correct' interpretation, use and misuse of Duchamp."[46]

Contrary to Siegelaub's objections, Kosuth interpreted Buchloh's text as a provocation to further dive into precisely this right-or-wrong dispute. In his critique, Kosuth seemed particularly keen on defending his own position and obtaining an active role in his own history-making. He made a project out of negotiating with the organizers; the amount and length of letters that he sent to the museum do not compare to the issue at hand. In a letter to Laffon from June 2, 1989, he wrote:

> [I] was in shock to learn that the two people least sympathetic to my work [Buchloh and Harrison] were invited to write in the catalogue. I appreciate your assurances that an attempt will be made to re-balance the catalogue. Enclosed you will find my text from Artforum (March 1988), which attempts to clarify, philosophically, the difference between my work and the work of others I have been associated with. This text is titled: "No Exit."[47]

This text by Kosuth, a rather idiosyncratic revision of conceptual thought through fragments of his earlier writings, was eventually not republished in the exhibition's catalogue.[48] Various documents in the museum's archives relating to the production of the catalogue show that it was the intention to republish Kosuth's text "Art after Philosophy." In a correspondence with Charles Harrison on August 7, 1989, Laffon asked for a less specific analysis of "Art as idea (as idea)" in his catalogue contribution, since Kosuth's seminal text would be included. This was not approved by Kosuth, however, because he later realized that "this is because Buchloh wants it in since he attacks it."[49] In a very offensive letter to both

46 Siegelaub, in exh. cat. Paris 1989, p. 258.

47 Archives MAMVP (Box 524/9).

48 Joseph Kosuth, "No Exit," *Artforum* vol. 26, no. 7 (March 1988), pp. 112–115.

49 Letter of January 11, 1990, Archives MAMVP (Box 524/9).

Pagé and Laffon, dated January 11, 1990, he further expressed his disappointment in not being permitted to read Buchloh's text until three days before the installation and the organizers' rescinded promise to include "No Exit" in the catalogue, which was the reason he had agreed to participate in the show.

There is no record of this, but the museum did include an essay by Gabriele Guercio at the request of Kosuth, "to balance the texts by Harrison and Buchloh." Ironically, Guercio's text, even more than Buchloh's, confirmed the cliché of conceptual art being a New York initiative of four artists—and one in particular.[50] But if this gesture was not enough for Kosuth; he insisted on having the statement that he wrote as a comment on Buchloh's text included in the catalogue, as was promised to him, and threatened to "not permit my work to be exhibited," and moreover that he would "go to court to block the catalogue's sale if these conditions, in writing and signed, are not met."[51] After a further extensive correspondence his statement was finally published in the second edition of the catalogue, strangely enough, after Harrison's and not Buchloh's critical text, and he got the chance to counter the "attack" he felt had been directed at him.[52]

In his response to Buchloh, however, Kosuth mainly focused on two footnotes in his essay, in which Buchloh questions specific claims made by the artist regarding the influence of certain artists in his work, or the dates of certain works.[53] Kosuth tried to demonstrate Buchloh's lack of credibility by criticizing the latter's confusion about the correct name of the Lannis Gallery (Museum of Normal Art) that he founded in New York in 1967, after which he tried to tackle Buchloh in his presumed confusion about the dates of his *First Investigations*,[54] which he claimed to have made during

50 Ibid. The museum had agreed to include a text in the catalogue by Gabriele Guercio, who was recommended by Kosuth, to balance the specific approach of Buchloh and Gintz.

51 Ibid.

52 Kosuth, in exh. cat. Paris 1989, p. 60.

53 In footnote 6 in his text, Buchloh makes reference to Kosuth's text "Art after Philosophy (Part II)," in which he stated that he was "certainly much more influenced by Ad Reinhardt, Duchamp via Johns and Morris, and by Donald Judd, than I ever was specifically by LeWitt." Buchloh argues, "The list would seem complete, if it were not for the absence of Mel Bochner's and On Kawara's name, and its explicit negation of the importance of Sol LeWitt. According to Bochner, who had become an instructor at the School of Visual Arts in 1965, Joseph Kosuth worked with him as a student in 1965 and 1966. Dan Graham mentioned that Kosuth was also a frequent visitor to the studios of On Kawara and Sol LeWitt during that time. Kosuth's explicit negation makes one wonder whether it was not precisely Sol LeWitt's series of so-called "Structures" (such as *Red Square, White Letters,...* produced in 1962 and exhibited in 1965) that was one of the crucial points of departure for the formulation of Kosuth's *Proto-Investigations.*" In footnote 18 Buchloh states, "By contrast these claims were explicitly contested by all the artists I interviewed who knew Kosuth at that time, none of them remembering seeing any of the *Proto-Investigations* before February 1967, in the exhibition *Non-Anthropomorphic Art by Four Young Artists*, organized by Joseph Kosuth at the Lannis Gallery. The artists with whom I conducted interviews were Robert Barry, Mel Bochner, Dan Graham, and Lawrence Weiner."

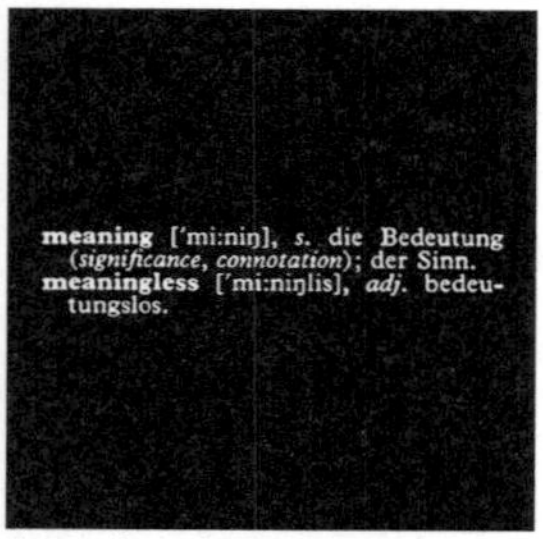

54a Joseph Kosuth, *Titled (Art as Idea as Idea) The Word "Meaning,"* 1966–1968.

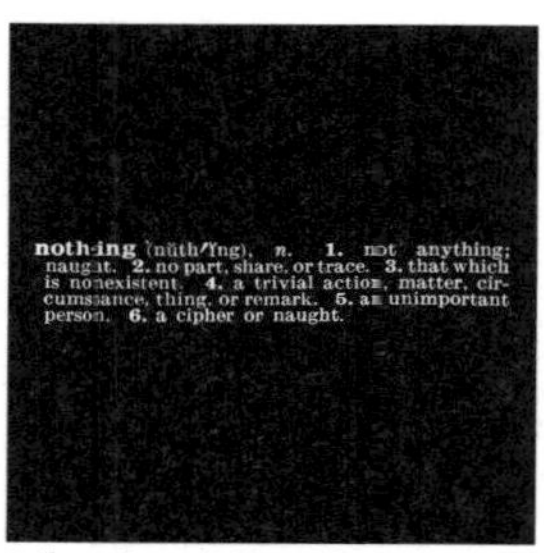

54b Joseph Kosuth, *Titled (Art as Idea as Idea) The Word "Nothing,"* 1966–1968.

his show *Fifteen People Present Their Favorite Book* at the Museum of Normal Art in 1967. Buchloh found no records of the supposedly early dates as claimed by Kosuth—and these records were also not provided by the artist—a fact that was certainly not corroborated by Kosuth's frail reference to his position within the School of Visual Arts, claiming that "the director of the school, Silas Rhodes, put me on the faculty at the age of 22."[55]

The discussions between Buchloh, Siegelaub, and Kosuth continued in *October* 57 (Summer 1991) at the request of Kosuth, following Buchloh's republished and slightly rewritten text in *October* 55 (Winter 1990). In his response, Kosuth added another comment on one of the footnotes in Buchloh's text to his critique, in which he concentrated on Buchloh's assumed misinterpretation of his *First Investigations* as paintings.[56] Siegelaub's contribution to the discussion is his republished and unaltered catalogue text. In turn, Buchloh replied once more to both Kosuth and Siegelaub and had a final say about the reception of this dispute on the catalogue and exhibition in Paris. Buchloh expressed he was less surprised by Siegelaub's critique, although the latter's choice to specifically defend Kosuth does not fit with his more sociopolitical commitment to conceptual practices, since he is "of all participants in the Siegelaub group certainly the least convincing candidate for the political causes of Conceptual Art, *then and now*."[57]

Buchloh admitted and rectified the small mistakes in his text, but refused to believe that these footnotes had triggered Kosuth's defiant response, one that not only addressed the author *ad hominem* but also the museum in the threat to withdraw his work if they would not meet his demands.[58] He comments on Kosuth's argumentation, writing, "It seems that in the mind of artists like Kosuth, artistic practice is a matter

55 Kosuth, in exh. cat. Paris 1989, p. 60.

56 In footnote 28 Buchloh states, "Paradoxically even Kosuth's work from the mid-1960s—while emphasizing its departure from painting's traditional object status and visual/formal design—continues to display the definitions of words on large, black, canvas *squares*."

57 Benjamin Buchloh, "Benjamin Buchloh Replies to Joseph Kosuth and Seth Siegelaub," *October* vol. 57 (Summer 1991), p. 160.

58 This is not only mentioned in Buchloh's text but also confirmed by the documents of correspondence found in the MAMVP Archives.

of image control and product protection, of territorial strategies, networked or, if necessary, extorted in the various institutional and commercial venues that facilitate the work's continued circulation and guarantee its mythical status."[59] Although Buchloh stated that his essay "does not in fact contain any accusations or polemics directed especially at Joseph Kosuth or his work," in his reaction he took the opportunity to do just that, and continued with the suggestion that "[Kosuth] could not resist the temptation to display once again his status as a *master* by deploying the institutional power of the museum to stage a public retaliation similar to the famous Guggenheim affair when he co-initiated the censoring of Daniel Buren's work from the Guggenheim International Exhibition in 1971."[60]

It is in a way incomprehensible why Kosuth objected so much to Buchloh's interpretation of conceptual art as a lineage starting with Duchamp, since the artist himself also sketched this lineage of conceptual art in his text "Art after Philosophy," a lineage that was followed by historians such as Ursula Meyer—and was in fact adopted once more in the Paris exhibition.[61] Why did Kosuth not counter Harrison's text of Art & Language and elaborate on his role in this group? His objections against Harrison were even more serious than those against Buchloh, as can be read in his letter to Laffon:

> Art & Language, as it is historically understood, ended in about 1975 at the time of The Fox.... After we all left the two of them [Michael Baldwin and Mel Ramsden] rather dishonestly continued to use the name, although it had, by then, almost nothing to do with Art & Language's earlier contribution. Mr. Harrison remained with them as a kind of public relations agent. Abusing

59 Buchloh 1991, p. 158.
60 Ibid., p. 159.
61 See Kosuth 1969.

> his background as an "objective" art historian he has been re-writing the history of Art & Language ever since. Ala Stalin [*sic*], they have erased my name from the history of the group.[62]

Although Kosuth's latter accusation may be true, his correspondence and public reaction to Buchloh bespeaks a preoccupation with ascribing his own artistic practice as a prologue to the movement, as well as incapacity to place the process of writing history in a broader perspective. Since this discussion has dominated the subsequent discourse surrounding *L'art conceptuel,* other aspects of the Paris exhibition have been largely ignored. As the preface of the catalogue started with a reference to Lippard and dematerialization, which is based upon a tradition stemming from minimal art and highly influenced by LeWitt's theoretization of conceptual art, this perspective on conceptual art, and thus the dialectic between object and non-object, was not further elaborated in the Paris exhibition.[63] Therefore, the objective of the retrospective *L'art conceptuel* remained particularly contained in its theorizing/historicizing effort, without taking the actual works on exhibition into consideration.

Discourse versus Exhibition

Following the lively discussions that surrounded the process of the catalogue's realization, the compilation and installation of the exhibition was not a smooth operation either. With regard to the fact that the artists associated with conceptual art never wanted to be positioned as a movement, and all had individual ideas about their positions, there was considerate debate about their inclusion or exclusion with respect to the

62 Kosuth, in his letter of June 2, 1989, Archives MAMVP (Box 524/9).

63 This remained a subject for the next large retrospective exhibition on conceptual art, organized at the Museum of Contemporary Art in Los Angeles in 1995 and 1996. Titled *Reconsidering the Object of Art: 1965–1975*, it was more specifically involved in the intrinsic problematic of exhibiting conceptual art. As James Meyer has adequately observed, it focused on the discourse that surrounded the dematerialization of the object—the basic principle of conceptual art. See James Meyer, "Reconsidering the Object of Art, 1965–1975," *Artforum* vol. 34, no. 6 (February 1996), p. 78.

show. Carl Andre, for instance, as mentioned before, charmingly declined to take part in a retrospective exhibition on conceptual art.[64] According to Laffon, all of the artists were immediately contacted when the decision to do the exhibition was made, and they were provided with lists of selected works and asked to give their comments.[65] As a matter of fact, the artists, galleries, and critics linked to the conceptual movement were only contacted when they were in possession of the selected works, and only when their direct involvement was necessary to loan these works or locate others.[66] In this regard the organization and installation of the retrospective conceptual art exhibition was not any different than that of a traditional museum exhibition. It was the response of the artists—similar to their initial radical positioning in the late 1960s—that made it a controversial one.[67]

The crucial question that the organizers of the show faced was how a museum can actually "present mental processes as works of art and to make the audience understand that the artwork is essentially a question of how they experience it," as Mollet-Viéville had posed.[68] The fact that most of the selected works were traced through their documentation in early anthologies, such as the ones by Lippard and Meyer, and were nonexistent or "dematerialized" at the start of the project, challenged the endeavor to assemble a physical exhibition.[69] Pagé recognized the problem of how to "present 'dematerialized' artworks that are foreign to the traditional forms and contents of representation. How do you get people to realize that they can do more than read the works?"[70] In her elaboration of this question, however, she addressed the dilemma of exhibiting conceptual art, something that was already known since its beginnings: "We did our best to present the works the way they were presented originally.... Despite our efforts, visitors will go on reading the works, but

64 See footnote 33 for Andre's note in which he declined his participation in the show.

65 Laffon, in an interview with Mollet-Viéville 1989, p. 102.

66 Adrian Piper, for example, sent a letter to the museum on February 10, 1990, stating, "Dear Claude Gintz, I understand I have been included in your exhibition, *L'Art Conceptuel, Une Perspective*, as well as in the catalogue. I would appreciate if you could send me a copy of the catalogue at the following address..." Archives MAMVP (Box 524/1).

67 In the interview with Mollet-Viéville, Laffon stated, "Our discussions with them rekindled quite a few controversies, many of which are as relevant today as they were twenty years ago!," p. 102

68 Ibid., p. 101.

69 The confusion of documentation and work had been a very important discussion for many artists at the start of conceptual practices. See Alberro and Norvell 2001.

70 Pagé, in an interview with Mollet-Viéville 1989, pp. 101–102.

that was also the case twenty years ago."[71] The efforts that were made to install a physical presentation in the upper ground floor (level 2) of the Musée d'art moderne—an "experimental floor" where the contemporary art program "Animation, Recherche, Confrontation" (ARC) was and remains situated—were considerate.[72] A large amount of communication about the loan of many works dominates the museum's archives of the show, which represents the intention to not only historicize conceptual art but also to stimulate its appreciation by a broader audience.[73]

Pagé must have had a clear idea of how such an exhibition should be envisioned; most remarkably, in her introduction to the show in the catalogue, she points out the aesthetic appreciation of conceptual art, "Undoubtedly, from a current perspective, in all of these works we might find, due to a shifting in the terms of what we are prepared to receive mentally and perceptually, a certain form of aesthetic seduction, an undeniable visual and formal dimension."[74] Given the fact that many conceptual artists were very ambivalent about the presentation of their work, Pagé's last point suggests a reevaluation of this positioning and at the same time anticipates the subsequent appreciation of conceptual art as art documentation.[75] It is remarkable that none of the artists who had expressed such skepticism with regard to the documentation of their work in the late 1960s commented on this specific matter. As Patricia Norvell uncovered in her early interviews with the conceptual artists, as well as with Siegelaub, in the late 1960s the historical presentation of their works from the 1960s and 1970s was something the artists themselves had difficulty dealing with.[76]

Gintz considered the idea of conceptual art untenable in this respect: "I don't think you can rely on a strict sense of conceptualism for too long when you are speaking of visual

71 Ibid.

72 ARC had been founded in 1966 and was a rather independent "area" within the Musée d'art moderne, where new methods of presentation (mainly educational) were experimented in order to reach new audiences. Suzanne Pagé directed the ARC program from 1973 until 1988, the year before *L'art conceptuel* opened, and, given her specific ideas about a retrospective exhibition on conceptual art, might have intended to curate this show herself. For further information about the role and position of the ARC within the Musée d'art moderne, see <www.mam.paris.fr/en/node/607> (8-6-2012).

73 See also Landry 1990, n.p. Laffon stated, "We also tried to see that a wide audience would find the exhibition accessible, through the notes written for each work, and would grasp the process involved in producing the works."

74 Pagé, in exh. cat. Paris 1989, p. 11.

75 As Jean-Marc Poinsot commented on the ambivalent positioning of many of the core conceptualists, "How is it possible to make an exhibition, to show something, and simultaneously deny its existence as a work of art?," Poinsot 1999, p. 104.

76 See Alberro and Norvell 2001.

77 Conversation with Gintz, 2011.

78 Interesting also is that, according to Gintz, the design for the presentation of the work was done by Kosuth. Conversation with Gintz, 2011.

79 Mollet-Viéville 1989, pp. 101–102.

80 See, for example, Lawrence Weiner.

81 Conversation with Gintz, 2011.

arts; it is more the moment in the artistic discourse than anything else."[77] In regard to the artistic discourse, he emphasized the strategy of Art & Language. "It was their idea to build up a theory, and that was enough. Each of them in accordance with the theory started building works, visual works. So conceptual art was just a step or a phase in their own working process. That is the danger of labeling. When you name something it goes outside and then it is restricted to something."[78] In contrast to Pagé, Gintz could hardly have been thinking of a physical presentation when he stressed that the "conceptual artists were not interested in visual effects. Indeed, they were adamantly opposed to them. Art & Language attempted to transform the passive viewer, whose traditional role was to admire things like talent and taste, into a reader. They insisted that their only public was the people who participated in their discussions, debates, and so forth."[79] This specific approach of conceptualism, also emphasized by Kosuth in his text "Art after Philosophy," however, was not shared by all of the artists who affiliated with conceptual art. Many of them had different ideas about the presentation of their work in regard to primary or secondary information and held a broad public responsible for the "completion" of their works.[80]

Gintz stated that it was difficult to clearly implement his ideas of conceptualism within the context of the exhibition: "My definition of conceptual art is difficult to represent… the site was always a compromise."[81] The fact that he considered the catalogue more important than the exhibition and positioned himself as a theorist of conceptual art rather than the curator of its exhibition seems to be a way to dissociate from the final result of the exhibition—a rather dogmatic translation of discourse into a physical exhibition. His initial ideas about what the exhibition at ARC should be about were more straightforward.[82] In an early correspondence with Daniel Buren he wrote, "I am preparing for the next spring at ARC a retrospective exhibition around conceptual art. The idea is not to present any static things, but on the contrary to try set up the upheaval that it gave rise to, in the form of a recontextualization of the work of art. This is why I have thought to enclose in the exhibition works by Hans Haacke, Michael Asher and, of course, Daniel Buren."[83] In later correspondence with other artists, however, there is no record of the further elaboration of this plan.

It could be for this reason that Gintz was particularly engaged with Michael Asher's contribution, as can be read from a letter he sent to Pagé to try to convince her to keep Asher's project in the show, something that was apparently uncertain.[84] Asher had initially proposed to redistribute posters that were made for the publicity of exhibitions with conceptual artists between 1962 and 1972, specifically addressing an audience of seventy-five years and older (what was then the mean age of the supposed public at the time of conceptualism). With this proposal he wanted to question the idea of a retrospective exhibition on conceptual art, a project that he considered contradictory to its dictum:

> Yet, both the quest for reproduction and the quest for nostalgia seem totally inimical to conceptual art practice whose program included a constant request for radical change and an analysis of how that might be effectively carried out. Simultaneously, the strategies which this practice employed, consistently attempted to subvert its very own institutionalization. The question that lingers at this moment is: will this retrospective be experienced and even used as a tool to problematize aesthetic practice just as the practice it represents managed to do?[85]

82 In my conversation with Gintz in 2011 he stated, "I did not approach the artists at first, I was free to choose whoever I wanted."

83 Gintz, in a letter to Buren on April 28, 1988. On March 16, 1988, he had already sent a letter to Hans Haacke to meet in New York and discuss the exhibition. Archives MAMVP (Box 524/9). ("Je prépare pour le printemps prochain à l'ARC une exposition rétrospective autour de l'art conceptuel. L'idée est de ne pas présenter cela comme quelque chose de statique, mais au contraire d'essayer de montrer le renversement auquel il donna lieu sous la forme d'une recontextualisation de l'œuvre d'art. C'est pourquoi, j'ai pense faire figurer dans l'exposition des travaux de Hans Haacke, Michael Asher et, bien entendu, Daniel Buren.")

84 On September 29, 1988, Gintz wrote to Pagé: "Chère Suzanne, J'ai appris par Juliette Laffon que vous aviez des doutes quant à la faisabilité du projet de Michael Asher. Soit. Mais n'aurait-on pu s'en assurer en sondant quelques-unes des institutions concernées? La participation de Michael Asher me parait indispensable a l''économie' du projet et ce serait a mon sens très dommage qu'il n'en fasse pas partie. Je le rencontrerai probablement le 15 octobre à l'occasion d'une exposition de groupe à Marseille avec Daniel Buren et John Knight. Comment faire pour ne pas lui opposer une pure et simple fin de non-recevoir? Bien a toi, Claude Gintz," Archives MAMVP (Box 524/9). In the interview with Pierre Landry, Gintz specifically points out Asher's contribution to the exhibition: "We should not overlook the participation by Michael Asher. He refuses to have his work from that time 're-presented' and hence historicized. In his logical, consistent way, he wanted the subject of his involvement to be the very existence of this retrospective exhibition." Landry 1990, n.p.

85 Michael Asher, in an undated letter to Claude Gintz, Archives MAMVP (Box 524/8).

86 Letter from Laffon to Asher on March 15, 1989, Archives MAMVP (Box 524/9).

87 Undated letter from Michael Asher to Claude Gintz, Archives MAMVP (Box 524/8).

Because of the difficulties encountered when trying to acquire the posters from different institutions—there were barely any posters left, and the institutions were not ready to give the few remaining ones away—the museum sent a letter to Asher with the suggestion to abandon the project and come up with another proposal.[86] As can be read in the continued correspondence with Gintz and Laffon, the artist struggled to find a project befitting the exhibition. In an undated letter to Gintz he wrote:

> I think it's possible to construct a work that would address similar issues as my works before 1972. I have considered the material and theoretical context to a retrospective; but I cannot figure out what that work would be without recapitulating ideas which to me seem to be a bit redundant. I think I should have it as such; please don't depend on my participation or plan my participation and I will keep working on this project and will write you if I have a work which seems suitable. Further, I will understand it if I cannot participate due to timing or funding.[87]

Asher nevertheless came up with a different plan and proposed placing announcements for the exhibition in several magazines for seniors and retirees:

> Many times a retrospective of a prior art movement can serve as a means of recapturing the past, such as if members of the elder part of our art community and its institutions realize a historical need to introduce the movement's constituent issues to a younger generation in order to somehow insure the reproduction of these issues. Furthermore, a retrospective can represent a sense of nostalgia or a long mixed rendering of the past,

> as often used to substitute what we feel is missing as well as confirming what we have chosen to believe.[88]

Ultimately the announcements were not published in senior magazines but in a selection of art historical journals, including *Apollo, Art History, Daidalos, The Journal of Aesthetic and Art Crticism, La Revue du Louvre et des Musées de France, Romagna Arte e Storia,* and *Simiolus,* with which Asher intended to notify separate groups of historians that a new historical perspective was being mapped out for conceptual art practices.[89] It is not clear why Asher made this change, but in one of his letters he wrote of his happiness with the result of the project.

Although Asher clearly sketched what he wanted to address in the exhibition in his correspondence and catalogue text, the final result of his laborious project does not seem to represent his intention. The dry representation of the various journal advertisements within the exhibition did not manage to resolve the dilemma that Asher had already foreseen in the public exhibition of his project: "I realize I run the risk of people thinking that perhaps this work is a joke. I might want to write a small thing so this doesn't happen."[90] In a short text that is also published in the catalogue, Asher emphasized the role that the museum/institution assumes in the historical analysis of conceptual art: "Historical objectification ought to be accelerated while there is still a collective experience and memory which can assist in the clarity of an analysis simultaneously, opening up a space to ask fundamental questions regarding history-making."[91] In regard to the effort that preceded this conclusive statement, Asher seemed to have subjected the curators of the exhibition to a process of creating awareness. Asher's contribution to the exhibition reveals like none other the complexity that a curator faces when trying to

88 Michael Asher, in an undated letter to Claude Gintz, Archives MAMVP (Box 524/8).

89 See Asher's contribution in exh. cat. Paris 1989, p. 112.

90 "It will probably point to the democracy of the conceptual art practice and the contradiction of who got short-circuited in this democracy. It will also point to how the senior citizen represents a sector of society who must rearrange their thoughts about their community at a time when it is most difficult and what has to be confronted in doing this." Letter from Michael Asher to Gintz. Archives MAMVP (Box 524/8).

91 Asher, in exh. cat. Paris 1989, p. 112.

make a retrospective on conceptual art, which Gintz underlined by saying, "It is a very complex dialectic in a sense between the object and non-object and how it was coped with by different artists. I think that is really the basis of conceptualism: it is something unresolved."[92]

Instead of making this key characteristic of conceptual art visible in the exhibition, progressive projects like Asher's were represented in the exhibition in a rather static manner. The conversion of primary information into a spatial presentation, however, was an important aspect in the work of several of the artists in the show. In the case of the wall drawings by Sol LeWitt, the spatial execution of the work was relatively easy. LeWitt contained the essence of his works in certificates that are used for the further installation of the works. Concerning the inclusion of *Wall Drawing #28* (1969),[93] loaned from a private collection in Cologne, the museum received an enlightening letter by the collector: "I am pleased to lend out the piece to your proposed exhibition. But there is no need to send you a loan form; the work, as you know, will be realized without the need of an original drawing. If you need a copy of the certificate please let me know."[94] Although the realization of the piece did not require the participation of LeWitt himself, it is clear that the organizers had contacted the artist to ask for directions on how to install the work. In a postcard from Spoleto (Italy), LeWitt asked when the show would be opened and instructed the museum that two assistants would be needed to come to Paris "to do the work" (i.e., to execute the wall drawings).[95] The museum subsequently solicited two "draftsmen" in the Netherlands, Ton van der Laaken and Wim Starkenburg, who realized several of LeWitt's drawings in the exhibition.[96]

Not many conceptual artists have so meticulously recorded the execution of their work as LeWitt. For most of

92 Conversation with Gintz, 2011.

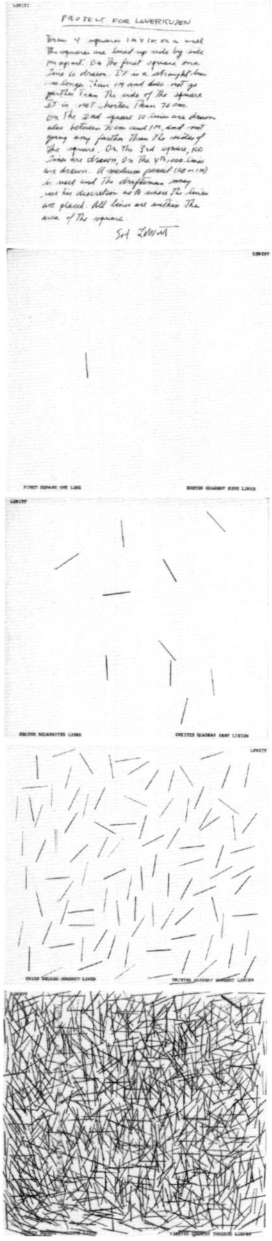

93 Sol LeWitt, *Wall Drawing #28* in its primary manifestation in the catalogue of *Konzeption—Conception* (Leverkusen: Museum Schloss Morsbroich, 1969), consisting of instructions only, and titled "Project for Leverkusen." The realization of the drawing is added.

94 Letter from Hans Böhning to Suzanne Pagé on May 17, 1989, Archives MAMVP (Box 524/9).

95 Postcard from Sol LeWitt to ARC Paris, July 16, 1989, Archives MAMVP (Box 524/9).

96 By the time *L'art conceptuel* was organized, Van der Laaken and Starkenburg had realized many wall drawings by LeWitt in the Netherlands; for example, at Martin Visser's residence in Bergeijk. In their correspondence they refer only to the numbers of the wall drawings, which are #12, #28, #44, and #46. These correspond with the following titles/descriptions in the catalogue: *Series I 1 (A & B) and III 1 (A & B)*, 1969; *One four adjacent squares, 1: one line, 2: ten lines, 3: 100 lines, 4: 1,000 lines. All lines are straight and drawn at random*, 1969; *Straight lines less than 10 inches (25 cm) long, not touching, uniformly dispersed with maximum density, covering the entire surface of the wall*, 1970; *Vertical lines not straight, not touching, uniformly, dispersed with maximum density, covering the entire surface of the wall*, 1970. Besides the wall drawings, two of LeWitt's structures and his "Sentences on Conceptual Art" were included in the exhibition. Exh. cat. Paris 1989, pp. 208–209.

the artists, *L'art conceptuel* was a first opportunity to think about the retrospective aspect of their work. This is illustrated in the correspondence of the museum with the two remaining members of Art & Language, Mel Ramsden and Michael Baldwin, about the presentation of their *Index 001* ("Documenta Index," 1972).[97] The museum intended to present the work as eight filing cabinets stacked on top of each other, an installation that was based on a photograph of the work in a magazine.[98] The artists, however, rejected this installation of the work, and scarcely held to the initial display of the work, as can be read from a letter sent to the museum. "Instead, it should be shown as in the photograph and Xerox copy I have enclosed: two cabinets each on four grey painted plinths with an extensive wall-mounted index. Otherwise it is not the work. It takes up space. At Documenta 5 it occupied a whole room."[99] The eventual installation of the work, however, did not provide the wall-mounted index, since it was installed in the central room of ARC, which is enclosed by large windows. Furthermore, the information in the drawers was not accessible to visitors due to security policies.[100]

Mel Bochner, who received a personal letter from the director regarding the loan of several of his works, also requested particular installation conditions for two of his seminal conceptual works, *Working drawings and other visible things on paper not necessarily meant to be viewed as art* (1966)[101] and *Measurement Room* (1969).[102] The first consisted of four identical ring binders with works/sketches on paper by fellow artists, which Bochner exhibited at the (influential) exhibition at the School of Visual Arts in New York in 1966. Bochner stressed that each of these binders should be mounted (screwed down) on a white wooden sculpture base of 12 × 25 × 36 inches. For the second work he required "a clean, empty white room. No other art works can be seen

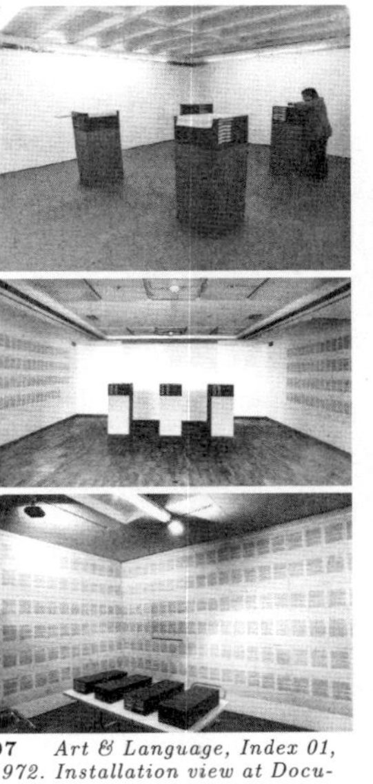

97 *Art & Language, Index 01, 1972. Installation view at Documenta Kassel and other venues.*

98 A copy of the photograph from a magazine was kept in the archives of MAMVP; however, it is not clear which magazine it is taken from.

99 Letter to Juliette Laffon by Mel Ramsden and Michael Baldwin on June 3, 1989, Archives MAMVP (Box 524/13).

100 Ironically, since the work was not to be touched/used, it was in fact transformed into an empty showcase. See John Bentley Mays, "Conceptualism: The Legacy and the Lessons," *The Globe and Mail*, August 25, 1990.

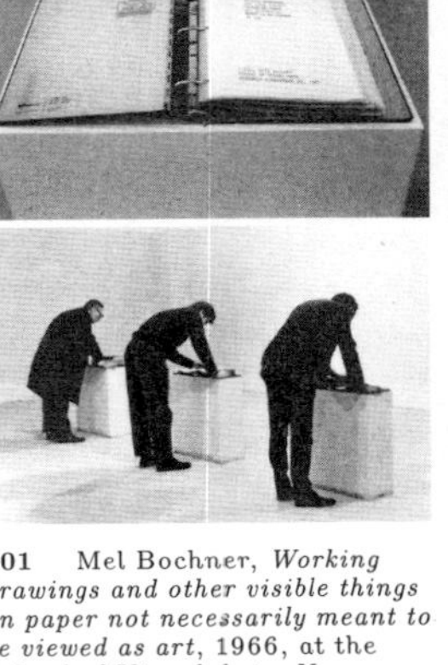

101 Mel Bochner, *Working drawings and other visible things on paper not necessarily meant to be viewed as art*, 1966, at the School of Visual Arts, New York.

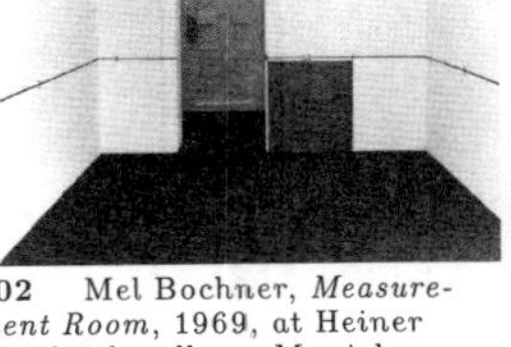

102 Mel Bochner, *Measurement Room*, 1969, at Heiner Friedrich gallery, Munich.

inside the room. The room should be at least 6 × 6 meters and must have windows."[103] Because of the limited space and Bochner's request to install the work himself, for which he charged the museum a fee of $2,500 ("installation as well as preparation tasks"), the museum abandoned the plan to include this work in the exhibition.

Douglas Huebler proposed including in the exhibition a "reexecution of a historical work from 1969," *Duration Piece #6*.[104] It would consist of a corner with sawdust on the floor that should be photographed during the opening for one to two hours at specific intervals, as a kind of "demonstration." The original work was executed in Siegelaub's *January 5-31* exhibition in New York, and the documentation of the piece was in his possession. Since the historical document of the original piece, loaned by Siegelaub, was included in the exhibition (as illustrated in the catalogue), it seems that the work was not reexecuted as Huebler requested. In an elaborate correspondence with the curators of the exhibition, Huebler tried to explain that the "originality" of his works is not of great importance. According to the artist, many of the works selected for the exhibition could be represented by copies: "The pieces you are interested in would be 'copies.' My copies (authentic as replications) 42nd Parallel and Location Piece #11 are owned by Malcolm (or Alan) Power, London, and they won't loan pieces. But, all will be available, one way or another."[105]

Since the beginning of his conceptual practices, Huebler most often exhibited his work in the form of "artist's copies," and proposed to do the same with a few works requested for the Paris exhibition, such as *Location Piece #11, Variable Piece #1*, and a work he referred to as the "Drawing."[106] The suggestion to use copies, however, was not accepted by the museum, since the eventual exhibition (as illustrated in the

103 Letter from Bochner to Pagé, April 17, 1989, Archives MAMVP (Box 524/9).

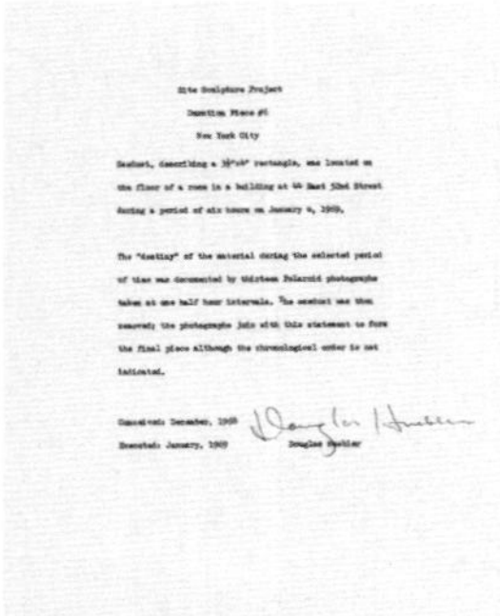

Site Sculpture Project

Duration Piece #6

New York City

Sawdust, describing a [illegible] rectangle, was located on the floor of a room in a building at 44 East 52nd Street during a period of six hours on January 4, 1969.

The "destiny" of the material during the selected period of time was documented by thirteen Polaroid photographs taken at one half hour intervals. The sawdust was then removed; the photographs join with this statement to form the final piece although the chronological order is not indicated.

Conceived: December, 1968

Executed: January, 1969

Douglas Huebler

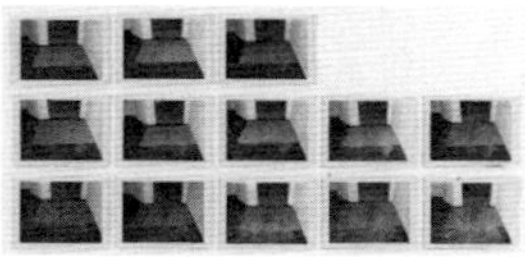

104 Douglas Huebler, *Duration Piece #6*, 1969.

105 Huebler in a reply to Gintz on May 27, 1988, Archives MAMVP (Box 524/9).

106 Ibid.

catalogue) included only "original" works. In a subsequent letter, Huebler therefore proposed that the curators include two other "original" works that were still in his possession, *Duration Piece #11* (1969) and *Site Sculpture Project, Cape Cod Star Shape Exchange* (1968). He regarded the latter to be an appropriate alternative to *42nd Parallel* (1968),[107] which he presumed could not be loaned in its original version.[108]

By the time Huebler agreed on the works to be included in the exhibition and wanted to send the loan forms back to the museum, he started to have doubts about the presentation of these works in a large group show. In a comment placed between parentheses in his last letter he wrote, "However the original piece is not especially large and might not be visually impressive next to Joseph Kosuth's neon things so I would be happy to show it, along with the other five works. Twenty years ago I deliberately made small-scale pieces because the idea was important, not the visual aspect, but in a group exhibition the scale of other pieces could dwarf my work. I want to be informed if other exhibits in the show are installed as large-scale wall works because that was not the original thrust of the conceptual enterprise."[109]

The above cases illustrate that there were several individual considerations of the participating artists about the proper installation of "original" works of conceptual art within a new historical continuum. The museum obviously struggled to meet the requests of the artists, but was not able to deal with the specific demands that come with the re-exhibition of works of conceptual art. Eventually, this inability to meet the demands of reexecution of conceptual artworks in a new exhibitionary setting led to the withdrawal of several "impermanent" works that, in their reexecution, could have more accurately demonstrated the conceptual endeavor. Conversely, the ultimate selection of works in the exhibition

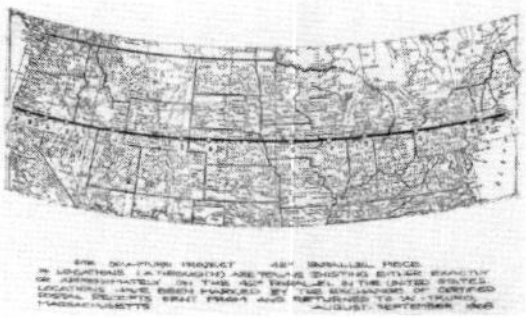

107 Douglas Huebler, *42nd Parallel*, 1968.

108 In the end the organizers succeeded in obtaining this specific work, since it is included in the catalogue as a loan from the collection of Alan Power.

109 Letter from Douglas Huebler to Juliette Laffon, February 12, 1989, Archives MAMVP (Box 524/9).

included many "original," more documentary, works that were displayed in frames on the walls. That the traditional setup of museums conflicted with the new art was already pointed out by conceptual art practices in the late 1960s, but that these procedures had hardly changed by 1989 is emphasized by the curatorial approach and eventual production of *L'art conceptuel*.

(Institutional) Critiques

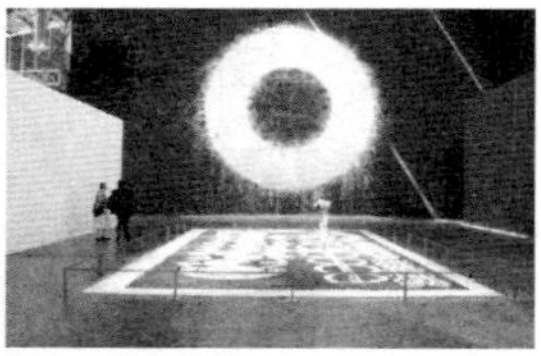

110 Exhibition overview of *Magiciens de la terre*, Centre Pompidou and Grande Halle de la Villette, Paris, 1989.

111 Conversation with Gintz, 2011. The exhibition *Magiciens de la terre* was extensively reviewed in the professional art press throughout 1989, which obviously left little room for other interests.

112 Pascaline Cuvelier, "Une certain idée de l'art," *Liberation*, December 8, 1989, p. 45 ("Tous travaux passionnants qui ne se laissent pas approcher sans une grille de re-lecture.") My translation.

In contrast to the discussions that surrounded both the production of the catalogue and the installation of the exhibition, the professional reception of *L'art conceptuel, une perspective* is virtually negligible. Dominating the debate was the group of people that had been affiliated with conceptual art from the very beginning and, even though the intentions of the curators were otherwise, the exhibition seems not to have succeeded in breaking out of this inner circle. The sparse reviews by the press could be explained, as Gintz suggested, by the success of the exhibition *Magiciens de la terre*[110] earlier that year, and as a sign of the time.[111] Certainly the exhibition, as Pascaline Cuvelier ironically pointed out in *Libération*, was not understood in its autonomous appearance: "All those fascinating works cannot be approached without guidelines for reinterpretation."[112] But that the proper understanding of conceptual art was complicated by the format of exhibition, which merely represented the conceptual movement as a series of works brought together without considering the translation of "information" into a spatial exhibition, was a point of reference in its reception.

German art critic Thomas Wulffen emphasized these curatorial aspects in his short review in *Kunstforum*

International, published when the exhibition in Paris had almost ended. According to Wulffen, the exhibition did not succeed in its initial intentions; both the suggestion to provide a "perspective" rather than a "retrospective" on conceptual art and the question what conceptual art means for contemporary artistic production were left unanswered.[113] Gintz explained his approach as a broad understanding of conceptualism that went beyond the American pioneers and also included European practices, but how this approach differed from the historical representation of conceptual art that already existed at the time is not made clear.[114]

Furthermore, Wulffen asserts, the *contemporary* perspective on conceptual art was missing; not only in its relation to contemporary artistic production but also in relation to a contemporary exhibition of historical conceptual work. Especially within conceptual art the simple assembly of works does not give any insight into its methods, which Wulffen categorized in three progressive origins of the concept: as artistic discourse, as a departure from the material-object paradigm, and as a reflection on the market system of art.[115] In this respect the curators of the exhibition missed the opportunity to approach the format of a retrospective exhibition in an innovative manner, which is provoked by the residue material of conceptual practices, as well as the commitment of the artists. According to Wulffen:

> It is possible to question every paradigmatic change that was asserted by conceptual art, but shouldn't this question itself become the subject of exhibition? How does a retrospective exhibition relate to its material? What conditions give rise to the necessity to re-present a particular phase of art history? How do objects in an exhibition "speak"? What status do they occupy within a sequence

113 Thomas Wulffen, "L'Art Conceptuel: Une Perspective," *Kunstforum International* no. 106 (March/April 1990), pp. 298–299.

114 Conceptual art had already been regarded in this perspective in the exhibition *Konzeption* in Leverkusen.

115 Wulffen 1990, p. 298 ("Wenn man spezifische Inhalte innerhalb der konzeptuellen Kunst benennen will, so stehen drei Themen in Vordergrund: Konzeptualisierung als künstlerisches Arbeiten in Begriffen, Minimalisierung als Abkehr vom material-objekthaften Paradigma, Metaierung als Reflexion auf das Betriebssystem Kunst.") My translation.

of objects? Those who shift the answers to these questions solely to the catalogue make it too easy for themselves.[116]

Wulffen's accurate critique did not have much effect on the sequence of the exhibition at the other venues. By the time the exhibition traveled to Montreal his comments were either not yet received by the French-speaking organizers of the show or not understood, since the same issues arose there.[117] In an interview with Gintz and Laffon in *Le journal du Musee d'art contemporain de Montréal*, Pierre Landry, the responsible curator of the museum of contemporary art in Montreal, discussed the installation of the exhibition in regard to its curatorial strategy—although in a slightly different understanding.[118] Landry specifically addressed "the aspect of the hanging," following a certain chronology, in relation to the exhibition's plan. In their explanation of how the installation of the exhibition came about, it becomes clear that the curators were mainly concerned about how to "hang" specific groups of works in terms of historical reading:

> We… first tried to show a number of works that could be described as "pre-conceptual"…. We then see some thematic orientations or trends emerge, as there is a transition from the visual to the linguistic—from a system of representation using visual signs to a system of linguistic signs—along with that other characteristics of conceptual art, namely the notions of time and space, of temporalization of space and spatialization of time. Next, within conceptual art itself, among its leading figures, we can detect certain contrasts, certain dialectical connections between artists we could identify as heirs to the New York School… and those who introduced a thematic orientation that is no longer the purity of art but,

116 Ibid., p. 299 ("Es ist möglich, jene paradigmatische Veränderung, die von der konzeptuellen Kunst behauptet wurde, in Zweifel zu ziehen, aber sollte dieser Zweifel nicht selber zur Darstellung kommen? Wie verhält sich eine retrospektive Ausstellung zu ihrem Material? Welche Bedingungen erzeugen die Notwendigkeit, eine bestimmte kunsthistorische Phase wieder darstellen zu müssen? Wie 'sprechen' Objekte in einer Ausstellung? Welchen Status nehmen sie in der Abfolge der Objekte ein? Wer die Beantwortung dieser Fragen allein auf den Katalog verschiebt, macht es sich zu einfach.") My translation.

117 Contrary to the exhibition in Paris, the Montreal version of *L'art conceptuel* was largely reviewed in the (local) papers.

118 Landry 1990, n.p.

> on the contrary, a connection between art as an autonomous cultural activity and the works in which this art functions and fits.[119]

Gintz's thorough art historical approach resulted in a formative catalogue/publication, in which the definite categorization of conceptual art is problematized and the different works that were selected to illustrate this perspective are contextualized in detail. However, in a spatial configuration of conceptual artworks, this problematization and contextualization cannot be explained in the same manner—something that was recognized by Gintz himself when he pointed out that his perspective on conceptual art was difficult to represent.[120] Whereas the historical approach determined the format of the catalogue, Gintz emphasized that for the exhibition it was important "to respect the physical presentation of this form of art, as it might have been shown during that time. We therefore tried, as much as possible, not to change it into something that would be seen differently by 1990 eyes."[121] Curiously, the fact that the lacking historical context would inevitably change the understanding of the exhibited works was completely ignored.

This changed status of the conceptual artwork was observed in a rather tenacious review in the Canadian *Globe and Mail* with the startling headline: "Montreal retrospective seems designed to confer high-art status on objects and texts made during the movement's opening phase."[122] The author of the article, John Bentley Mays, compares the contemporary art market in its dependency on art historical validation to the dog market that requires pedigrees as assurance that the product will hold its value over time: "Museums and *haut-bourgeois* private collectors alike have shown their willingness to pay hundreds of thousands of dollars for individual

119 Ibid. In the last phrase of this citation, Gintz is specifically referring to the work of Dan Graham, Daniel Buren, Marcel Broodthaers, and Hans Haacke.

120 Conversation with Gintz, 2011.

121 Landry 1990, n.p.

122 John Bentley Mays, "Conceptualism: The Legacy and the Lessons," *The Globe and Mail*, August 25, 1990.

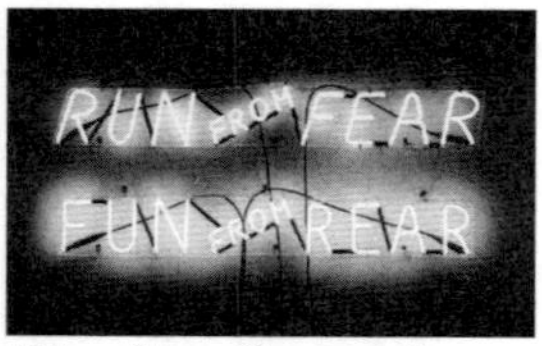

123a Bruce Nauman, *Run from Fear, Fun from Rear*, 1972.

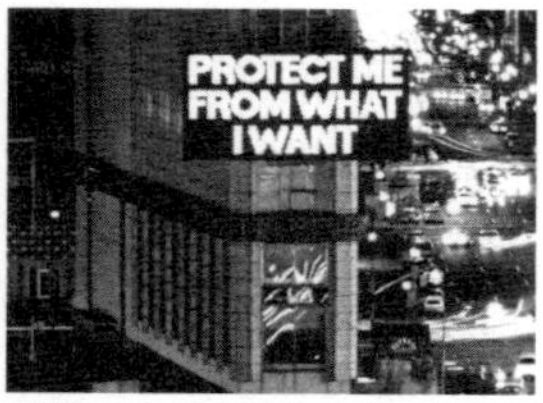

123b Jenny Holzer, *Protect Me From What I Want*, from *Survival* series (1983–1985), Times Square, New York, 1985.

works by, say, Bruce Nauman or Neo-conceptualist Jenny Holzer[123]—hence the urgency behind exhibitions of this [kind]."[124] The suggestion that the exhibition would be sponsored by the art market is somewhat exaggerated, but the effect of a retrospective exhibition of conceptual art by an important museum on the value of the works exhibited is evident, as has been analyzed in the previous chapter. That this validation in turn also had a great effect on the setup of diverse works in the exhibition is illustrated in the following observation:

> Among the most intriguing works featured here is an elaborate installation originally constructed by Art & Language for the 1972 Documenta.... Involving complex charts and many scraps of information sorted in filing cabinets, the piece is something of a vast game, to be *played* rather than merely viewed.... But as soon as I opened the first file drawer, a guard swooped down on orders from above to advise me that the drawers were to stay firmly *fermé*. Thus did the game become a traditional art object, to be cherished by the institution like any Henry Moore sculpture, and thus was the would-be player turned back into a traditional viewer—all in the twinkling of an eye.[125]

The specific approach of historicity within the execution of *L'art conceptuel* in fact could have been a stimulating factor in the process of commodification regarding the conceptual artworks in the exhibition. Because of the restrictions that valuable works loaned from (private) collections demand in a public exhibition, the final presentation of these challenging and discursive works was rather static. Artists like Huebler and Asher were consciously trying to implement the spirit of the conceptual endeavor in the exhibition, but they were

124 Mays 1990.

125 Ibid.

confronted with institutional procedures meant to "protect" the artists' work. Yet most of the artists seemed to have accepted this fact, and disregarded seriously discussing or criticizing the actual installation of the works in the spaces of ARC. This is no doubt because at a time when conceptual practices were for the first time historicized by an important museum, and (in the Duchampian tradition) thus validated as proper artworks, it was not opportune to criticize museum politics.

In 2001, however, in an interview with Hans Ulrich Obrist, Siegelaub retrospectively turned out to be particularly critical about the museological setup of the show:

> The "authority" of museum spaces makes everything so "museum-like." This was the case, for example, of the exhibition *L'art conceptuel, une perspective* [1989] organized by Claude Gintz at the Musée d'art moderne de la ville de Paris, the first institutional look at the period. No fault of his, but it really looked dead. But isn't this one of the more important functions of museums, to kill things, to finish them off, to give them the authority, and thus distance them from people by taking them out of their real everyday context? Even over and above the will of the actors involved with any given museum, I think the structure of museums tends towards this kind of activity: historicization. It is a sort of cemetery for art.[126]

Although Siegelaub's bold critique meets the ideas and projects of conceptual art that he instigated in the late 1960s, it is remarkable that he waited more than ten years to express his thoughts about the exhibition—something that would have befitted his critique on Buchloh's text. Gintz assumed it only natural that Siegelaub was very critical towards the

126 Obrist 2001, p. 220.

exhibition, saying, "He was more concerned about the context of how art functioned.... In a sense you should admit or accept the idea that it is true that the founding person and advent of conceptual art as such were Seth Siegelaub and his *January* show, even if historically speaking it also comes from Fluxus and Henry Flint."[127] Gintz also points out the inconsistency in the initial conceptual practices in this respect, stating, "I don't think that when Siegelaub tried to make the artist contract the follow up was really between artists and galleries; it was not something concretely existing; it was conflicting the show from the beginning. There was a difference between what Siegelaub represented and what European artists, Broodthaers[128] or Buren, were representing."[129]

But the real critique that Siegelaub expressed related to the functioning of the museum, a contextual aspect that many conceptual artists addressed. Although the will of the MAMVP to meet the artists in their specific wishes for the presentation of their work was certainly there, the challenge to engage with a discourse that conflicted institutional methodology and the exhibition as such was just too much to handle for the museum curators.[130] The focus on "a very discreet hanging device," as Laffon stressed, instead of on "the problematization of the exhibition itself," as Wulffen had suggested, indicates how the intentions that had initiated the project of *L'art conceptuel* were not applied to their ultimate consequence, or were gradually neglected in the installation of the final exhibition. This can largely be explained by the art historical validation of the "originality" of the work of art.[131] Since the notion of originality is highly problematized by conceptual art, as was illustrated through the specific case of Huebler's participation in the Paris exhibition, the curators overcame or simply ignored this problem by sticking to the "original" (i.e., authentic resumes of the works).[132] Although

127 Interview with Gintz, 2011.

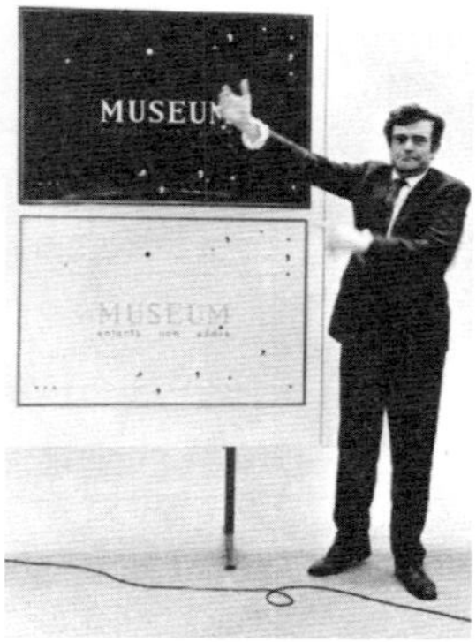

128 Marcel Broodthaers at his exhibition *Musée d'Art Moderne, Département des Aigles*, Kunsthalle Düsseldorf, 1972.

129 Interview with Gintz, 2011.

130 This is also illustrated in the interview with Mollet-Viéville, who emphasized, "Did you consult the artists? How did they react to your choices? Although many of them are now working in different directions, I imagine they all wanted to make sure you did not underestimate their role in the movement!" Mollet-Viéville 1989, p. 102.

131 See, for example, Rosalind Krauss, "The Originality of the Avant-garde," in *The Originality of the Avant-Garde and other Modernist Myths* (Cambridge, MA: MIT Press, 1985). "But the formula that specifies a print as a photographic original made close to the 'aesthetic moment' is obviously a formula dictated by the art historical notion of period style and applied to the practice of connoisseurship. A period style is a special form of coherence that cannot be fraudulently breached. The authenticity folded into the concept of *style* is a product of the way style is conceived as having been generated: that is, collectively and unconsiously." p. 157.

132 The problem of originality is much more significant within conceptual art than that which is suggested here. Since I will revisit this theme in detail in the next chapter, I allow myself to leave the subject to this too brief notion.

this method of work sometimes meant that the curators had to compromise—for security reasons the most accurate presentation (e.g., tacking a piece of paper directly onto the wall) was impossible—they still gave preference to a traditional framing and hanging of documents instead of creating a "design side," as they stated, which was considered a form of "betrayal" to the audience.[133]

133 Laffon, *in* Landry 1990, n.p.

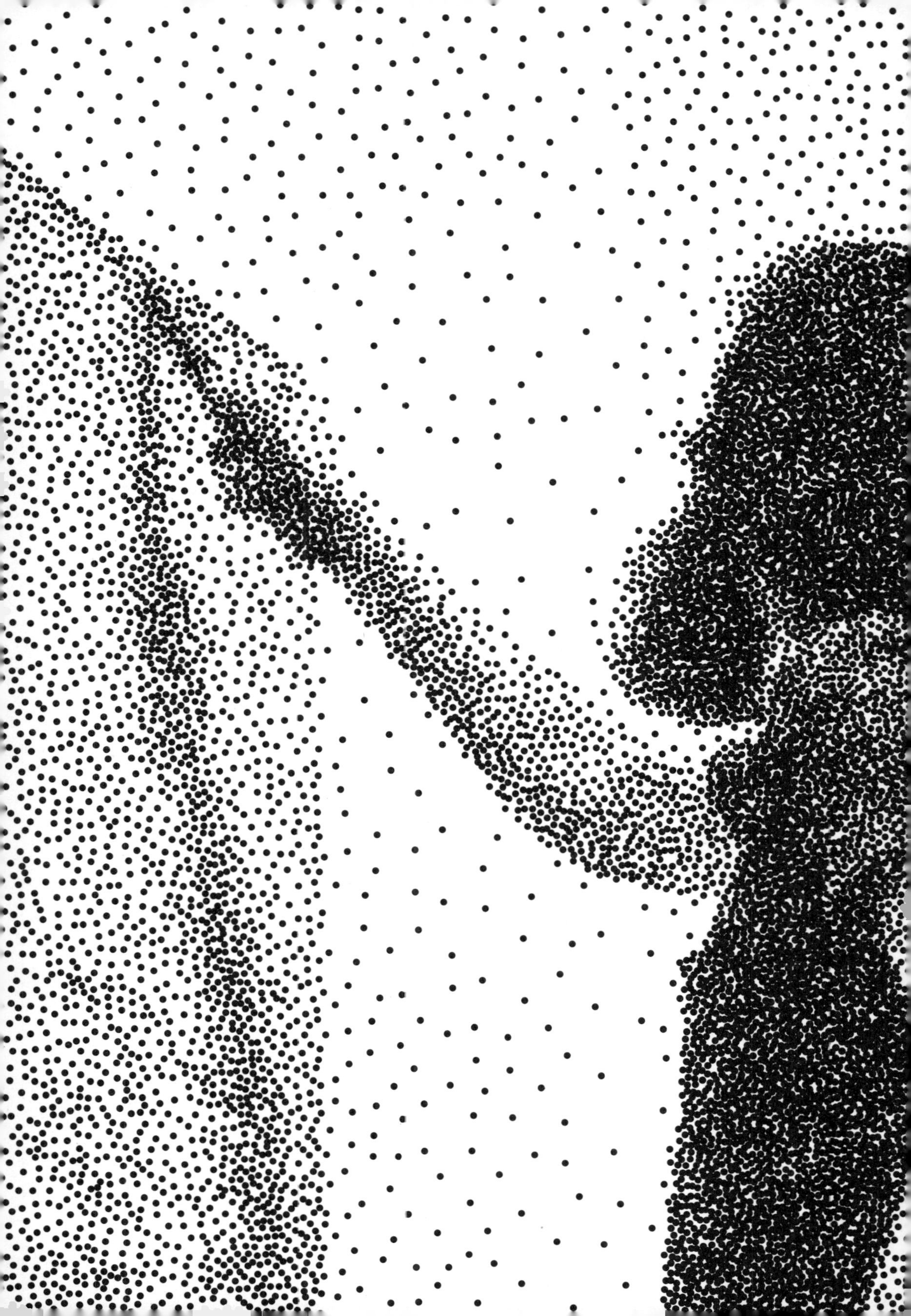

Chapter 4
Case Study

When Attitudes Become Form Bern 1969/Venice 2013 at the Fondazione Prada in Venice (2013)

The exhibition space has moved a long way from being a "temple to art," and beyond being "a place for art activity." It is one site in a string that aims to become a "creative commons." In such circumstances, what happens to the curator's responsibility to art's history, and to the processes of social memory in her or his culture?
— Terry Smith[1]

1 Terry Smith, "Artists as Curators/Curators as Artists: Exhibitionary Form Since 1969," in *When Attitudes Become Form Bern 1969/Venice 2013*, ed. Germano Celant, exh. cat. Venice (Fondazione Prada) 2013, p. 528.

Reconsidering the Exhibition of Conceptual Art

Parallel to the opening of the 55th Venice Biennale in 2013, entitled *The Encyclopedic Palace*, which reflected on psychological subversions in art-making, the Fondazione Prada in Venice restaged an exhibition that has been paramount to the conceptualization of artistic thought. Harald Szeemann's 1969 exhibition *Live in Your Head: When Attitudes Become Form: Works-Concepts-Processes-Situations-Information*, studied and described in-depth over the past two decades, hardly appears to need additional consideration, and yet it

Image appropriated from Lawrence Weiner constructing *A 36" × 36" Removal to the Lathing of Support Wall of Plaster or Wallboard from a Wall* at the Kunsthalle Bern in 1969. See also p. 156.

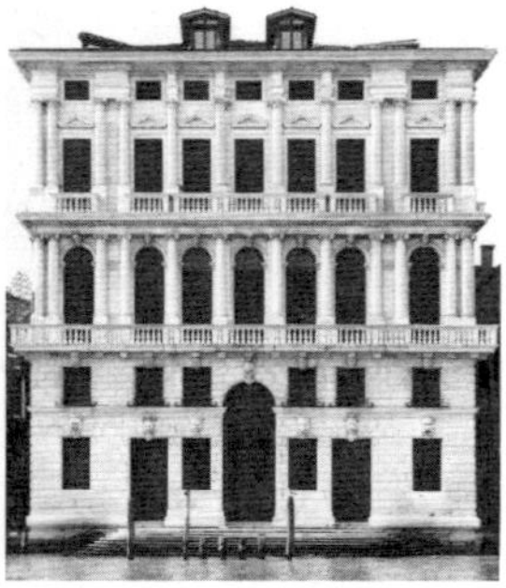

2 Ca' Corner della Regina in Venice.

was precisely this legendary exhibition that was systematically reconstructed in the eighteenth-century Venetian palace Ca' Corner della Regina[2]—the exhibition venue of the Fondazione Prada.[3] According to the foundation's president, Miuccia Prada, who also initiated the project, *When Attitudes Become Form Bern 1969/Venice 2013* was an effort to "verify the possibility of reestablishing the relationship… between the works and the public."[4] The Bern exhibition that contributed to a turning point in art history was not seen by many, and the reconstruction of such an important moment could be regarded as another opportunity to convey the 1969 experience in this respect.

Whether the project eventually succeeded in this precise objective can be questioned, but the reconstruction of the historical exhibition, accomplished by the shared efforts of curator Germano Celant, architect Rem Koolhaas, and artist Thomas Demand, certainly challenged existing ideas about art historical research, transmission of knowledge, and curation.[5] The "remembering exhibition," as Reesa Greenberg framed it, has become a recurring genre within curatorial practice today, and to reconstruct a historical exhibition as a "site of memory," a place where memory can be (re-)activated, is not a novelty in that respect.[6] The Venice exhibition fits Greenberg's typology of the "replica," most explicitly in its "leap-in-time approach"; reconstructing as identically as possible, although at a different site, the original *mise-en-scène* of the Kunsthalle Bern.[7] While the replication of entire exhibitions did not come about before the early 1990s, replicas of "environments" within museums can be regarded as a preparatory practice, as Celant has pointed out. The "reconstruction proposals" that he developed for the Venice Biennale in 1976, such as ensembles by El Lissitzky, Piet Mondriaan, and Lucio Fontana, can therefore be considered

3 Before Bruce Altshuler coined it as one of the canonical exhibitions of the contemporary in his book *Biennials and Beyond: Exhibitions that Made Art History, 1962–2002* (London: Phaidon Press, 2013), *Live in Your Head: When Attitudes Become Form* was already considered seminal, and was extensively described in *Die Kunst der Ausstellung* (1991) and in *Exhibiting the New Art: 'Op Losse Schroeven' and 'When Attitudes Become Form' 1969* (2010), among others. The original as well as the restaged exhibition included works by Carl Andre, Giovanni Anselmo, Richard Artschwager, Thomas Bang, Jared Bark, Robert Barry, Joseph Beuys, Mel Bochner, Alighiero Boetti, Marinus Boezem, Bill Bollinger, (Daniel Buren), Michael Buthe, Pier Paolo Calzolari, Paul Cotton, (Adam II), Hanne Darboven, Walter de Maria, Jan Dibbets, Ger van Elk, Rafael Ferrer, Barry Flanagan, (Philip Glass), Ted Glass, Hans Haacke, Michael Heizer, Eva Hesse, Douglas Huebler, Paolo Icaro, Alain Jacquet, Neil Jenney, Stephen Kaltenbach, Jo Ann Kaplan, Edward Kienholz (and Jean Tinguely), Yves Klein, Joseph Kosuth, Jannis Kounellis, Gary B. Kuehn, Sol LeWitt, Bernd Lohaus, Richard Long, Roelof Louw, Bruce McLean, David Medalla, Mario Merz, Robert Morris, (Hidetoshi Nagasawa), Bruce Nauman, Claes Oldenburg, Dennis Oppenheim, Panamarenko, Pino Pascali, Paul Pechter, Michelangelo Pistoletto, Emilio Prini, Markus Raetz, Allen Ruppersberg, Reiner Ruthenbeck, Robert Ryman, Frederick Lane Sandback, Alan Saret, Sarkis, Jean-Frédéric Schnyder, Richard Serra, Robert Smithson, (Michael Snow), Keith Sonnier, Richard Tuttle, Frank Lincoln Viner, (Aldo Walker), Franz Erhard Walther, William G. Wegman, Lawrence Weiner, William T. Wiley, and Gilberto Zorio. The names in parentheses participated but were left unmentioned in the original exhibition, which was rectified in the (catalogue of the) restaged exhibition.

4 Miuccia Prada, "Foreword," in exh. cat. Venice 2013, p. 377.

5 Hal Foster discussed the reconstruction of *When Attitudes Become Form* with Helmut Draxler, who declared such an endeavor "a total fake." Hal Foster, in conversation with Helmut Draxler, "On Collecting Critical Art," in Folie, Holz, and Lafer 2013, p. 251. In the reviews of the exhibition, the failure of recreating the 1969 experience was mentioned by, among others, Klaus Honnef, "When Attitudes Become Form," *Kunstforum International* no. 223 (October/December 2013), pp. 30–33, and Franco Fanelli, "In Fruitless Search of Lost Time," *The Art Newspaper* vol. 22, no. 248 (July/August 2013), p. 25.

6 Greenberg 2009. In 2000 Whitechapel Gallery in London organized an exhibition under the title *Live in Your Head: Concept and Experiment in Britain, 1965–1975* that reexamined the artistic legacy of the 1960s and '70s, and attempted to clarify the points of origin of a formative generation in British art; in 2012 Jens Hoffmann curated a show entitled *When Attitudes Became Form Become Attitudes* at the CCA Wattis Institute for Contemporary Arts in San Francisco, presented as a "sequel" to and a reevaluation of Szeemann's exhibition.

7 Greenberg distinguishes three different types of the remembering exhibition; besides the "replica" these are the "riff" and the "reprise," which, respectively and in brief, denote the reconstruction of a historically significant exhibition in the original form (either at the original site or in an alternative form at a different site), the rethinking of an exhibition in a new exhibitionary form, and the online representation of an exhibition. Greenberg 2009; exh. cat. Venice 2013, p. 377.

as anticipating the specific curatorial approach of the *Attitudes* remake.[8]

The choice to remake an exhibition that is iconic in its representation of a new art that was created in-process at the exhibition site, and consequently had a certain nonchalance in its installation, is precarious or even ambiguous in many respects. Not all of the "original" works from the Bern exhibition have been kept; many of these works were demolished after installation, or are absent for other reasons. These "deficiencies" were overcome in the Venice remake with the production of replicas or, if that was not possible, the photographic representation of the original work.[9] In its meticulous replication of the entire historical setting of the Kunsthalle Bern as a 1:1 scale model implemented into the architecture of the Ca' Corner della Regina, the replica exhibition can be considered a unique showcase within its genre. The precise physical reconstruction of the *Attitudes* show was realized through the study of more than one thousand photographs of the original exhibition in Bern, as well as the extensive analysis of documents and correspondence of the Harald Szeemann Archives at the Getty Research Institute in Los Angeles, emphasizing the influence of documentation.[10] In this respect the exhibition is more than a replica, and could also fit Greenberg's typology of the "riff," recognizing the importance of the exhibition or exhibition phenomenon and rethinking it in a new exhibition format.[11]

Whereas much effort was put into revitalizing the historical setting, it was in the constant friction between the implemented model of the Bern Kunsthalle and the spaces of Ca' Corner della Regina, as well as the historical context that was generated through the presentation of documents from the archives, tablets with photographs, selected television interviews, and the extensive catalogue, that the project

8 Thomas Demand and Rem Koolhaas, "Why and How: A Conversation with Germano Celant," in exh. cat. Venice 2013, p. 395.

9 In the cases that the works did become part of important art collections, the original, nonchalant manner of installation of these pieces in a current setting was certainly challenging in terms of security and insurance.

10 There is no other exhibition so extensively documented as this one by Szeemann, which no doubt contributed to its reputation. The conscientious research that preceded the endeavor in Venice is outstanding, and it is worth mentioning that it could probably not have been realized by a public art institution depending on external funding. Furthermore, due to incomplete documentation, the works that were originally exhibited in the Schulwarte, an adjoining building of the Kunsthalle, were not exhibited within a recreated setting of the interior of the Schulwarte, but on the third floor of the palazzo.

11 Greenberg 2009.

reached its full potential. As Celant stressed, it has been one of the project's intentions to reclaim the analysis and comprehension of the history of modern and contemporary art through the study of the relationships that works of art have established within the context of other works and architecture rather than their autonomous status.[12] Although this objective does not directly pay attention to the broader sociopolitical commitment that the artists in the original show proclaimed, it is a means to provide deeper insight into the artistic and curatorial strategies that were applied to engage with the transformations within the larger society at the time.[13]

In a strict sense the original *When Attitudes Become Form* was not a conceptual art exhibition, as I have argued in my second chapter, yet it is generally regarded within the context of conceptual art, since many of the works in the 1969 exhibition were proclaimed within the trend of dematerialization. The reconfiguration of these works in a replica exhibition is therefore indicative of a number of questions related to the curatorial representation of conceptual art. It is for this specific reason that I have chosen to analyze specifically this exhibition as the last case study of this thesis, and not one of the many conceptual art retrospectives that were compiled over the past few years (e.g., *In & Out of Amsterdam: Travels in Conceptual Art, 1960–1976* at the MoMA in New York [2009]; *With a Probability of Being Seen, Dorothee and Konrad Fischer: Archives of an Attitude* at the MACBA in Barcelona [2010]; and *A Bit of Matter and a Little Bit More: The Collection and Archives of Herman and Nicole Daled 1966–1978* at Haus der Kunst in Munich [2010]).[14]

As opposed to the exhibition in Venice, these exhibitions were particularly focused on (private) collections of conceptual art in which the singularity of the autonomous works rather than the relational component of works in an exhibition

12 Celant, in exh. cat. Venice 2013, p. 394.

13 Although an important new approach in the assembling of an exhibition, the relational aspect between the works and the surrounding architecture was not the most radical quality of Szeemann's project; the break with the "triangle in which art operates—studio, gallery, and museum" and the engagement of many of the artists with the counterculture of the 1960s were cathartic. As Szeemann declared in his introduction to the catalogue, "It was inevitable that hippie philosophy, the rockers and the use of drugs should eventually affect the position of a younger generation of artists." Szeemann, in exh. cat. *When Attitudes Become Form* (Bern 1969), as published in Rattemeyer et al. 2010, p. 192.

14 More than twenty years after the retrospective *L'art conceptuel, une perspective* in Paris, a sequel of exhibitions on conceptual art has been organized in various places around the world. Issues of stretching the canon of conceptual art were, for example, addressed in *Global Conceptualism: Points of Origin, 1950s–1980s* at the Queens Museum of Art in New York in 1999. Expanding conceptual practices in contemporary art have been addressed in several exhibitions at the Generali Foundation in Vienna, like *Concept Has Never Meant Horse* in 2006, and in a series of exhibitions that resulted in *A Book about Collecting and Exhibiting Conceptual Art after Conceptual Art* (2013).

dominated. This underlines the acceptance of the "object" of conceptual art, documentary remains of works that cannot simply be identified as (final) works, instead of reconsidering the "open-ended" status of conceptual art that is problematized in its spatial-temporal exhibition.[15] The "recuration" of an exhibition that is a textbook example of the temporality of the new art in its full spatial and temporal dimensions offers the possibility to productively rethink its aspects of historicity, site-specificity, and presentation.[16] These aspects are key for the understanding of the present-day exhibition of historical works of conceptual art, and will be further analyzed in this chapter.

15 As the title suggests, this was the case with the exhibition by Anne Rorimer and Ann Goldstein, *Reconsidering the Object of Art, 1965–1975* (1995) at MOCA in Los Angeles, but this exhibition asserted the conceptual art object rather than problematizing it—notwithstanding Jeff Wall's critical contribution to the catalogue in which he, according to Luke Skrebowski, distinguished a "pure or linguistic conceptualism" from photoconceptualism that prepared the return of pictorialism. Skrebowski, in Folie, Holz, and Lafer 2013, p. 132.

16 Terry Smith coined the revision of historical exhibitions in order to accentuate contemporary topics as a practice of "recuration." See Smith 2012, p. 194.

(Re-)Curating Art History

Compared to the five months in which the original exhibition was conceived and organized, the remake of *When Attitudes Become Form* was a highly structured assignment that had been elaborated two years in advance.[17] Since *Attitudes* was an "anti-exhibition" that emphasized the attitude and mentality of the artist, the included works did not have or were deliberately rejecting commodity value, consequently leading to the destruction or loss of many of them.[18] As a curator working parallel to Szeemann at the time that *When Attitudes Become Form* was conceived, as well as being involved in the original project, Celant was well aware of the pitfalls of such an endeavor to reassemble an exhibition with works that declined to be conventional artworks.[19] He describes the momentum of the late 1960s as "a cathartic process, aimed at a rebirth... beginning to sweep away inequalities and exalt differences... the obvious sign of this equalization was the abolition of plinths.... All that counted was the

17 The idea for the project came about in 2010, when Celant and his team had a discussion about remakes of works of art, such as editions and multiples, culminating in the exhibition *The Small Utopia* that took place at the Fondazione Prada in 2012. See Celant, in exh. cat. Venice 2013, p. 393.

18 For instance, the works by Saret, Alighiero Boetti, Neil Jenney, Richard Artschwager, Robert Morris, Mario Merz, Sarkis, and Sol LeWitt were lost or destroyed. See exh. cat. Venice 2013, p. 413.

19 As the initiator and representative of Arte Povera in the late 1960s, Celant was associated with Szeemann. In constant dialogue with Szeemann about their shared interests in the art of those days, he had been involved in setting up the show in Bern, and was asked to conduct the opening speech.

trace, material or immaterial, left by the person in the setting."[20] Nonetheless, Celant, under the auspices of Prada, met the challenge to reenact these material and immaterial traces.

With the help of the artists who participated in the 1969 event—or their estates, if they were no longer alive—all the still existing works were traced and (most of) the collectors were convinced to allow the original mode of installation.[21] To bring together the original works was one thing, but to be authorized to show them in exactly the nonchalant way they had been previously was another. Quite a number of the works, conflicting the commodity status of artworks at the time, were acquired by important museum collections, among which the Museum of Modern Art and the Guggenheim Museum in New York, Tate Modern in London, the Stedelijk Museum in Amsterdam, the Van Abbemuseum in Eindhoven, Museum Ludwig in Cologne, and Castello di Rivoli in Turin, and now represented the eminent market values that could be secured. Furthermore, the most challenging part of the remake of the Bern exhibition was how to exhibit the works that were not or no longer available. The register of curatorial inventions that was applied in this respect was impressive, and encouraged a broad perspective on the exhibition of art from the 1960s. In joining forces with Rem Koolhaas and Thomas Demand, as well as a team of researchers, Celant covered curatorial questions and decisions within the architectural, artistic, and art historical domains.

As a model for the remake venture, Celant referred to his own experience in reconstructing projects of "environmental situations" and complete ensembles, which he applied in the exhibition *Ambiente/Arte: dal futurismo alla body art* [Environmental Art: From Futurism to Body Art], part of the Venice Biennale in 1976.[22] According to Celant, the

20 Celant, in exh. cat. Venice 2013, p. 402. See also p. 404.

21 It took a great deal of persuasive power to convince the collectors and, in terms of security, the organizers had to submit to current regulations for the protection of artworks, including a limited amount of visitors at the time, under guidance of a security guard. E-mail conversation with Chiara Costa, associate researcher of the Fondazione Prada, May 13, 2014.

22 Celant, in exh. cat. Venice 2013, p. 395.

reconstruction is an important contribution to the history of knowledge. He sketched a prehistory of the remake exhibition, starting with the reconstruction of environmental situations by artists such as Vladimir Tatlin, El Lissitzky, Alexandr Rodchenko, and Kurt Schwitters that had been done by museums.[23] The earliest "exhibition proposals" in this regard are ascribed to Jean Leering, former director of the Van Abbemuseum in Eindhoven, who commissioned the reconstruction of El Lissitzky's *Proun Room*,[24] as well as a stage set by Mondriaan as early as 1964, Theo van Doesburg's *Flower Room* and two scale models of the Café Aubette in 1968, and László Moholy-Nagy's *Light-Space Modulator*[25] in 1970.[26]

To position the *Attitudes* remake within the domain of these reconstructions of environmental works adds a historical component to the recent trend of remembering/replica exhibitions since the early 1990s that Greenberg observed, and puts emphasis on the artistic value of the project and the exhibition as a total work of art. Although the Venice exhibition meets the criteria of a replica—in its precise reassemblage of the original exhibition's contents, in its archival documentation supplement, and even in its homage to the original—the focus is on the relational aspect of works in an exhibition that exceeds the prevalent modernist tradition to exhibit autonomous artworks in museums of contemporary art.[27] Celant declares that the relational component of art is now finally receiving serious attention: "Today we understand that recreating a situation and a relationship between objects of art is a way of communicating a history that, while it has shaped the developments of the last fifty years, has been lost at the level of experience."[28]

The emphasis on experience suggests that the project was merely reactivating or celebrating the historical

23 Ibid., p. 415. In conversation with Thomas Demand, Celant asserts, "Personally, I think that reconstructions—or remakes, reenactments and so on—are an important contribution to the history of knowledge. By this I mean the knowledge of a 'whole' that our society has dismantled, exactly as the wholeness of environments has been destroyed. That is why I think it is important to remake something that existed in the past, not only as an object or room, but as a whole. It has no kitsch intent: the idea is to reintroduce it historically, in our accelerated, image-based contemporaneity."

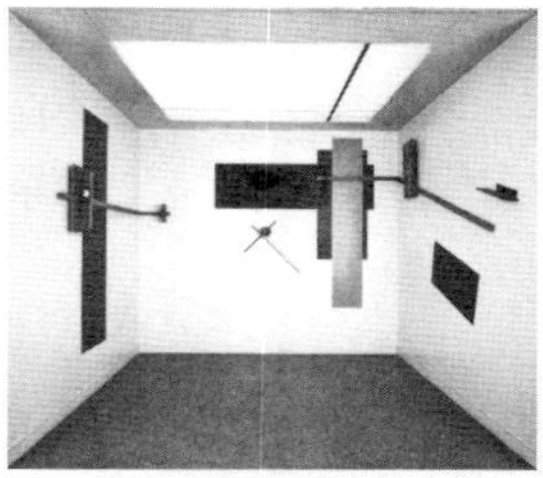

24 El Lissitzky, *Proun Room*, 1923/1965 (Stedelijk Van Abbemuseum, Eindhoven)

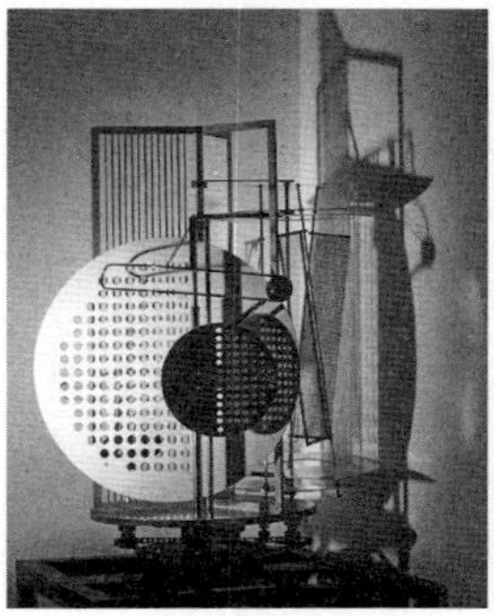

25 László Moholy-Nagy, *Light-Space Modulator*, 1922–1930/1970.

26 Leering was highly concerned with the absorption of the arts into the larger social context or society, of which the reconstruction of important "contextual works" can be considered exemplary. The Van Abbemuseum's current director, Charles Esche, in taking up Leering's approach has since executed several new reconstructions of works by El Lissitzky and Rodchenko, among others, as well as reconstructed several historically important exhibitions. Esche considers "the urge to reproduce the canon of exhibitions," together with the newly developed disciple of exhibition histories "a motor for understanding the social interface of art, and even its future political potential today through analyzing what public presentations achieved and how they functioned in their own time and place." See Charles Esche, "A Different Setting Changes Everything," in exh. cat. Venice 2013, p. 471. See also René Pingen, *Dat museum is een mijnheer: De geschiedenis van het Van Abbemuseum 1936–2003* (Eindhoven: Van Abbemuseum/Amsterdam: Artimo, 2005).

27 See Greenberg 2009.

28 Celant, in exh. cat. Venice 2013, p. 395.

moment—which it did—but it also offered the possibility to experience the historical exhibition in a contemporary perspective, which is captured in its rehabilitated spatiotemporal installation. Celant in this respect points out "the exhibition setting," a definition by Terry Smith, "in which meaning can be found not only in the isolated artifact but also in the dialogue and connection sought and constructed in the process of mounting and displaying it along with other works of art in a specific space."[29]

The most reliable information about how the works were installed in the environs of the Kunsthalle Bern[30] was obviously represented in the more than 1,000 photographs of the original exhibition.[31] The remake of the historical show was therefore largely based on the study and interpretation of these documents—a task in which the participation of Thomas Demand was significant, and which the artist approached from his own artistic understanding: "We have to operate on a 1:1 scale, which means the surrounding is less speculative, and that is something I always try to make a feature in my own work.... To find a balance between abstraction and distraction, it seems key to find the right depth of detail."[32] Remarkably, the type of detail the artist refers to is quite literary, emphasizing the importance of doorframes, floorboards, the white of the wall, etc., according to Demand, "not because the physical Kunsthalle played such a big role in the exhibition, but just to have a space within which the artworks can be experienced as a reaction to their surroundings."[33]

The architectural surroundings of the Kunsthalle were in fact defining for the exhibitionary form that the works in *Attitudes* took, since most of them were made directly at the site. As Christian Rattemeyer has pointed out, the most interesting and compelling aspect of the new art for Szeemann

29 Ibid., p. 394. In the catalogue of the exhibition, Celant explains, "Analysis and comprehension of the history of modern and contemporary art has generally passed through the single and compact artifact that can range from the object—picture or sculpture—to the environment, but very rarely through study of the relationships that the works of art have established with the context formed by other works of art or their interactions with architecture. It is time to reclaim this fundamental relational component of the story, which Terry Smith has defined as "the exhibition setting," in which meaning can be found not only in the isolated artifact but also in the dialogue and connection sought and constructed, in the process of mounting and displaying it along with other works of art in a specific space." See also Terry Smith, "What is Contemporary Curatorial Thought?," in Smith 2012, p. 30.

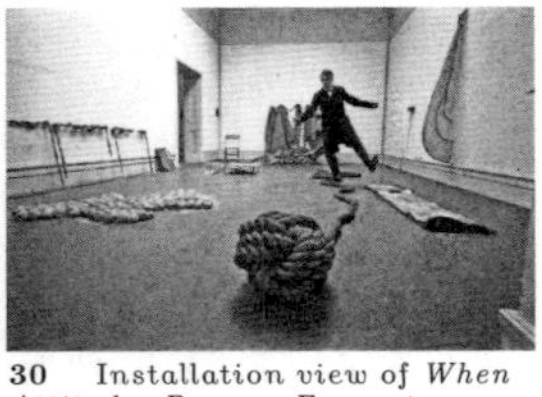

30 Installation view of *When Attitudes Become Form* at Kunsthalle Bern, 1969 (Works by Mario Merz, Robert Morris, Barry Flanagan and Bruce Nauman).

31 The catalogue checklist was not entirely correct, or was even incomplete, since many of the works that were initially selected by Szeemann were replaced with others at the moment of installation—while the catalogue must have been in the process of printing. E-mail conversation with Chiara Costa, 2014.

32 Demand, in conversation with Celant, in exh. cat. Venice 2013, p. 399.

33 Ibid.

was the tension between dematerialized gestures and their material residues—which held the works in a state between finished and unfinished.[34] Szeemann intentionally avoided the expressions "object" and "experiment" to make clear that "the newest art" exhibited did not fit any traditional art historical category.[35] Consequently, according to Rattemeyer, the central issue of *When Attitudes Become Form* was "how to exhibit a gesture," which "takes literally the idea that exhibiting attitudes must mean deemphasizing the object—locating the radicality of new artistic practices in the 'dematerialization of the art object.'"[36]

In a corresponding way, the central problem that Szeemann was confronted with—how to exhibit a gesture—remains as big a challenge in the task of the remake exhibition. To recreate the essence of the original exhibition—its indefinite, in-progress character relating to several sociopolitical changes at the time—is more complicated than the simple reassemblage of the material remains of the "dematerialized works" from the original exhibition. The re-curation of such an exhibition comes with a responsibility that goes beyond the traditional tasks of the curator. Jean-Marc Poinsot considers this a responsibility that the curator shares with others, like the conservator, the collector, the art critic, and even the viewer, who "have to bring together disparate elements of a work in order to produce effects and meanings, and to contribute to the sustainment of the work outside the attendance and period of activity of the artist."[37] In this respect the reenactment of works "without a permanent material structure" can be considered a participatory practice.[38]

While many of the artists were still alive at the time of the installation of the show in Venice, Celant and his team applied several strategies indicative of "recurating" in direct dialogue with them. Some of the artists in Szeemann's

34 Christian Rattemeyer, "How to Exhibit a Gesture: The Innovations of When Attitudes Become Form," in Jens Hoffmann, ed., *Life in Your Head: When Attitudes Became Form Become Attitudes: A Restoration—A Remake—A Rejuvination—A Rebellion*, exh. cat. San Francisco (CCA Wattis Institute for Contemporary Art) 2012, n.p. "Without 'becoming form' such immaterial gestures remain unpresentable in an exhibition, and Szeemann acknowledged that by including several artists and their works only via what he called 'information' in the catalogue. Without 'attitudes,' the 'forms' would be just conventional sculptural objects. Szeemann made sure to create definitive images—iconic moments—that would allow the exhibition to be read as an object—a formed, formal object—while still being ostensibly about gestures of dematerialization, process, concept, and information. Attitude *and* form created the exhibition's historical success."

35 Harald Szeemann, "About the Exhibition," in exh. cat. Bern 1969, n.p., as published in Rattemeyer et al. 2010, p. 193. Translator unknown. Celant, like Szeemann, sees the role of the curator as that of a (film) director, see exh. cat. Venice 2013, p. 394.

36 Rattemeyer, in exh. cat. San Francisco 2012, n.p.

37 Poinsot, p. 130 ("Ce que les énoncés performatifs, les récits autorisés et les énoncés théoriques ainsi que la prise en charge de la présentation investissent, ce sont des fonctions qui maintiennent la structure de l'œuvre quand celle-ci n'a pas de structure matérielle permanente. Loin d'être repoussé l'observateur, l'organisateur d'exposition, le conservateur, le collectionneur ou le critique se voient investis de nouvelles responsabilités. Ils doivent mettre ces éléments disparates en œuvre pour produire les effets et le sens et contribuer à la pérennisation de l'œuvre au-delà de la présence et au-delà de la période d'activité de l'artiste.")

38 Ibid.

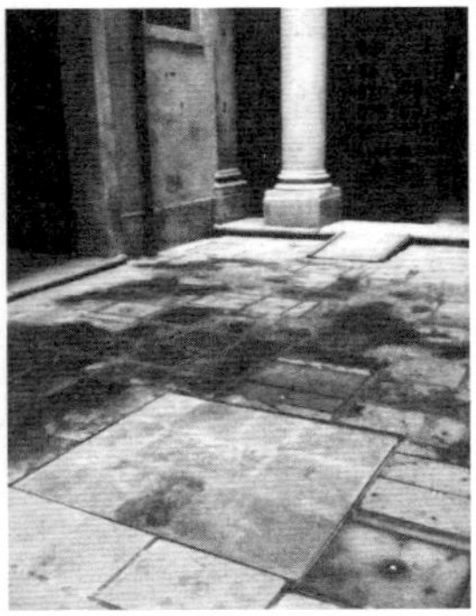

39 Ger van Elk, *Replacement Piece*, 1969/2013.

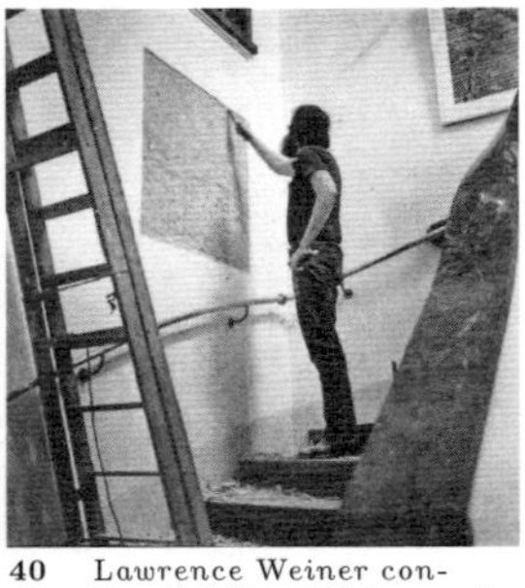

40 Lawrence Weiner constructing *A 36" × 36" Removal to the Lathing of Support Wall of Plaster or Wallboard from a Wall* at the Kunsthalle Bern in 1969.

41 Zorio's contribution to the catalogue of the Bern exhibition actually reads as an instruction: "Collare di gomma bianca. Trasciando il lavoro ottengo una traccia umida sul pavimento. Il mio cervellue in cielo e la cenere lava la terra. Cenere bagnata e foglie di lauro. Tela bianca semi impermeabile." Gilberto Zorio, in exh. cat. Bern 1969, n.p. Dutch artist Ger van Elk died on August 17, 2014, while this text was being written.

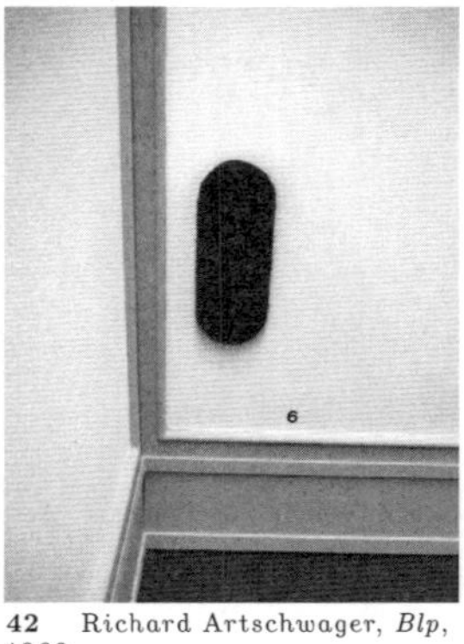

42 Richard Artschwager, *Blp*, 1968.

exhibition already anticipated the future remake of their work in the late 1960s. LeWitt's wall drawings, which can be reexecuted in different spatial situations by means of the certificates preserved with descriptions and diagrams, are the most evident of such works and, because of the artist's clear instructions, need no further justification. Other artists actively engaged in the reenactment of their work, like in the case of Ger van Elk's *Replacement Piece* (1969),[39] Keith Sonnier's *Mustee* (1968), Weiner's *A 36" × 36" Removal to the Lathing of Support Wall of Plaster or Wallboard from a Wall* (1968),[40] or Gilberto Zorio *Let's drag a little…* (1969).[41] Reconstructions of conceptualist works from artists who were no longer alive, however, like Richard Artschwager's *Blp* (1968),[42] Joseph Beuys's *Fettecke* (Fat Corner) (1969),[43] or Alain Jacquet's *Electric Wires* (1968), were approached following the same methodology, and were reexecuted in Celant's remake with the help of the artists' estates. Another category of reconstruction distinguished in the Venice exhibition is the "exhibition copy," or works reproduced for exhibition only, like Mario Merz's *Appoggiati* (Leaning Against) (1969/2013),[44] Robert Morris's *Felt* (1967/2011), and Bruce Nauman's *Neon Templates of the Left Half of My Body Taken at Ten Inch Intervals* (1966/2007),[45] the latter already a copy in the 1969 exhibition.[46]

Although the reexecution, reenactment, or reconstruction of many indefinite works was fairly straightforward, the most prominent or radical recreation in the *Attitudes* remake was undoubtedly the architectural intervention of the Kunsthalle Bern in the building of the Ca' Corner della Regina.[47] As Celant explained, "Overlapping the Bern spaces with the eighteenth-century Ca' Corner della Regina spaces involves both an architectural and temporal tear. A dramatic and spectacular graft where two sets intertwine in a third spatial and

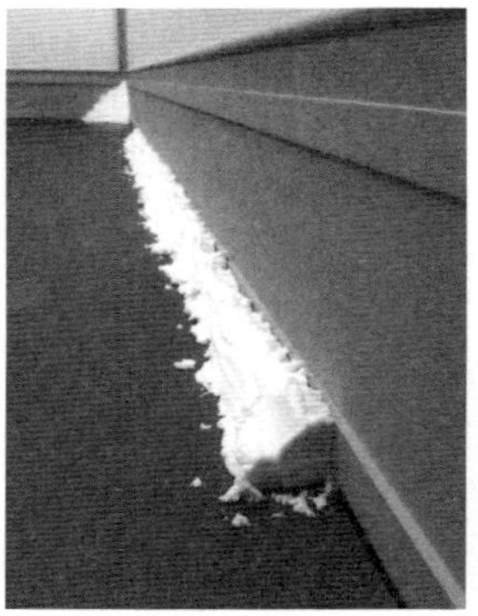

43 Joseph Beuys, *Fettecke*, 1969.

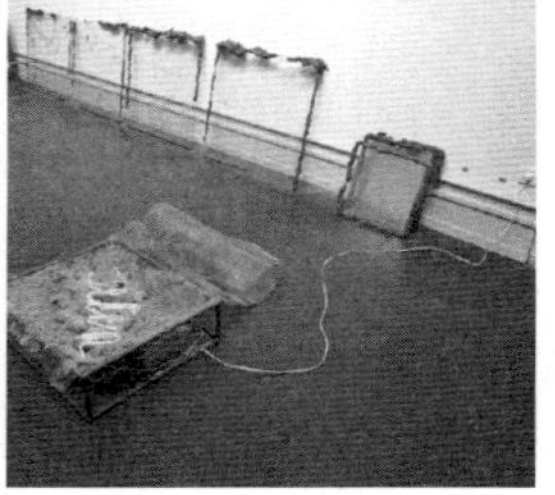

44 Mario Merz, *Appoggiati*, 1969/2013.

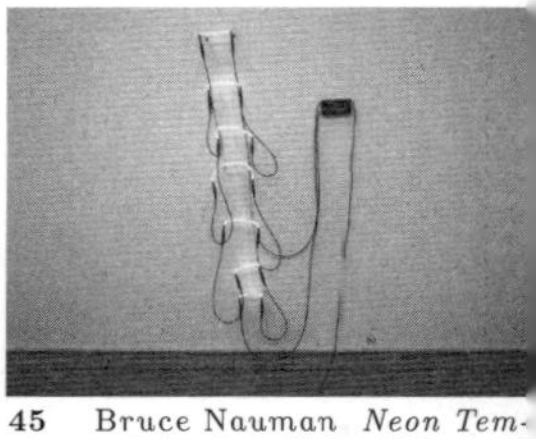

45 Bruce Nauman *Neon Templates of the Left Half of My Body Taken at Ten Inch Intervals*, 1966/2007.

temporal case."[48] The intention to graft the exhibition in its totality—inserting on a full-size scale the modern rooms of the Bern Kunsthalle, with its white walls, distinct floors, and all the artworks included in their relative positions—into the ancient frescoed and decorated rooms of the Venetian palace was an unusual, as well as ambitious project. As Koolhaas emphasized in a conversation with Celant, it was not clear from the start that they would eventually succeed to reconstruct the historical exhibition in its totality: "Initially we were resigned to the fact that only fragments, or physically reduced spaces that would create a weird relationship with the existing building would work. But when we printed Bern's plans on transparent film we discovered that the whole building actually fit exactly inside the architecture of Ca' Corner della Regina."[49]

To experience the *Attitudes* exhibition in its totality, or to correspondingly understand the original exhibition's routing within the reconstructed spaces of the Kunsthalle Bern, was in fact far from self-evident. When visiting the exhibition in Venice, one would enter the Ca' Corner della Regina and go up the stairs to the second mezzanine floor, first encountering Jannis Kounellis's *Untitled* (jute sacks with different contents, including coal, peas, rice, and lentils)[50] in the stairways. Subsequently, a rather small room with works by Dibbets (*Museum-socle with Angles of 90°*, 1969) and Sarkis (*Waiting Tray [with Underwater Lighting + Neon]*, exh. copy 2013, and *Waiting Roll [with White Neon]*, 1968)[51] could be entered, whereas reconstructed works by Zorio (*Giunchi con arco voltaico*, 1969) and Neil Jenney (*The Siegmund Biederman Piece*, 1968)[52] were placed in the adjacent room.[53] In Bern all of these works would have been situated in the same room, but the existing walls of the palace prevented the exact reassembly of the whole scenery.[54] Moreover, the works

46 Bruce Nauman had already made exhibition copies of his works in the 1960s, used for (traveling) exhibitions. Morris has been reexecuting his works from the 1960s and 1970s more recently, in a museum as well as a (commercial) gallery context. He recurated his 1971 exhibition *Bodyspacemotionthings* in 2009 at the Tate Modern, but more recently reexecuted earlier works in the *Unlimited* exhibition at Art Basel 2012, for the Berlin gallery Sprüth Magers. Remarkably describing himself as a "choreographer and dancer" in the Bern catalogue, Morris stated that the "object-type work is not based—as has been supposed—on a particular, limiting, geometric morphology or a particular, desirable set of materials. Lumps are potentially as viable as cubes, rags as acceptable as stainless steel rods." Robert Morris, exh. cat. Bern 1969, n.p.

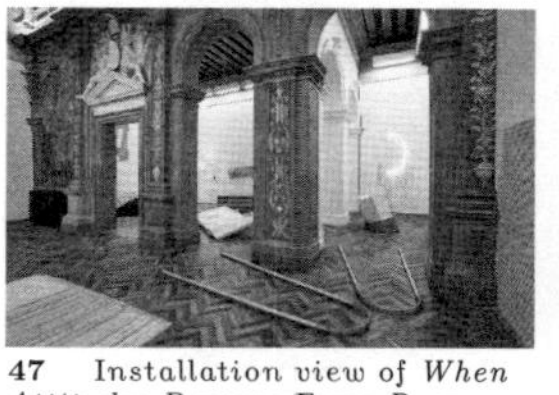

47 Installation view of *When Attitudes Become Form Bern 1969/Venice 2013*.

48 Celant, in exh. cat. Venice 2013, p. 416.

49 Ibid., p. 414.

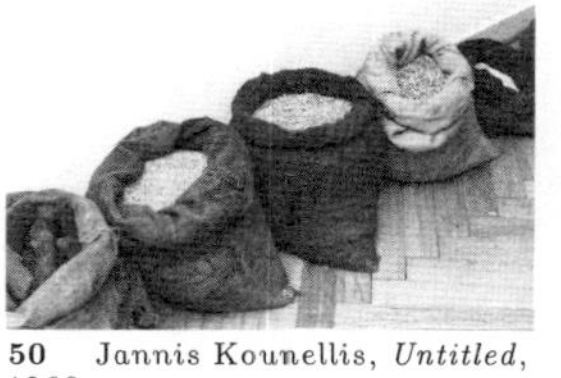

50 Jannis Kounellis, *Untitled*, 1969.

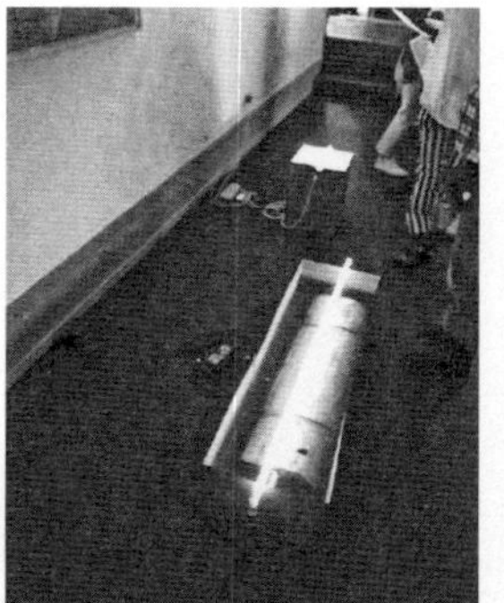

51 Sarkis, *Waiting Tray (with Underwater Lighting + Neon)* and *Waiting Roll (with White Neon)*, 1968/2013.

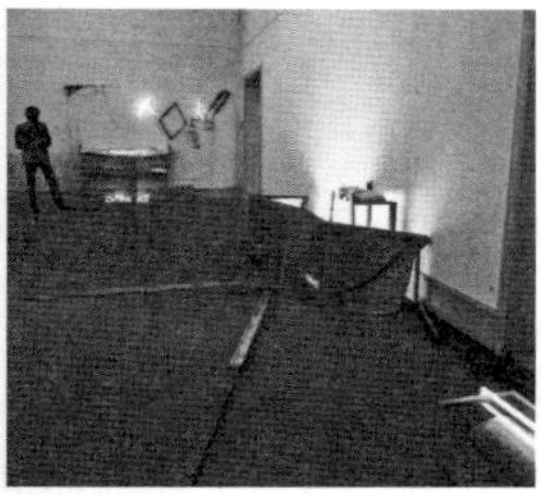

54 Exhibition view of *When Attitudes Become Form*, Kunsthalle Bern, 1969, with works by Jenney, Sarkis etc.

53 In the original show this work was also in the stairways, as other works that were missing here (except Weiner's square and Jacquet's wires). Zorio's work, like the original, was electrified several times a day, but unlike in the original show it was placed behind a rope and could not be approached.

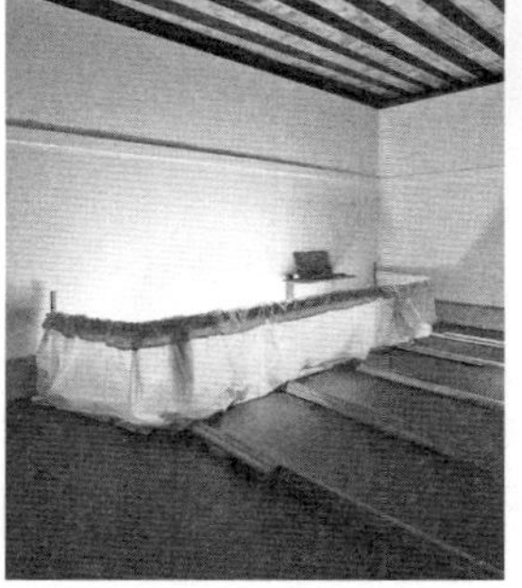

52 Neil Jenney, *The Siegmund Biederman Piece*, 1968.

in these rooms were originally located on the lower floor of the Kunsthalle Bern and would not have been encountered first.[55] The entry to the original show was via the big entrance hall of the Kunsthalle Bern, where Richard Serra's *Splash Piece* (1968–1969) and *Belts* (1966–1967) were installed on the facing wall—quite a different sequence of events.[56]

The reconstruction of the entrance room of the exhibition in Bern was situated on the *piano nobile,* further up the stairs, first engaging a small hallway with a black-and-white tiled floor and photographs on the facing wall. Since the staircase of the palazzo took up almost half of the original entrance room, the precise reenactment of the exhibition setting was disturbed. Due to enhanced health and safety regulations, Serra's *Splash Piece,* an *in situ* work that the artist made with (highly poisonous) hot lead "splashed" against the floor and plinth, could not be reenacted. The same concerned Hidetoshi Nagasawa's *Ghiaccio Secco* (1969), a small cube made of dry ice, which is now under prohibited materials legislation.[57] Serra's work *Belts,* in the collection of the Guggenheim Museum in New York (Panza Collection), which hung above *Splash Piece,* was too fragile to travel and could not be installed.[58] The absence of these works was recaptured in the demarcation of the location at the exhibition site, as if a crime scene, accompanied by black-and-white photographs of the original setting—a peculiar intervention, which nevertheless effectively emphasized their actuality within the historical time frame.[59]

Regarding the still existing works in this room, a series of minimalist works by Serra, *Close Pin Prop, Shovel Plate Prop,* and *Sign Board Prop* (all 1969, in the collection of the Guggenheim) were exhibited in a more or less original setting, loosely leaning towards the wall and close to one another, directly placed on the replicated black-and-white

55 Jenney's piece was somewhat altered and bigger than the original. Unfortunately, the more exciting *The Curtis Mayfield Piece* (1968), a shrine covered with aluminum foil and colorful neon signs, was not reenacted. Jenney included a short statement in the Bern catalogue, "My sculpture is theatrical. The activity among the physical presences of the items and events they realize, provided they exist together, is theatrical. This goes beyond the visual image. Ideally my sculpture exists unseen," suggesting the temporary existence of the pieces.

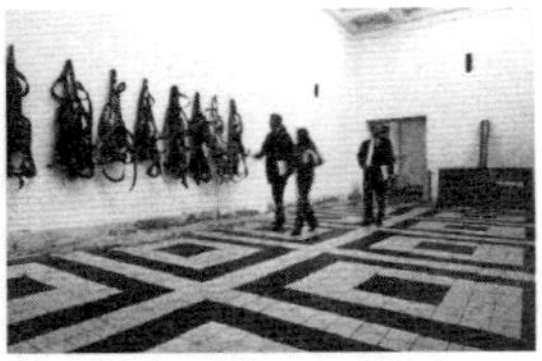

56 Richard Serra, *Splash Piece*, 1968–1969, and *Belts*, 1966–1967, Kunsthalle Bern, 1969.

57 Serra executed this piece earlier in the exhibition *Nine* at Leo Castelli's warehouse in December 1968, and in Wim Beeren's exhibition *Op losse schroeven*, directly against the facade of the Stedelijk Museum in Amsterdam, where it was vandalized by opponents of the event soon after installation. Some artists did not agree to reexecute their work within the historical context of *Attitudes*; Jean-Frédéric Schnyder decided not to reenact his work *Schreibbrett* because he considered it an early work in his development as an artist and no longer interesting in a contemporary perspective. In these rare cases, similar works were selected. E-mail conversation with Chiara Costa, 2014.

58 Photographic documentation of Michael Heizer's *Dissipate II*, 1968, and *Ground Incision (Loop Drawing)*, 1968, were also missing in the reconstruction of the Kunsthalle's entrance room. In fact, none of Michael Heizer's work was included in the remake exhibition in Venice; Celant explains in the catalogue that his Land art interventions could not be reenacted in Venice because of "Heizer's aspiration to actually break down museum boundaries." Why the documentary works, considered documents and not originals at the time, were not exhibited remains unclear. See exh. cat. Venice 2013, p. 406.

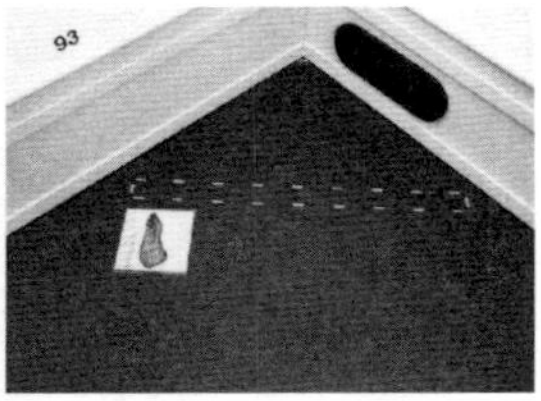

59 Installation view of *When Attitudes Become Form*, Venice, 2013.

tiled floor that cut through the architecture of the Ca' Corner della Regina.[60] Surprisingly, this specific installation took away the neutrality of these formal works, but it was unfortunate that, because of the staircase, they had to be relocated in between two doors of the palazzo and guarded by a thick jute rope, which left the 1960s desecration of the autonomous object status of the artwork in a contradictory juxtaposition. Because of these hindrances and adjustments, the reassemblage of the entrance hall of the Kunsthalle did not to give a full perspective of the original installation—despite the meticulous replication of architectural details, like the tiled floor, the grey wooden paneling and plinths, its typical doors, windows, and radiators, which provided an almost cinematic "décor." Rather, it showed the extent to which the "survived works" from this specific room of the Bern exhibition were suffering their "confiscation."

In comparison, the reconstruction of the central room of the Kunsthalle, with distinctive works by Bill Bollinger, Eva Hesse, Gary Kuehn, Reiner Ruthenbeck, and Keith Sonnier, can be considered more successful.[61] All of the works—either in original, exhibition copy, or reenacted—were reassembled on the exact robust herringbone floor and large white walls of the "original's" space, divided by only a few columns of the palazzo underneath.[62] With the biggest and most complete works brought together here, the reconstructed central room of the Kunsthalle was the most convincing in the experience of a historical ambiance, where one could actually taste some of the excitement that the original show must have generated.[63] The (historical) artworks that were jumbled throughout the room, with every wall covered and spread across the floor—where one had to step carefully in between and across them—directly engaged in interaction with the visitors. To experience the accumulation of the entire exhibition in this

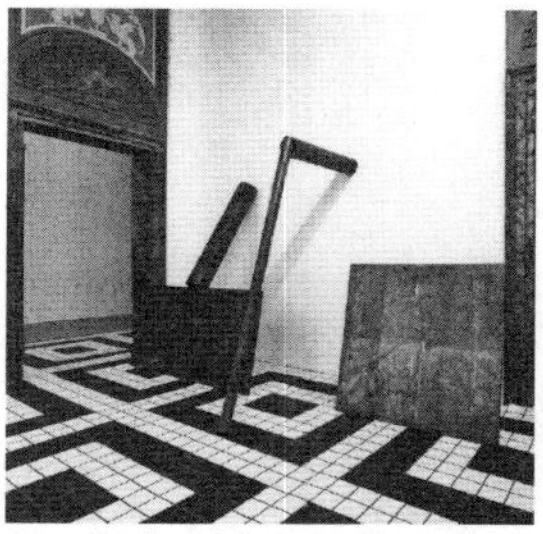

60 Richard Serra, *Close Pin Prop*, *Shovel Plate Prop*, and *Sign Board Prop*, all 1969, as installed in Venice.

61 The distinctive works referred to in this room included *Pipe Piece* (1968), *Screen Piece* (1968), and *Rope Piece* (1969/2011) by Bill Bollinger; *Augment* (1968), *Sans III* (1969/2013), and *Vinculum II* (1969) by Eva Hesse; *Untitled (Wedge Piece)* (1968) by Gary B. Kuehn; *Aschenhaufen III* and *Möbel I* (both 1968) by Reiner Ruthenbeck; and *Mustee* (1968/2013), *Untitled (Neon and Cloth)* (1968), *Flocked Wall* (1969), and *Neon Wrapping Neon and Incandescent Bulbs* (1969) by Keith Sonnier.

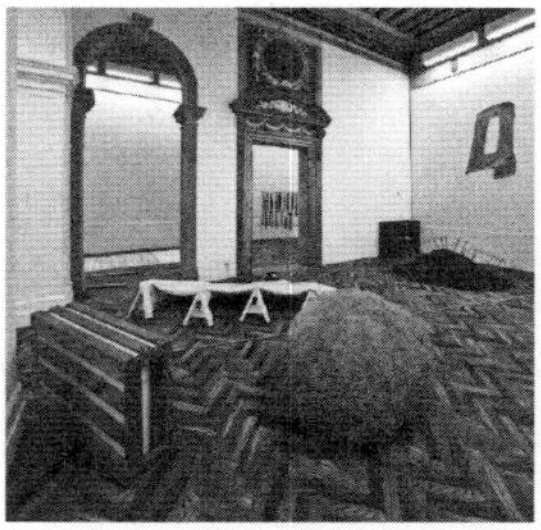

62 Installation view of central room of *When Attitudes Become Form*, Venice, 2013.

63 Franz Meyer, director of the Kunsthalle Bern before Szeemann, stated that, "The 'Attitudes' exhibition, unlike the contextual group shows before, overwhelmed me. It was an event with a palpable inner necessity, an uncertainty maybe that was felt beneath the skin, but one that was also immensely pleasurable and inspiring." See Rattemeyer et al. 2010, p. 36.

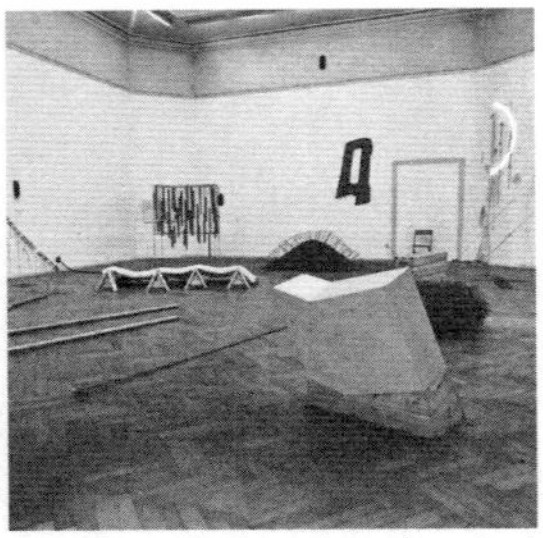

64 Installation view of central room of *When Attitudes Become Form*, Kunsthalle Bern, 1969.

central room[64] was striking, and revealed the precise spatial choreography that Szeemann applied to his exhibition.[65]

Within this careful reassemblage and reconstruction of works and setting, it was somehow surprising that visitors were not more explicitly guided to first enter the upper floor of the Ca' Corner della Regina, in order to walk through the exhibition as Szeemann had intended. The works, concepts, processes, situations, and information that he wanted to present in the *Attitudes* exhibition were in their process-based configuration developed in immediate dialogue with the site and routing of the Kunsthalle Bern—an aspect that is also particularly stressed with this project. Koolhaas described the reconstructive venture as "an archeological project to be entangled by the viewer," which puts emphasis on the "receivership" of the project.[66] It seems the architect is referring to the active or participatory role of the viewer, or the "receiver" according to Lawrence Weiner's terminology, which was foremost in the understanding of conceptual art in the 1960s.[67] But the small audience of artists, art dealers, and art collectors that were affiliated with the new art practices in the 1960s and 1970s can hardly be compared to the increasing number of contemporary art lovers that regularly visit contemporary art manifestations around the world—akin to the Venice Biennale's (professional) audience, which the Fondazione Prada was clearly referencing.[68]

The responsibility for the reenactment of these "new art practices" today is therefore primarily restricted to the "delegated receivership" of the curator, to borrow a definition by Camiel van Winkel, "who receives the work on our behalf, reads, interprets, and assesses it, and communicates the results to us, the audience."[69] In this respect the information provided in the adjoining handout and catalogue was essential; comparing the enclosed floor plans and (photographic)

65 It is interesting that the amount of available work is so considerable in this central or main gallery of the exhibition, which emphasizes the importance of the works from the youngest generation of (mainly) American artists brought together here. For a precise description of the spatial choreography of Szeemann's exhibition, see Rattemeyer et al. 2010, pp. 37–39.

66 Celant, in conversation with Koolhaas, in exh. cat. Venice 2013, p. 414.

67 See, for example, Jean-Marc Poinsot, in conversation with Lawrence Weiner, *Beaux-Arts Magazine* no. 65, 1988, p. 35. "The existence of the work also depends on the decisions of recipients. In this assertion Weiner indicated clearly that art's existence derives from shared decisions and responsibilities. Whilst rejecting the notion, which was very much in vogue at the time, of participatory art in which the recipient puts the finishing touches to the work, he emphasised that whilst the onus for interpretation is on the viewer: 'It's not the idea of "laisser-faire," it's the idea of the limits of the artist's responsibility.'"

68 Joseph Kosuth even claimed that "an audience seperate from the participants doesn't exist." Kosuth, "Introductory Note to Art-Language by the American Editor," 1968, p. 39, as cited in Alberro and Stimson 1999, p. xvii.

69 Camiel van Winkel, "Global Concept: Applications and Embodiments," in Folie, Holz, and Lafer 2013, p. 95.

views of the original exhibition in the Kunsthalle Bern with those of the remake exhibition in the Ca' Corner della Regina stimulated recalling the artworks in their original context and simultaneously added an objectifying historical layer to this experience. In an interview with the "team of the Fondazione Prada, journalists and friends" published in the catalogue, Celant stressed the importance of addressing different layers of historicity, elaborating not only the spatial, physical, and artistic but also discursive representation of the original exhibition:

> Instead of adapting the works nostalgically to fit into Ca' Corner della Regina, the curatorial, artistic and architectural choice was to plug the whole of "When Attitudes Become Form" into the container.... The intention was not to go back and adapt history to our space, but to bring back the past exactly as it was. And so, without breaking down the exhibition and diluting it in streams of objects, the novelty lay in putting together the before and the after, the yesterday and the today of the exhibition, obliging them to coexist in a time, context and place that are not the ones in which it was held.[70]

While the disruption of the implemented model of the Bern Kunsthalle by the architecture of the eighteenth-century palazzo constantly frustrated a simple reviving or remembering of the past, it can be questioned whether the remake of *When Attitudes Become Form* was meant to function as a genuine replica (i.e., reproduction of the original exhibition). Moreover, the frustration it provoked encouraged rethinking the values of art from the 1960s in a contemporary perspective, and revealed several problems related to the historical relevance of exhibitions and the so-called "authenticity" of artworks.[71]

70 Celant, in exh. cat. Venice 2013, pp. 405–406.

71 Aileen Burns and Johan Lundh, in their "Review When Attitudes Become Form Bern 1969–Venice 2013," *Kaleidoscope Web Specials*, stated, "Like the show, the publication is geared towards art professionals, for whom no detail is insignificant. 'When Attitudes Become Form: Bern 1969/Venice 2013' has taken the phenomenon of the curator as pilgrim to a whole new level," <http://kaleido-scope-press.com/web-specials/reviewwhen-attitudes-become-forms-bern-1969venice-2013words-by-aileen-burns-johan-lundh/> (21-8-2014).

72 Miuccia Prada, "Foreword," in *exh. cat.* Venice 2013, p. 377. Emphasis mine.

73 Fanelli 2013.

An exhibition that is so legendary and canonized as a turning point in art history is intriguing in the sense that one wants to (re-)experience the importance of the original event. For Prada, this even explicitly stipulated the remake venture in Venice, stating in the foreword to the catalogue that it wanted "to verify the possibility of reestablishing the relationship… between the works and the public; *moreover to recreate the emotion and passion which one perceives in the original photos from 1969.*"[72] To move in between the works exactly as they were originally installed, however, did not generate the same encounter as the one represented in the historical photographs. In fact, to approach the remake exhibition in search of a lost time could be rather disappointing, as the review by Franco Fanelli testified: "The Celant-Demand-Koolhaas trio, in reproducing a myth, have only managed to produce a faithful but lifeless copy. And in this devitalisation of a great and justly famous exhibition, works that were born out of creative energy come across as taxidermied fetishes, juju-less idols, as snuffed out as the torches by Gilberto Zorio in one of the most gloomy rooms of the claustrophobic sequence."[73]

The problem of re-exhibiting works of art that are the remnants of counter-positioning the art system as it existed in the 1960s, as well as the exhibition format itself, is particularly articulated within this observation. Although seemingly obvious, it is important to stress that the legacy of the exhibition, which is created by several not necessarily correlated events, is not the same as the spatial (re-)configuration of the exhibition, or the exhibition as a materiality. Moreover, the documentation of the original exhibition in Bern, as Rattemeyer pointed out, at the time already projected an image of Szeemann's project that could not be communicated through the actual exhibition. Knowing that the flexible and indefinite character of the artworks was difficult to grasp at the moment of display, Szeemann cautiously emphasized the site-specific, in-process character of the project in photographs as well as film/video registrations as a means to consolidate his idea of *Attitudes*.[74] In this manner he created a representation of the exhibition that effectively generated an overall interest, in addition to its reception in the professional art world.

This aspect was also pointed out in the accompanying documentary presentation at the ground floor of the Fondazione Prada. The more than 1,000 photographs of the original show in Bern were viewable on a number of iPads spread around on big tables in a separate room with comfortable chairs. A program of television interviews with Szeemann and the artists, essentially showing the activity at the site of the Kunsthalle Bern, were projected in another room, and documents from the Szeemann Archives, shown in a small room with vitrines, contextualized the replica show. Paraphernalia related to the setup of the original show were displayed here, including a worn-out list with telephone numbers of the participating artists that Szeemann carried with him, transportation budgets for the works, Szeemann's sketches for the poster of the exhibition, and, most peculiar, a handwritten letter by Szeemann's mother in which she begged her son to stop making shows that infuriate the press and cause her to fear repercussions. The off-putting review by the Swiss press and a number of ridiculing cartoons were displayed as well, illustrating the turmoil that surrounded the original show, which in turn confirmed the exhibition's image as an anti-establishment venture.[75] Functioning as a "parallel exhibition," this documentary presentation elaborated on the

74 For instance, the famous photograph in which Weiner is holding a chisel in front of his work *A 36" × 36" Removal to the Lathing or Support Wall of Plaster or Wallboard from a Wall* (1968), which was (clearly) staged because the work was already finished at the moment the picture was shot. See Rattemeyer, in Hoffmann 2012, n.p.

75 See also Lange 2013.

importance of archives for the writing of (art) history, but simultaneously showed how much the historical reception of the exhibition contrasts its actual experience in a spatial configuration.[76]

Szeemann had been extremely aware of the "politics of publicity." As Charles Esche pointed out, he was a "charming impresario with an eye for the press and media," by which means he successfully launched the careers of the participating artists in the art market and museum world.[77] The recent development of curatorial studies, according to Esche, has created an urge for the canonization of exhibitions, in which Szeemann's *When Attitudes Become Form* has subsequently gained "the aura of an exemplary curatorial strategy."[78] Esche has certainly played his part in the canonization of *Attitudes*; as one of the editorial directors of the Exhibition Histories series by Afterall Books, he commissioned an extensive case study on both *When Attitudes Become Form* and *Op losse schroeven* (2010) for its inaugural publication.[79] According to Esche, the concentration on this exhibition is not without a reason, since it had an avant-garde quality that foreshadowed the most significant developments in the art that followed, while simultaneously being representative of the moment: "It was speculative yet it took a clear position, proclaiming this new art to be the art of the future as well as a discovery of the present."[80]

This reflection of the exhibition has been confirmed time and again in several other studies, most recently in Bruce Altshuler's anthology, *Biennials and Beyond: Exhibitions that Made Art History, 1962–2002* (2013).[81] Also, reinterpretations in exhibition format have both celebrated and adapted its legendary status (to create their own), such as *Live in Your Head: Concept and Experiment in Britain, 1965–1975* at Whitechapel Gallery in London (2000), and *When Attitudes*

76 Curator Glenn Phillips of the Getty Research Institute stated in the *New York Observer* that "'[t]he material from "Attitudes" was in 300 different locations within an archive that stretches a kilometer long. You can't just go to the "Attitudes" box.' Mr. Phillips, who calls the Szeemann archive 'probably the greatest 20th-century art archive in the world,' happens to be a veteran of what he calls 'exhibition remakes,' mostly ones involving performance art. The Prada Foundation show's 'detective work,' as Mr. Phillips put it, took the Getty—Mr. Phillips, along with a research assistant, five cataloguers, three conservators and four photographers—a year to complete." See Sarah Douglas, "Bad Attitudes: Harald Szeemann's Landmark Exhibition Was a Scandal in Its Day," *New York Observer*, June 1, 2013, <http://observer.com/2013/06/bad-attitudes-harald-szeemanns-landmark-exhibition-was-a-scandal-in-its-day/> (21-8-2014).

77 Charles Esche, "A Different Setting Changes Everything," in exh. cat. Venice 2013, p. 473.

78 Ibid. The methodologies used in the construction of an exhibition canon, however, have been criticized to the same degree as art history has been criticized for its imperialistic, Western-centered approach; for example, by Okwui Enwezor. See my report on the Former West Conference, Utrecht, November 6, 2009, <www.formerwest.org/ResearchCongresses/1stFormerWestCongress/Text/Report-Day2> (19-10-2016).

79 Rattemeyer et al. 2010.

80 Esche, in exh. cat. Venice 2013, pp. 473–474.

81 See also Alison Green, "When Attitudes Become Form and the Contest over Conceptual Art's History," in Corris 2004, pp. 123–143; Klüser and Hegewisch 1991.

Became Form Become Attitudes at the CCA Wattis Institute for Contemporary Arts in San Francisco (2012). The first, curated by Clive Phillpot and Andrea Tarsia, reexamined the artistic legacy of the 1960s and 1970s in British art, to clarify the points of origin of this "formative generation"; the second, curated by Jens Hoffmann, was presented as a "sequel" and a reevaluation of Szeemann's exhibition. Hoffmann focused on the potential influence of the historical exhibition in artistic practices today, presenting artists working in relation to the history of conceptual art, or responding directly to the 1969 event. A large part of this exhibition was devoted to the representation of the original show, including floor plans, photographs, and a large-scale model of the Kunsthalle Bern with miniature replicas of the artworks.[82]

Important to point out is that both the exhibitions in London and San Francisco also appropriated the distinguished design of the *Attitudes* catalogue, following the model of an office binder that contained introductory texts on the exhibition, alphabetical files of all the participating artists with bio-bibliographical information, as well as documentation and several "works" that could not be included in the exhibition.[83] This catalogue format was an indispensible component in Szeemann's show; it stressed the information-based quality of many of the works and served, as was accustomed at the time, as an alternative space in which projects that were too immaterial or conceptual to fit into the physical exhibition could nevertheless be "exhibited."[84] It is remarkable that Celant did not specifically address this aspect of *Attitudes* in his remake, especially since he himself had been so concerned with the format of the book as an alternative exhibition space in the early 1970s.[85] Instead, the catalogue of the Venice exhibition,[86] an extensive, 600-page publication, focused on the remake endeavor as such, in which the

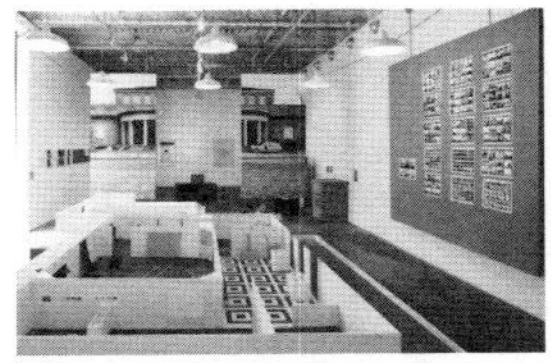

82 Installation view *When Attitudes Became Form Become Attitudes* at the CCA Wattis Institute for Contemporary Arts in San Francisco, 2012.

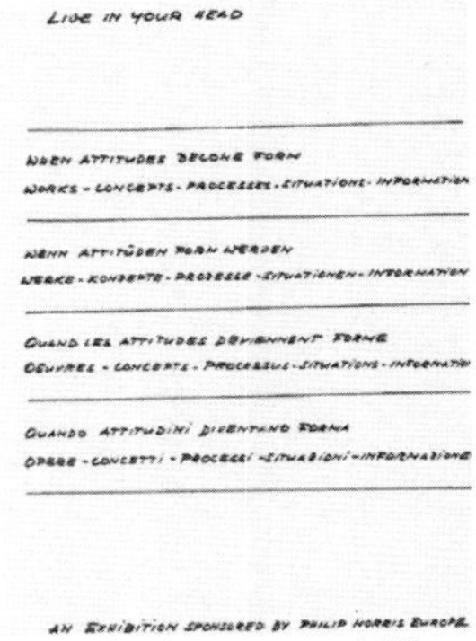

83a Catalogue cover of *When Attitudes Become Form*, Bern 1969.

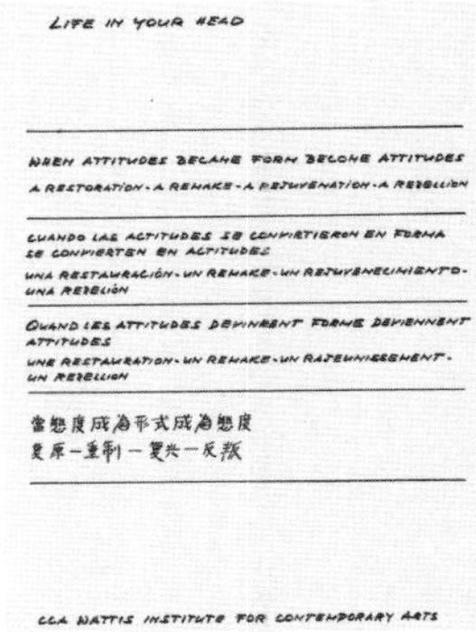

83b Catalogue cover of *When Attitudes Became Form Become Attitudes* at the CCA Wattis Institute for Contemporary Arts in San Francisco, 2012.

84 These were the contributions by Jared Bark, Ted Glass, Douglas Huebler, Jo Ann Kaplan, Bernd Lohaus, Bruce McLean, David Medalla, Paul Pechter, Michelangelo Pistoletto, and William Wegman.

85 See Celant 1972.

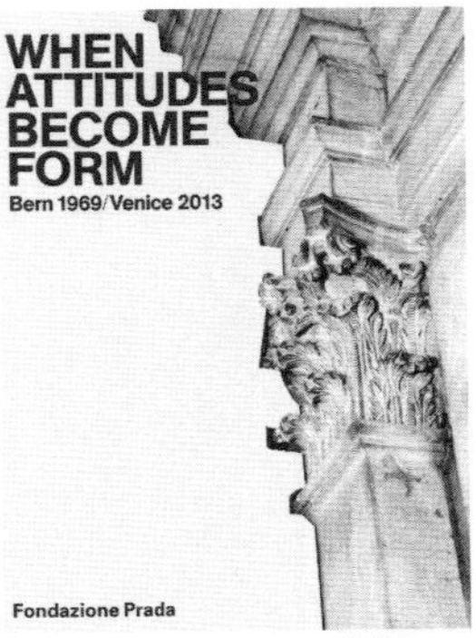

86 Catalogue cover of *When Attitudes Become Form*, Venice 2013.

historical documentation of the Bern exhibition, together with the floor plans, marked the overture to the detailed description of the reconstruction through interviews with Celant and his team.[87] Additionally, contributions by renowned art historians and curators, such as Benjamin H. D. Buchloh, Charles Esche, Boris Groys, Jens Hoffmann, Chus Martínez, Terry Smith, and Mary Anne Staniszewski, among others, emphasized either the significance of the historical exhibition or the implications of its "re-materialization" in a contemporary perspective.

In his catalogue interview, Celant anticipated the future reception of the *Attitudes* remake, arguing, "If the exhibition is going to have an effect on criticism it will be through a reinterpretation of the methodologies used in exhibitions and museums in the past and present."[88] According to Celant, the current market values assigned to art make it almost impossible to show art in the unhindered manner of when it was first produced and shown, an aspect that is certainly stressed with the reconstruction venture. Esche, in his catalogue essay, considered the exhibition's relevance to be particularly found in its essential opposition to modernist tenets such as originality and uniqueness, "tenets that have been fundamental to maintaining the value of artworks in the art market."[89] He declares the potential significance of the repeated exhibition in Venice:

> If it shapes not only a desire to memorialize a strand of Modernism that is more compatible with the present but also to challenge the construction of Modernism in museums and collections, then it will be of real importance. If it further disrupts the contemporary art world by showing its inadequacy as a successor to the ambitions of "When Attitudes Become Form," then this 2013

87 See also Henry Andersen, "Exhibition: When Attitudes Become Form: From Bern 1969 to Venice 2013," Berlin Art Link, October 8, 2013, <www.berlinartlink.com/2013/10/08/exhibition-when-attitudes-become-form-from-bern-1969-to-venice-2013/>. "The catalogue which accompanies the exhibition takes great care to let us know that every piece has been installed with the utmost cooperation with the artists involved (or with their estates), but is it important that we are seeing Alain Jacquet's wires rather than someone else's? Not really. In the right frame of mind, certainly, Jacquet's wires are beautiful—but no more than any others. Rather, the piece's great achievement is one of directing the viewer's focus, in placing parenthesis around an everyday banality and in doing so making it beautiful."

88 Celant adds, "It will be possible to deduce their positive and negative sides. Certainly it raises questions about the current limitations and defenses required by the market values assigned to art, which makes necessary the systems of isolation that transform perceptions of the works, to the point where museums and collections are being turned into bunkers and strong rooms! It suffices to note the freedom with which the public in 1969, however uninformed... strolled around works located just a few centimeters from one another." Celant, in exh. cat. Venice 2013, p. 412. Although the critique on the current market system of art seems fairly hypocritical in regard to the costly Venetian event that would not have been possible without a big sponsor like Prada (just as the original event would not have been possible without the sponsorship of Philip Morris), this aspect of the exhibition is certainly relevant and will be further discussed in the last subchapter.

89 Esche, in exh. cat. Venice 2013, p. 474.

> version will go down in art history, and some art historians yet to be born might be restaging this Venice version somewhere else in the world in 44 years' time.[90]

Employing this kind of discourse, the remake venture in Venice naturally adds to the already legendary status of *Attitudes*. In addition, Esche's perspective on the exhibition's potential makes clear that the project is specifically addressing a professional art audience, as critic Holland Cotter has vigilantly noted: "The majority of the audience queuing to get in during the biennial's preview days were curators and art historians. In a young field such as curating, it is little wonder that we are all entranced by this dual offer: to walk through an exhibition curated by a canonized figure and to visit a remarkable and innovative curatorial endeavor orchestrated for and in the present."[91] Nevertheless, the highly stage-managed replica exhibition also instigated an irritable response by some of its (art historical) reviewers, criticizing "the lack of willingness to engage with the selective, antiseptic, undeniably fetishistic return to this particular exhibition."[92]

The most forthright but also premature critique was expressed by the German art historian and critic Helmut Draxler, prior to the exhibition in a conversation with Hal Foster, who asked his opinion on the mode of representation addressed in reenactments of past performances, or in remembering exhibitions, referring to the one in Venice. Draxler criticized the specific approach of the *Attitudes* remake, questioning the historical correctness of the project: "In general, I would say of course this is a total fake, that you can't represent history like that if you try to reinstall the Harald Szeemann show *When Attitudes Become Form* in Venice now. It's a totally different event doing it now; and artistic ways of dealing with the past are interesting only

90 Ibid., pp. 475–476.

91 Holland Cotter, "Art's Future Meets Its Past: Prada Foundation Remounts a 1969 Exhibition," *New York Times*, August 13, 2013, <www.nytimes.com/2013/08/14/arts/design/prada-foundation-remounts-a-1969-exhibition.html?pagewanted=all&_r=1&> (21-8-2014).

92 Catherine Spencer, "When Attitudes Become Form: Bern 1969/Venice 2013," This is Tomorrow, September 2, 2013, <http://thisistomorrow.info/articles/when-attitudes-become-form-bern-1969-venice-2013> (21-8-2014).

93 Draxler, in Folie, Holz, and Lafer 2013, p. 251.

94 Spencer 2013.

95 Ibid.

96 Ibid. For an articulated examination of the turn of museum practices towards business models since the 1990s, see Rosalind E. Krauss, "The Cultural Logic of the Late Capitalist Museum," in Krauss et al. 1998, pp. 427–441.

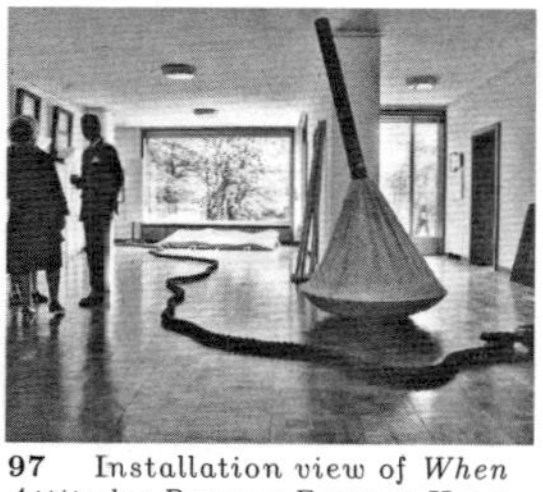

97 Installation view of *When Attitudes Become Form* at Haus Lange in Krefeld, 1969.

when they try to precisely address the difference between then and now in one way or another. In doing so they may become critical."[93]

Art historian Catherine Spencer asserted that even though the accompanying pamphlet stated that the intervention in the Ca' Corner della Regina is not connected with a fetishistic and nostalgic dimension, "nostalgia's seductive spectre is both irrepressible… and the most interesting element in the whole enterprise."[94] While Spencer rightly questions how nostalgia affects the writing of history, and whether this is necessarily a negative thing, she herself makes the mistake of uncritically adapting the historical picture of the exhibition, which "makes for an experience that feels like a lot of missed opportunities" in comparison with its remake.[95] In both Draxler's and Spencer's observations, there is a principle distance to the historical event, a historical "correctness" that prevents a direct interaction with the curatorial proposition in which the historical setting is reenacted. The presumption that the 1969 exhibition was a chaotic enterprise in which "artists made small but significant essays on the museum fabric" (a hole in a floor here, a shaky wiring project there), and the rejection of the 2013 version as "stage-managed, even Disneyfied," is indeed based on a nostalgic sentiment for the past.[96] That the original exhibition might have been as stage-managed as its remake is something that the exact replication of the exhibition's *mise-en-scène* presents: writing history can in fact be a mythologizing practice.

In its curatorial reevaluation the *Attitudes* remake emphasized how a legend comes into being, which added to a critical perspective of the exhibition and the process of historicization in general. German art historian Klaus Honnef, author of the book *Concept Art* (1972), who saw Szeemann's exhibition in 1969 in Haus Lange in Krefeld,[97] accurately described the nostalgic feeling linked to the historical show and the inevitable disappointment that followed after seeing the remake in Venice. His critical observation reads, "Through John Ford's formidable 'Liberty Valance' film, we know that 'truth' in the age of media does not stand a chance against the legend. And thus went the winding road of the reconstruction into a nostalgic trip through the labyrinth of one's own memory and, ultimately, to disappointment. With the sinking feeling that seizes the narrator in Marcel Proust when, after a long absence, he recognizes his beloved grandmother only as an old woman."[98]

Honnef's remarkable assessment of the remake venture is that it would have been better had Demand made a scale model of the exhibition in Bern and photographed it, since "it is photographic and cinematic images that, contrary to Walter Benjamin's view, lend a mythical aura to certain events and persons."[99] Demand, however, did make photographs of the exhibition setting within the Ca' Corner della Regina, which are included in the exhibition's catalogue and actually have the opposite effect. Compared to the vibrant photographs of the original exhibition in the beginning of the catalogue, these unambiguous photographs of the life-size scale model squeezed within the Venetian palace emphasize the artificiality of the project. It becomes evident, even more than in the actual experience of the exhibition, that the specific curatorial approach of this project dismisses the replica as an attempt to simply revive the past. As Esche claimed in his catalogue essay, the remake exhibition cannot even be regarded a genuine reproduction of the original; whereas its curator is no longer alive and the artists' projects are now static objects, the replica in Venice becomes "a phenomenon totally independent of the original exhibition."[100]

Consciously or not, the Venice remake is playing with

98 Honnef 2013, pp. 31–32 ("Durch John Fords formidablen 'Liberty Valance'-Film, weiss man, dass 'Wahrheit' im Medienzeitalter gegen die Legende chancenlos ist. So geriet der Weg über den verwinkelten Parcours der Rekonstruktion zu einem nostalgischen Trip durch das Labyrinth der eigenen Erinnerung und am Ende zur Ent-Tauschung. Mit dem flauen Gefühl, das den Erzähler bei Marcel Proust ergreift, als er die geliebte Grossmutter nach langer Abwesenheit nur noch als alte Frau erkennt.") My translation.

99 Ibid. ("Fotografische [und filmische] Bilder sind es, die entgegen Walter Benjamins Ansicht bestimmten Ereignissen und Personen erst die mythische Aura verleihen.") My translation.

100 Esche, in exh. cat. Venice 2013, p. 472.

expectations and at the same time not fulfilling these expectations, instead creating a historical distance, which, through the format of the exhibition, gives insight into the critical aspects of historicity. As Cotter has pointed out, the curatorial strategy that Celant and his team applied in a way demythologized the status of the original exhibition:

> The hyper-presence of two competing spaces and many temporalities pushes back against the immediacy of the '60s display techniques. The curatorial strategy is not subtle and does not pretend to transport viewers back into a great Szeemann exhibition. Instead, Celant expertly layers references, which gives the audience an intangible sense of a past exhibition, relying on the ability of the audience to experience the show as it is, and as it was simultaneously. At the same time, the Prada's nesting of architecture inside architecture is itself a disruption, and a clever one. It turns replication into a form of rethinking about art's past and present, and about how myths are made.[101]

According to Cotter, the show's reputation as improvisatory and chaotic is "ill founded"; Szeemann made a careful planning of the exhibition's setting, in which certain rooms were devoted to more established artists who could be considered progenitors of the younger artists, like Joseph Beuys and Edward Kienholz, while other rooms were assigned to new art tendencies, like the Italian Arte Povera (e.g., Giovanni Anselmo, Alighiero Boetti, Mario Merz, and Gilberto Zorio), and post-minimal and conceptual art (e.g., Carl Andre, Mel Bochner, Hanne Darboven, Sol LeWitt, and Franz Erhard Walther).[102] As noted previously, the exhibition culminated in the largest room of the Kunsthalle, which was devoted to the "emerging" American artists, among them Bill Bollinger, Eva

101 Cotter 2013.

102 Ibid. That the exhibition was politically radical, as is usually assumed, is another aspect that Cotter regards as being contradicted in the remake. "Little of the work was topical. The artists were almost exclusively white and Euro-American. Only three—Hesse, Jo Ann Kaplan and Hanne Darboven—were women. In addition, far from being a counter-cultural bootstrap affair, the show floated on a cloud of money."

Hesse, Keith Sonnier, and Walter De Maria. By using the stairways as an additional exhibition space, with documentary (De Maria, Flanagan, Smithson) as well as site-related works (Weiner, Jacquet), Szeemann created a *Gesamtkunstwerk* in the environs of the Kunsthalle wherein the whole was greater than the sum of its parts (the individual artworks).[103]

The result of the remake effort in Venice goes beyond a simple reconstruction of the exhibition, while the whole exercise of making an exhibition was taken into serious consideration, as Celant explained, "to remake something that existed in the past, not only as an object or room, but as a whole. It has no kitsch intent: the idea is to reintroduce it historically, in our accelerated, image-based contemporaneity...."[104] The consequences for (the interpretation of) the works of art within this constellation are commanding. According to Pierre-Yves Desaive, "Celant forces us to wonder whether it makes sense to display these historical pieces in this way, putting the emphasis on the freedom of the curator. His gesture seems iconoclastic at first glance, but produces the exact opposite effect; even under these conditions, the works maintain their integrity."[105] The Venice exhibition explicitly addressed, although did not explicitly mention, the problem of dealing with "original" works from the 1960s and 1970s in an exhibitionary perspective and the role that the curator can play in this. In this respect integrity, or authenticity, is a significant point of discussion that also recurs in the reception of the remake exhibition. But how should the authentic (re)-curation of the historical exhibition and its works be determined?

103 Szeemann was in fact highly criticized on this approach, more specifically by Daniel Buren in regard to his artistic directorship of Documenta 5 in 1972. See Daniel Buren, "Where Are the Artists?," February 1972, <www.e-flux.com/projects/next_doc/d_buren_printable.html> (21-8-2014).

104 Celant, in conversation with Koolhaas, in exh. cat. Venice 2013, p. 415.

105 Pierre-Yves Desaive, "When Attitudes Become Form: Bern 1969/Venice 2013," *Flash Art* vol. 46, no. 291 (July/August/September 2013), p. 74.

106 Boris Groys, "On the Curatorship," in Groys 2008, p. 49.

107 Ibid., p. 50.

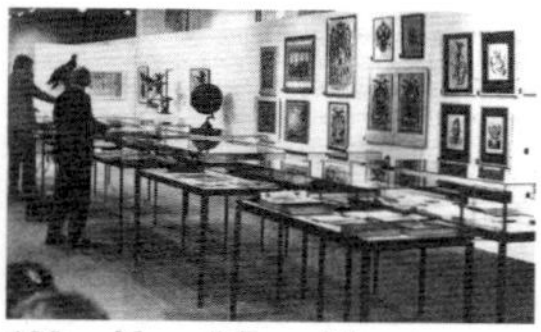

108 Marcel Broodthaers, *Musée d'Art Moderne, Departement des Aigles*, Kunsthalle Düsseldorf, 1972.

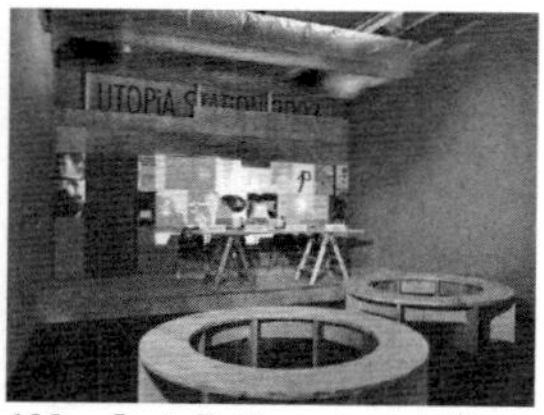

109 Installation view of *Utopia Station* at the Venice Biennale, 2003.

110 For a critical evaluation of *Utopia Station*, see also: Liam Gillick, "For a... Functional Utopia? A Review of a Position," in *Curating Subjects*, ed. Paul O'Neill (Amsterdam: De Appel, 2007), pp. 123–136.

The strategies used by many artists of the 1960s to demythologize the object of art can be considered, as Boris Groys has pointed out, an art-atheism in which artworks no longer posses autonomous status but are understood as "mere documents, illustrations, or signifiers of art."[106] The artistic projects, performances, and actions that took place during the 1960s and 1970s have been likewise documented, and are often represented in exhibition spaces and museums by means of this documentation. Such documentation, according to Groys, merely refers to art, without itself being art—in fact, it only confirms the absence of the artwork. He posits that, in bringing together different documents or illustrations and additional objects in an installation (or exhibition), the entire installation regains autonomous status.[107] Groys in this respect refers to Marcel Broodthaers's *Musée d'Art Moderne, Departement des Aigles* (1972), in which the separate objects are deliberately labeled "not a work of art," while the whole installation is a work of art.[108]

This principle, according to Groys, can also be applied to the contemporary independent curator who makes exhibitions comparable to artistic installations; the artworks take on the role of documentation of a curatorial project and do not aim to glorify the image's autonomous value, like in *Utopia Station*[109] by Hans Ulrich Obrist, Molly Nesbit, and Rirkrit Tiravanija at the Venice Biennale in 2003.[110] Szeemann's *Attitudes*, as one of the first curatorial projects to date, can be regarded within this same perspective. The role of the curator was employed by Szeemann as that of an "independent worker," as Florence Derieux has stated in her study of Szeemann's methodology, the "creator and author of the exhibition—he preferred to call himself an 'exhibition-maker,'" who positioned himself as a "free creative agent."[111] Consequently, the exhibition, in the words of Daniel Buren, no longer involved the display of artworks, but "the exhibition as the exhibition as a work of art," in which "the works presented are carefully chosen touches of color in the tableau that composes each section (room) as a whole."[112] Despite Buren's ironic comment, Szeemann's exhibition provided a context for the "invisible attitudes" of the artists in the late 1960s, by which means—one could posit—they were seen and understood by a (broader) audience. Consequently, the exhibition in its entirety created an autonomous status that its separate parts, the artworks, could not.

In his catalogue essay "Art Topology: The Reproduction of Aura," Groys claims that the artists of *Attitudes* did not create "new" (i.e., original or autonomous) objects or artworks like the avant-garde artists before them were accustomed to doing, but rather "new contexts," new "utopian, or at least heterotopian 'here and nows.'"[113] As an example of such works, one could think of Jan Dibbets's *Museum-socle with Angles of* 90° (1969), in which the artist excavated the corners of the Kunsthalle Bern, as well as those of the Stedelijk Museum in Amsterdam for the exhibition *Op losse schroeven*, by which means he literary revealed the foundations of the institution and, in a broader perspective, connected the two exhibitions. Michael Heizer's works *Depression* (1969), a wrecking ball that demolished the asphalt and was left in front of the Kunsthalle,[114] and *Cement Through* (1969), a nine-meter-long trench filled with cement in the lawn behind the Kunsthalle, are also works that have no particular meaning outside the specific context of the Bern exhibition.[115]

With regard to Benjamin, what guarantees these works their status of originality is their inscription in the "here and now"; the aura is determined by their topological context or

111 Florence Derieux, "Introduction," in *Harald Szeemann: Individual Methodology*, eds. Florence Derieux et al. (Zurich: JRP/Ringier, 2007), p. 8.

112 Buren 1972.

113 Groys, in exh. cat. Venice 2013, p. 455.

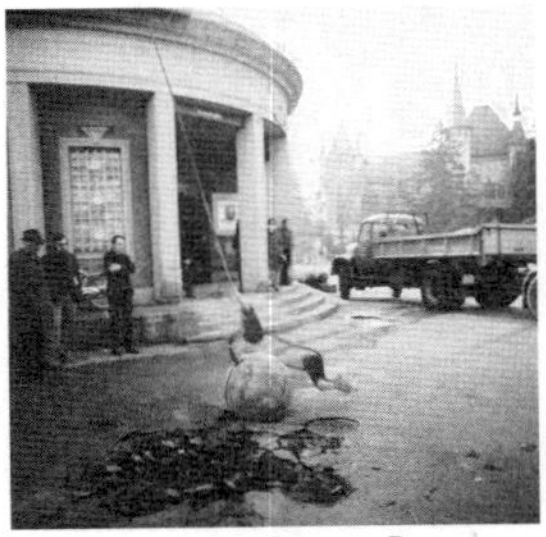

114 Michael Heizer, *Depression*, 1969.

115 Heizer, as one of the few artists who participated in the original *Attitudes* show, declined to participate in its remake venture in Venice for this reason.

historical site rather than their material characteristics.[116] The participating artists in *Attitudes*, according to Groys, produced "not the things themselves but precisely their auras. And the exhibition also produced its own aura—by creating the 'here and now' for their work."[117] Thus, the site-specificity of the works related to the context of the Kunsthalle Bern, as well as the other works in the show, generated an auratic experience; one that would be unavoidably destroyed at the moment that the original show was dismantled. Groys, however, claims that the reproduction of an exhibition like *Attitudes* also allows the "reproduction of aura." He considers this statement affirmed by the fact that the exhibition after Bern was similarly reproduced in Krefeld and London before entering its next episode in Venice. In the inimitable conclusion of his catalogue text he states, "The attitude must be utopian or at least heterotopian to be able to keep its aura through reproduction. The naturally emerged aura, as it was described by Benjamin, gets lost through the reproductive process, but an artificially produced aura allows itself to be reproduced again."[118]

Groys emphasizes that "the archive of art documentation" allows a more or less exact reproduction of an exhibition, especially an exhibition like *Attitudes* that is itself a form of documentation.[119] Analyzing the methodologies used by the Fondazione Prada to reproduce the *Attitudes* exhibition as close to its original as possible, however, illustrates how much the system of art is preventing an "authentic" manner of exhibition of works from the 1960s and 1970s. Although Groys's proposition could be made operational in theory, and has been in Venice, it is due to "the current limitations and defenses required by the market values assigned to art," that the "documents" from Szeemann's exhibition were difficult to reassemble in their original exhibition setting.[120] As Esche

116 Ibid. See also, Boris Groys, "Art in the Age of Biopolitics: From Artwork to Art Documentation," in Groys 2008, p. 62.

117 Ibid.

118 Groys, in exh. cat. Venice 2013, p. 456.

119 Ibid.

120 Celant, in exh. cat. Venice 2013, p. 412.

argued, to maintain the value of artworks in the art market, modernist tenets such as originality and uniqueness have been fundamental.[121] According to Celant, this "makes necessary the systems of isolation that transform perceptions of the works, to the point where museums and collections are being turned into bunkers and strong rooms."[122] Furthermore, Groys's perspective on "art documentation," as well as "reproduction" in regard to the *Attitudes* show, is ambiguous and not further elaborated in his catalogue text.

The fact that the original exhibition after Bern was also on show at Haus Lange in Krefeld, as well as at the ICA in London, both in a different setting because of the distinctive architecture, does not prove that the reproduction of the exhibition's aura is possible, but precisely marks the difference between the repeated historical exhibition and the Venice remake.[123] Whereas Szeemann was still the official curator of the exhibitions in Krefeld and London, in Venice it was Celant who chose to implement the entire Bern exhibition within the interiors of an eighteenth-century palace.[124] The "reproduction" of the *Attitudes* show in Venice was based on the historical documentation of the original show in Bern, photographs and archival information, as well as the reassemblage of the "original" works, but did not contain Szeemann's (original) curatorial methodology. Instead, the applied methodology offers an alternative to traditional art historical research by developing new information and knowledge through the process of reenacting, as Terry Smith has argued. Smith named the tendency "to revisit past exhibitions by restaging them or by designing a fresh one that reworks aspects of a previous exhibition," other than Greenberg's remembering exhibition, a practice of "recuration."[125]

The significance of curatorial practice as discursive and the creative role of the curator is underlined by Smith: "For

121 Esche, *in exh. cat.* Venice 2013, p. 474.

122 Celant, *in exh. cat.* Venice 2013, p. 412.

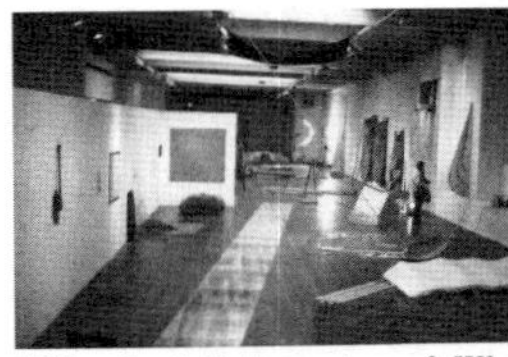

123 Installation view of *When Attitudes Become Form* at the ICA in London, 1969.

124 I deliberately write "official" in regard to Szeemann's curatorship of the two sequal *Attitudes* shows, since the exhibition in London was organized by Charles Harrison, and Lynda Morris has repeatedly asserted that it was Konrad Fischer who, behind the scenes, was responsible for the installation of the show in the ICA. See Morris, *in* Richard 2009.

125 Smith, *in exh. cat.* Venice, 2013, p. 529.

curators who think in and through exhibitions (as distinct from confining discursivity to speech or text, and from thinking primarily in art historical, art critical or theoretical terms)," the recuration of past exhibitions is a natural/logical consequence.[126] In this respect the Venice remake can be regarded a curatorial exercise in which solutions for the problems that site-specific or conceptually based works require in their re-exhibition had to be found through different methods of reproduction, as *Frieze* editor Christy Lange has pointed out:

> The result is a mixture of recreation, reconstruction and reenactment, and of absence and presence. It's possible to look at the show as a meta-show: a conceptual exercise or a curatorial readymade.... There are no straightforward solutions to the problems this presents: finding the right shade of grey paint for the baseboards, or attaining the proper shade of yellow to recreate Joseph Beuys's *Fettecke* (Fat Corner, 1969). But the show doesn't attempt to find perfect solutions; rather, it seems to embrace the imperfection of this venture. For that reason, among others, to me this recreation doesn't feel fetishistic or like a romanticization of the past.[127]

In the handout accompanying the exhibition, Celant, more unequivocally than in his catalogue text, elaborated on the creative aspect of the remake venture. He considered the approach of the project comparable to a "ready-made" in order to become reflective: "Taking the whole of 'When Attitudes Become Form' and inserting it as an 'archeological' citation into the exhibition spaces of Ca' Corner della Regina, according to a design by Rem Koolhaas and with a visual contribution from Thomas Demand, has created the same effect as the encounter between a bicycle wheel and a stool in

126 Ibid. Smith has seen this tendency appear "within biennials (Gwangju 2008, Whitney 2012), contemporary art spaces (Eastside Projects 2008) and in museums as temporary exhibitions or room installations, and in the overall programming of certain museums (most thoroughly at the Van Abbemuseum under the directorship of Charles Esche)."

127 Christy Lange, "55th Venice Biennale: Do Attitudes Still Become Form?," *Frieze Blog*, May 31, 2013, <http://blog.frieze.com/55th-venice-biennale-do-attitudes-still-become-form/> (19-10-2016).

Duchamp's *Bicycle Wheel* (1913)."[128] The specific curatorial strategy, incorporating the archeological composition of two separate realities, shows a similarity in approach with a project that Koolhaas developed in 1986 for the Milan Triennale, *La Casa Palestra*. The "whole" that Celant refers to replicates Koolhaas's former discourse in this project, which was the result of his critique of the 1984 reconstruction of Mies van der Rohe's Barcelona Pavilion (1929). Koolhaas addressed the problem of authenticity regarding the architectural reconstruction of Mies's pavilion, which he considered "a clone, not fundamentally differing from Disney," which had destroyed its aura.[129]

Instead, Koolhaas wanted, "in the name of higher authenticity," to research "the true history of the pavilion after the closing of the 1929 World's Fair and [to collect] whatever archeological remnants it had left across Europe on its return journey."[130] The oral, textual, and photographic tradition around the "lifeless, puritanical modern building" was considered an important aspect of its reconstruction in this respect: "Like a Pompeian villa, these fragments were reassembled as far as possible to suggest the former whole."[131] In his own "reconstruction" of Mies's pavilion within the Triennale building, Koolhaas provided a discursive spectacle that elaborated on the symbolic history, or perhaps "aura," of the pavilion, preserved in its photographic and narrative representation.[132] Similar to Honnef, the architect seems to persist in the "inversion" of Benjamin's notion of originality, in which the photographic (and cinematic) documentation does not copy or represent the original, thereby eliminating the original's aura, but instead contributes to the *creation* of aura.[133]

Whereas the pavilion was not designed to host an exhibition, but was merely an exhibit itself—apart from the purpose-designed furniture and a sculpture by Georg Kolbe,

128 Germano Celant, handout, *When Attitudes Become Form: Bern 1969/Venice 2013*, Venice (Fondazione Prada) June 1–November 3, 2013.

129 O.M.A., Rem Koolhaas, and Bruce Mau, *S,M,L,XL* (New York: Monacelli Press, 1995), p. 49. "In 1985, we were invited to participate in the Milan Triennale; the Palazzo della Triennale, subdivided neatly into rooms, had all the deadliness/charm of the treasure chamber of a belated pyramid.... OMA's room, projected in the curved exedra of the fascist Triennale building, was deformed—another misfit. By then, phobic about the duty to reveal, we decided to embody our resistance in an exhibit about exhibition. At the time, a clone of Mies's pavilion was being built in Barcelona. How fundamentally did it differ from Disney? In the name of higher authenticity, we researched the true history of the pavilion after the closing of the 1929 World's Fair and collected whatever archeological remnants it had left across Europe on its return journey. Like a Pompeian villa, these fragments were reassembled as far as possible to suggest the former whole, but with one inevitable inaccuracy: since our 'site' was curved, the pavilion had to be 'bent.'" Interestingly, Koolhaas suggests in a short story named "The House that Made Mies" that the idea for a 1:1 scale model was inspired by a 1:1 scale model that Mies made for Helene Kröller-Müller for her museum/house in Wassenaar to experience the project in its totality. The museum by Mies was never built; Koolhaas heard the story from Philip Johnson, who said it was a fake, but the 1:1 scale model of the house was really built; Sam Farnsworth discusses the "aura quality" of the pavilion that, contrary to Benjamin's definition of aura that is lost in the reproduction of an original, was generated through the photographic representation of the pavilion in a series of retouched black-and-white pictures. See "The Barcelona Pavilion: Barometer of Culture," <www.repetti.org/pdf/h1ujqu89_MIES_BP1.pdf>, p. 6 (11-8-2014).

130 O.M.A., Koolhaas, and Mau 1995, p. 49.

131 Ibid. See also <www.oma.eu/projects/1986/casa-palestra-the-domestic-project-/> (23-6-2014).

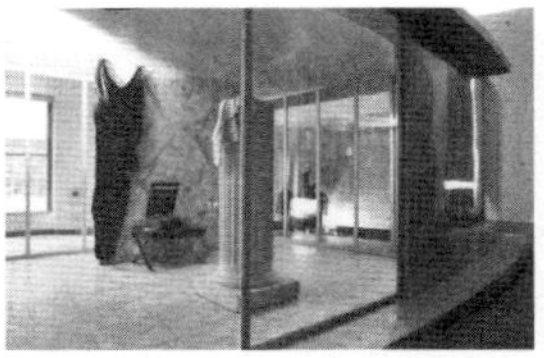

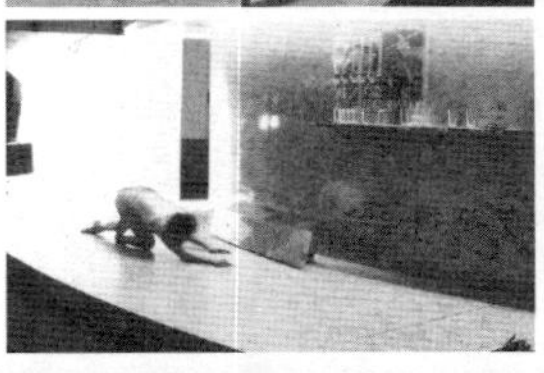

132 Installation views of Koolhaas's *La Casa Palestra* at the Milan Triennale, 1986.

133 See also Walter Benjamin, "The Work of Art in the Age of Mechanical Reproduction" (1935), in *Illuminations*, trans. Harry Zohn (London: Fontana, 1992), pp. 214–215.

134 O.M.A., Koolhaas, and Mau 1995, p. 49.

135 Groys 2008, p. 54.

136 Ibid.

it was empty—Koolhaas used its vacant opportunity to re-exhibit the building as a site where both its historical and current potential was explored. He referred to the project as "an exhibit about exhibition," recreating the Barcelona Pavilion in an exhibition setting.[134] In its critical reassessment of Mies's reconstructed pavilion, Koolhaas's project could be considered an early example of Greenberg's typology of the riff. Although the *Attitudes* remake in its meticulous replication of the original exhibition's *mise-en-scène* was less of a "rejuvenation" than Koolhaas's *Casa Palestra,* the intention to convey the symbolic history of the original exhibition rather than produce a genuine reconstruction is crucial.

In his plea for the reproduction of aura, Groys argued that there were in fact no original artworks produced in the Bern exhibition, but rather contexts, auratic experiences that were topical and temporal, which raises the question of how we should regard the "works" from various collections that Celant and his team reassembled. According to Groys, these works are rather "documents" or "signifiers of art," but it is important to further explicate their precise documentary status. In his essay "Art in the Age of Biopolitics: From Artwork to Art Documentation," Groys distinguishes between types of art documentation.[135] There is a significant difference between art documentation that refers to past art events—present and visible at a particular time—as a way of recollecting, and art documentation that merely represents artistic interventions, processes, explorations, or politically motivated activities within the context of daily life, which would otherwise remain invisible. In such cases, "art documentation is neither the making present of a past event nor the promise of a coming artwork, but rather… the only possible form of reference to an artistic activity that cannot be represented in any other way."[136]

Szeemann's exhibition certainly created a context for such works, like Robert Smithson's *Bern Earth—Mirror Displacement* (1969), which can be ascribed to the first category, and Douglas Huebler's *Duration Piece #9: Berkeley, California—Hull, Massachusetts, January—November 1969* (1969) or Richard Long's *A Walking Tour in the Berner Oberland* (1969),[137] which can be ascribed to the second, but not all of the works in the Bern exhibition can be considered art documentation. Other than Lippard's "suitcase exhibitions" or Fischer and Wedewer's *Konzeption, Attitudes* was strictly regarded as not being a conceptual exhibition (i.e., the plan of the exhibition was not based on the assemblage of artists' proposals or documents). Moreover, even in these exhibitions the "documents" that the artists provided needed some sort of adjustment to be exhibited in a spatiotemporal situation. Groys's perspective on the curated exhibition as a sort of artistic installation in which the artworks function as "documentation of a curatorial project" in this respect is a more appropriate tool to define the status of works from the 1960s and 1970s, in order to determine how to deal with such works in a contemporary exhibitionary context.

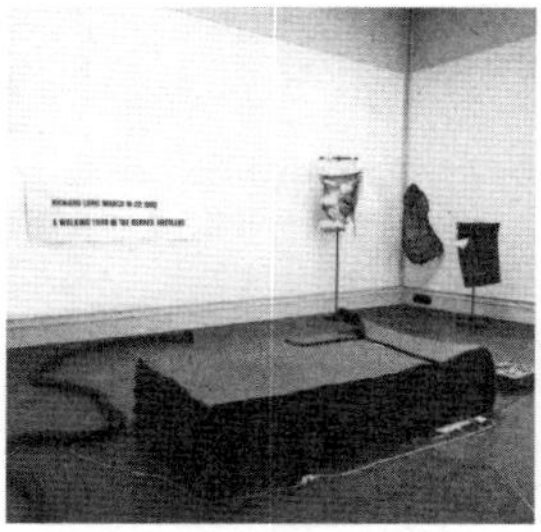

137 Installation view with Richard Long's, *A Walking Tour in the Berner Oberland*, Kunsthalle Bern, 1969.

The modernist tenets of museums of modern and contemporary art to store and preserve works according to the autonomous aspects of their visible form or materials rather than their relative implications has proved particularly ineffective for conceptual art—yet is precisely what the conceptual artists were trying to undermine. This does not mean that conceptual artworks have no material relevance, as Groys has emphasized: "Conceptual artists shifted the emphasis of art-making away from static, individual objects toward the presentation of new relationships in space and time. These relationships could be purely spatial, but also logical and political. They could be relationships among things, texts, and photo-documents, but could also involve performances, happenings, films, and videos—all of which were shown inside the same installation space."[138] Following Groys's argumentation, reactivating these relationships within the context of its (original) exhibition could also reactivate some sort of aura, which is something the Venice exhibition adapted to.

In bringing together all of the works or "documents" from Szeemann's *Attitudes*, the individual artworks from this exhibition were more authentically exhibited than in their "autonomous" presentation within the context of random (museum) collections for which they were once acquired. Despite the artificial or, according to many art historians, "Disneyfied" configuration of the project, this approach did provide a deeper understanding of the authentic significance of these works than any art historical writing or traditional modernist exhibition. Smith has argued that "in recent decades, most art museums have shifted their primary focus away from their historical purpose as scholarly repositories of collections, a selection of which was displayed to a limited range of publics for their edification, uplift, and occasionally glorification," and "have become sites of attraction within the cultural economy of a city, region or nation."[139] Within these new museological practices the remake of *When Attitudes Become Form* explored, in close collaboration with important public collections all over the world, the potential that the restaging, representing, and reenacting of artworks, performances, happenings, and total events can involve for new analysis and development of knowledge within the field of art's history and exhibition.

138 Groys 2011.

139 Smith, in *exh. cat.* Venice 2013, p. 519.

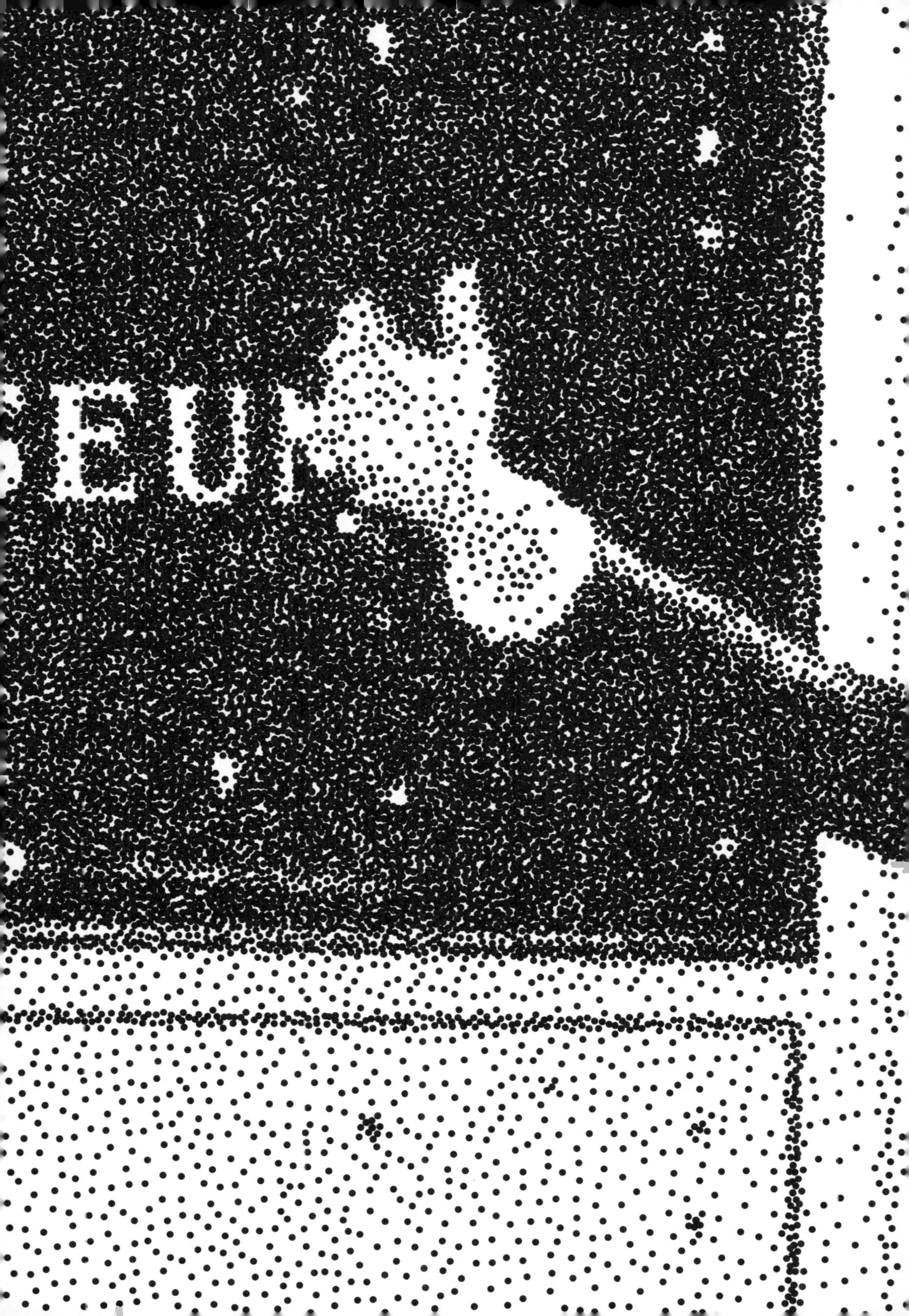

Conclusion

The curatorial has to do with research, in terms of art history and the (brief) history of the concept and practice of curating. However, perhaps, and more intriguingly, the curatorial could now be posited as a form of research, not just into exhibition-making but a specific mode of research that may or may not take on the spatial or temporal form of an exhibition.
— Simon Sheikh[1]

1 Simon Sheikh, "Towards the Exhibition as Research," in *Curating Research*, eds. Paul O'Neill and Mick Wilson (London: Open Editions, 2015), p. 33.

Corresponding to the principles of conceptual art, the (incomplete) exhibition history of conceptual art described in the three case studies of this book offers a perspective on the strategies and methodologies that curators, often in direct exchange with the artists involved, applied to publicly disclose works of conceptual art. As I have argued, the three exhibitions examined represent the transforming process of exhibiting conceptual art within a period of about five decades—from the beginnings of conceptual "practices" in the 1960s to the all-encompassing vista of contemporary art

Image appropriated from Marcel Broodthaers at his exhibition *Musée d'Art Moderne, Département des Aigles*, Kunsthalle Düsseldorf, 1972. See also p. 144.

today. Furthermore, the exhibitions are each indicative of shifts not only in the curation but also in the reception and historicization of conceptual art within this period. In regard to the latter, it should be emphasized that each of the exhibitions was also deliberately intended to influence the reception and historicization of the already defined trend of conceptual art. In 1969 Konrad Fischer and Rolf Wedewer intended to frame "a today's art tendency" with a first museum exhibition at the Städtisches Museum Schloss Morsbroich in Leverkusen. In 1989 Suzanne Pagé thought it was time, while most of the protagonists were still alive, to show conceptual art in a contemporary perspective at the Musée d'art moderne de la ville de Paris. In 2013 Miuccia Prada imagined that a remake of Harald Szeemann's famous *When Attitudes Become Form* at her eighteenth-century palazzo in Venice, Ca' Corner della Regina, would enable a younger generation of art enthusiasts to "reestablish" a connection with the historical works.[2]

2 Prada, in exh. cat. Venice 2013, p. 377.

Within art history, conceptual art has been generally described as a radical break with modernist traditions in the production, reception, and distribution of art, challenging institutional structures, art historical discourse, and the art market. As a refinement of this reading, my analysis of conceptual art within a curatorial perspective above all demonstrates that the exhibition of conceptual art practices has been a paradoxical or even opportunist undertaking from the very start—in which curators, dealers, and collectors have played a significant part. Although the role that curators, dealers, and collectors have adopted in the production, reception, and distribution of art in general may have been much larger than it is art historically acknowledged, it is with the advent of conceptual art that these respective roles have become ever more visible. Moreover, as I have argued, it is with conceptual art that specifically the role of the curator has come to the fore, and still remains an equally important part of the work when conceptual art (in public or private collections) is re-exhibited in a different historical time frame. The various positions of the curators, examined in the case studies in chapters two to four, reveal the formats, strategies, and methodologies that were, for better or for worse, applied to make visible the work of conceptual artists, or even, as Seth Siegelaub implied, to show that the artist "had done anything at all."[3] Whereas these formats, strategies, and methodologies can be derived from the theoretical definitions applied to conceptual art that I analyze in the first chapter of this book, the successive case studies demonstrate that they rather anticipated them. The curatorial histories of works of conceptual art are therefore considered significant points of reference for the determination of the current ontological status of these works in order to guarantee their continued exhibition.

While in the 1969 Leverkusen exhibition Lucy Lippard's 1968 principle of dematerialization was explicitly put to the fore in the reception of the exhibition at the time, the curators were in fact dealing with the predicament of what Siegelaub in 1972 had termed primary and secondary information—inviting the artists to send in proposals to be executed in both the catalogue and the exhibition. In Paris both guest curator Claude Gintz and museum curator Juliette Laffon, as well as the artists themselves, were struggling with the problem of art documentation, a notion which would not be framed until 1997 by Boris Groys.[4] The representation of the historical consequences of conceptual art in regard to the material reality of an exhibition was not yet sufficiently elaborated within the different spatiotemporal context of the Paris exhibition. The consequent engagement with the residue of conceptual art from the 1960s and 1970s that curator Germano Celant, in collaboration with Rem Koolhaas and

3 Siegelaub 1969, p. 202.

4 See Boris Groys. "On the Curatorship," in Groys 2008, p. 49.

5 Greenberg 2009.

6 See Smith 2012.

Thomas Demand, applied in the 2013 Venice exhibition made visible the historical positions and relationships of these works in a current perspective. Although the works were, paradoxically enough, engaged with the dematerialization of the art object, the use of the model of the remembering exhibition, as defined by Reesa Greenberg in 2009, provided a context to (re-)experience these works in an eloquent manner.[5]

The Venice case study illustrates that the model of the remembering exhibition has the potential to present historical works of conceptual art—familiar to many of us today mostly by the enigmatic descriptions in art history books—within the proper environs to continue to exist in the public context of museums and art institutions. The various typologies of replica, riff, and reprise that Greenberg defined can each in different ways contribute to a better understanding of works of conceptual art that in their initial presentation were often directly relating or committed to the social and political issues of the late 1960s and early 1970s. That is not to say that the original context of these works should always be recreated, but for curators dealing with contemporary art collections that include works of conceptual art it is important to accept that some form of recuration, to use Terry Smith's definition, needs to be applied.[6] In absence of both the context in which the works were conceived and the critical involvement of many of the artists, contemporary visitors require curatorial support to grasp the nature and content of the work, similar to but also other than the inherent logic of a book.

Another representative model of a remembering exhibition that took place after the instructive exhibition in Venice was *Seth Siegelaub: Beyond Conceptual Art* at the Stedelijk Museum in Amsterdam in 2015–2016. In this commemorative exhibition, curated by Leontine Coelewij and Sara

Martinetti, a large part was devoted to Siegelaub's early exhibition experiments. Making use of reconstructed spaces and reenactments of original exhibition settings, the show in Amsterdam attempted to provide a more complex representation of the context of the works of conceptual art exhibited by Siegelaub.[7] This specific approach supports my thesis that innovative forms of recuration that address the dilemma of exhibition within conceptual art can be integrated into the curatorial praxis of public museums of modern and contemporary art. It is, however, far from obvious how methods of recuration should be applied to various cases of exhibiting conceptual art. The three case studies that I examine provide, in relation to the theoretical concepts, the field of complexities and problems that arise from such exercises. They generate a perpetual arena of discussion from which I will nevertheless attempt to draw some concluding statements in order to stimulate a more flexible museological approach towards the exhibition of historical works of conceptual art today.

As Groys has argued, "the archive of art documentation" allows a more or less exact reproduction of an exhibition, especially an exhibition like Szeemann's *When Attitudes Become Form,* which is considered a form of documentation itself.[8] Groys's suggestion could in fact be more effectively applied to Fischer and Wedewer's *Konzeption-Conception: Documentation of a To-day's Art Tendency* in Leverkusen, which essentially or even solely consisted of documentation—as the subtitle also underlined. Unsurprisingly, in the aftermath of the Venice exhibition, the 1969 Leverkusen exhibition was also recurated in 2015 at the present-day Museum Morsbroich in Leverkusen under the title *More Konzeption Conception Now*. Because it presented the work of a younger generation of artists relating to the legacy of this historical

7 The exhibition ran from December 12, 2015, to April 17, 2016, and was developed in memoriam to Siegelaub, who passed away in 2013, in collaboration with his widow and former curator of the Stedelijk Museum, Marja Bloem. Coelewij is curator at the Stedelijk Museum, and Martinetti is a researcher working on a PhD thesis on the various activities of Siegelaub at the École des hautes études en sciences sociales (EHESS) in Paris. The exhibition design was made by APPARATA (Nicholas Lobo Brennan and Astrid Smitham).

8 Groys, in exh. cat. Venice 2013, p. 456.

exhibition, rather than reconstructing (the works from) the original exhibition, the show applied, to use Greenberg's terminology, the format of the "riff."[9] Although this specific format of the remembering exhibition provided an interesting perspective on the influence of the historical exhibition on current artistic practices, I believe that a more genuine recuration of the 1969 exhibition in the format of the replica (i.e., reworking the documentation in the catalogue as well as the exhibition's archives) could have provided more valuable insights regarding the contemporaneous misconceptions of the exhibition that I point out in my analysis.

In examining the remaining documents of Fischer and Wedewer's exhibition, I have demonstrated that the participating artists had, consequent to the dictum of conceptual art, little concern for the physical installation of their works. Primary was the idea, contained in the artists' proposals that were sent to Leverkusen by mail to be included as such in the "catalogue-book." According to the few historical records kept in the city's archive, these proposals were assumed to function in the same way in the exhibition within the spatial environs of the museum, which the curators termed the "space-catalogue." This approach, I would argue, constitutes the principle curatorial methodology of a conceptual art exhibition, both in a historical and present-day perspective. It makes use of artists' propositions (or concepts) that are to be directly transferred to any chosen venue, to any site besides the catalogue, and can be executed by anyone in addition to the artist—a methodology that was earlier applied in Lippard's Numbers Shows.[10]

The extensive critical review of the *Konzeption* exhibition in the local and national German newspapers implied that this approach lacked attention for the execution of the works within a spatial configuration. Many contemporary

9 Kreuzer 2015.

10 See Butler 2012.

critics—even sophisticated ones like Georg Jappe—were of the opinion that the works functioned better in the catalogue, which made the spatial exhibition an unnecessary addition. But the fact that the exhibition was nevertheless executed within the museum galleries was not without good reason. The choice of the curators to present the new, so-called conceptual type of art principally in a catalogue-book was based on the exhibition format of conceptual art that Siegelaub initiated the year before. But Fischer and Wedewer's format also differed from Siegelaub's in a few crucial aspects; not so much in its physical (re-)presentation—after the *Xerox Book*, Siegelaub made several spatial exhibitions that he defined as "a guide to the catalogue"—but rather in its traditional, art historical aspect of categorization.[11] In contrast to Siegelaub's explicit rejection of the museum and focus on places outside this dominating institution, Fischer and Wedewer accurately framed the new art tendency *within* the context of the museum. As a result, the newness of conceptual practices was diminished and the differences between respective practices of artists were mitigated to fit into a specific art historical category.[12]

Fischer's adapted role of curator-dealer, intermediating between the distribution of artworks and the production of knowledge through exhibitions, contributed to a large extent to the reception of conceptual art. More importantly, however, this intermediary role of the curator-dealer is essentially inherent to the exhibition of conceptual art, which, as I have argued, can be considered a curatorial project *a priori*. While it seemed more important to define conceptual art as a "movement" at the time—paradoxically conflicting with the motivations that initially urged the conceptualist assignment—the curatorial dilemma of exhibiting conceptual art was yet anticipated. There is little evidence that the execution

11 See The Siegelaub Collection and Archives, Stichting Egress Foundation: <http://egressfoundation.net/egress/index.php?option=com_content&view=article&id=62&Itemid=307> (19-10-2016).

12 Here I derive from Rosalind Krauss's definition of historicization. See Krauss 1979, p. 277.

13 It was only after Benjamin Buchloh's seminal essay, published first in the catalogue of *L'art conceptuel* and subsequently in *October* journal, that an increasing amount of studies and reevaluations of the 1960s discourse on conceptual art was published.

of the works within the spatial exhibition in Leverkusen was discussed with the artists. Furthermore, following the exhibition's reviews, it can be concluded that several of the exhibited works differed from the works printed in the catalogue. This substantiates my view that the artists' propositions were open to interpretation, hence, were adjusted on-site by the curator(s). Although the term "recuration" was not used in the late 1960s, it applies accurately to Fischer's approach in *Konzeption:* he *re*curated, in physical form, an exhibition that was already completed in the catalogue. This methodology was aimed at better transmitting the primary ideas of the works to the public and, for that reason, provides a major point of reference for all future curatorial iterations.

Gintz's exhibition *L'art conceptuel: une perspective*, in collaboration with Benjamin Buchloh, generated a revival of the conceptual project, which made, as I have argued, the historicization of conceptual art a fact in 1989.[13] Because many of the conceptual artists were still alive at the time, and some directly involved in the installation of the exhibition, there was plenty of opportunity to discuss with them the historical impact of the "conceptual movement." Ironically, the discussions centered not so much on the installation of the actual works or how to exhibit the idea-based art of the 1960s within a different historical time frame, but on the historical correctness of certain events, positions, and (self-acclaimed) ascriptions—which was mainly conducted in the thorough, scholarly catalogue that accompanied the exhibition. That the catalogue was regarded as the proper place for this, and the exhibition of secondary importance, in fact corresponded to the assignment of conceptual art in the first place. The format of the Paris catalogue, as well as that of the exhibition, did not, however, adopt the notion of primary and secondary information that was already anticipated in the 1969 Leverkusen exhibition and made, as Siegelaub had stressed, (the works in) *L'art conceptuel* look "dead."[14]

Twenty years after the historical momentum of conceptual art, the exhibition in Paris dealt with (the remains of) historical works, contained in certificates and art documentation. Yet the new exhibitionary setting did not always directly convey the primary idea of the selected works. The negation of this discrepancy created many problems, which were not—or could not yet be—properly resolved at the end of the 1980s. From the written correspondence with several of the participating artists, as well as representing galleries and collectors, it can be concluded that the museum personnel was thinking and operating in a traditional and modernist method of exhibition-making. The nonpermanent condition of works of conceptual art was not fully understood by Gintz's supporting curatorial staff, creating confusion about "originals" and "reproductions." Despite that several participating artists attempted to implement new versions of their primary ideas, the museum refused to include "copies" and stuck with the original art documentation. Whereas these documents did not anticipate interaction *per se*, they became rather trivial, like Art & Language's *Documenta Index* (1972), which remained inaccessible to the visitors of the exhibition.

Telling in this respect is also the execution of Michael Asher's proposition for the exhibition. Gintz, aware of the paradox of curating a retrospective exhibition on the "conceptual art movement," tried to get at the heart of conceptual practices by inviting Asher, Daniel Buren, and Hans Haacke. The direct participation of these artists had to demonstrate the disruption of traditions and methods in art production to which conceptual art gave rise.[15] This ambition, however, was not further elaborated; apart from Asher's project, as well as

14 Siegelaub in conversation with Obrist, 2011.

15 It was for this reason that Gintz titled his exhibition a *perspective* and not a *retrospective*.

16 Wulffen 1990.

some works that were reexecuted for this exhibition, such as the wall drawings by Sol LeWitt, newly produced works were absent in the final exhibition. Struggling to find a proper format to address the retrospective as a tool to problematize aesthetic practice—as works of conceptual art had done before—Asher eventually published an announcement of the exhibition in a number of art historical journals. Specifically focused on promoting the historicizing endeavor as such, it was the only work in the exhibition that functioned in a truly conceptual mode—existing outside the exhibition's framework, it was represented in both the exhibition and the catalogue only by the artist's statement. In the laborious completion of his proposal, moreover, Asher made a subtle institutional critique that could not be understood without secondary information.

L'art conceptuel fittingly illustrates that the continued exhibition of works of conceptual art is not a straightforward undertaking. As Wulffen argued, the examination of the paradigmatic shifts that conceptual art instigated should not be limited to the catalogue, but elaborated in the material reality of the exhibition as well.[16] The intention to historically convey the primary information and nature of the selected works was well served by the catalogue—making use of extensive secondary information—but the spatial exhibition did not similarly succeed in this. Apparently, it was the institutional division of tasks that caused the unbalanced junction between the catalogue and the exhibition, where different formats with different perspectives on historicity were applied. Besides the selection of works and the editing of the catalogue, curator Gintz in fact had little control over the final installation of the exhibition; this was the responsibility of museum curator Laffon. In this respect the curatorial responsibility was underestimated (i.e., the praxis of exhibition-making was taken for granted). As a result, *L'art conceptuel* failed to address the historical and theoretical issues of practices of conceptual art *by means of the exhibition*. To put it more bluntly, the lack of strong curatorial mediation caused the exhibition, as Douglas Huebler experienced, to be "far removed from the original thrust of the conceptual enterprise."[17] If anything, this case study shows that it was not about how to reconcile the public disclosure of works of conceptual art in 1989, not even for (most of) the artists; it was about how to settle the art historical discussion on the definition and contribution of the movement of conceptual art. As I have demonstrated, the discussions about the actual exhibition of the works that the curatorial staff conducted with the artists proved equally important, and could have been addressed in the exhibition as well. The question, therefore, remained: how can works of conceptual art and the respective historical discussions that they instigated be exhibited?

17 Douglas Huebler, in a letter to Juliette Laffon, December 2, 1989, Archives MAMVP (Box 524/9).

In a way, Celant, Koolhaas, and Demand's remake exhibition at the Fondazione Prada in Venice countered this dilemma. It successfully made use of the "replica" exhibition format to study the historical event at the Kunsthalle Bern in 1969, that is, the curatorial methodology of Szeemann and the ensuing installation of the artworks, many of which have become references in the art historical canon. The exhibition consisted of a precise reconfiguration of all the works included in the 1969 *Attitudes* exhibition within their "original" setting of the Kunsthalle Bern—although now located in an implemented, life-size model within an eighteenth-century Venetian palace. In accordance with my account that the exhibition practices of conceptual art have been historically opportunist in many aspects, the exhibition in Venice revealed the divergence of radical methods of curation within current museological frameworks. Since many of the works in the original exhibition were marked by the ambition to "dematerialize the art object," the problem of re-exhibiting these works within a contemporary context was not only challenged but also acknowledged and made visible. The curators researched appropriate formats of display through a variety of reproducing techniques, including reconstructions, reenactments, reexecutions, exhibition copies, and documentary representations, which were, as I have argued, truly advanced in comparison to the 1989 Paris exhibition.

Within the category of the replica exhibition, the exact reconstruction of the entire *mise-en-scène* of a historical exhibition is thus far unprecedented. Although the "repeat-remembering exhibition," as Greenberg termed it, is based on the reassemblage of all the original contents of the earlier exhibition in the same, unchanged space, exactly like before, so far no exhibition has consisted of the reconstruction of the entire original space within another space. Parts of exhibitions have been reinstalled at other venues, such as the 1937 exhibition *Entartete Kunst* at the Los Angeles County Museum of Art in 1991, or Frederick Kiesler's 1942 display for Peggy Guggenheim's *Art of This Century* in the same museum in 1997, but neither of these reconstructions matched the original architectural setting in scale or was entirely faithful to the disposition of the original exhibition.[18] In these cases it was rather the innovative exhibition design that stimulated a reenactment in terms of display. In the case of *Attitudes* the display of works was not predesigned for an existing collection of works, but took its final form at the time of installation on-site, anticipating the spatial characteristics of the Kunsthalle Bern. As a replica or genuine reconstruction of the 1969 exhibition, however, the remake in Venice was also not completely accurate. On the contrary, in

18 Greenberg 2009. The exhibition *Entartete Kunst* (Degenerate Art) was originally held at the Haus der Kunst in München in 1937; Kiesler's design for the display of Peggy Guggenheim's *Art of This Century* in New York was on show in 1942; the exhibition replicas were shown in Stephanie Barran's 1991 replica exhibition, *Degenerate Art: The Fate of the Avant-Garde in Nazi Germany*, and her 1997 *Exiles and Emigres: The Flight of European Artists from Hitler*, both at the Los Angeles County Museum of Art (LACMA). More recent examples can be found in the project *Time Machines Reloaded* at the Van Abbemuseum in Eindhoven (2011/2012). This program included a variety of presentations based on special museum models from the past, like an "ethnographic" installation in two galleries about the genesis of New York's Museum of Modern Art (MoMA, 1929–1936) by the Museum of American Art in Berlin and Lina Bo Bardi's 1968 design of "glass plinths" for the Museu de Arte de São Paulo (MASP), in which paintings and information could be displayed on either side.

regard to the recreation of the "auratic experience" of the original exhibition, it exactly showed the impossibility of reviving this historical momentum.

What I consider to be most remarkable about the *Attitudes* remake, however, is not that through the reproduction of this exhibition, as Groys claimed in the exhibition catalogue, the "artificially produced aura" of the original show is reproduced, but that the primary idea of the artworks was recreated through several discursive interventions in the context of the replica exhibition.[19] The highly stage-managed setup of the remake project stimulated the visitor to engage with the historical works in a manner one rarely encounters in traditional museum settings. The specificity of artworks and how to relate to them historically is an important aspect that is lost in the autonomous exhibition of singular works in most collection displays of museums of modern and contemporary art. It is in the recreation of no longer existing works—the nonchalant installation on-site, process-based works that have no permanent material structure—that the functions that keep the structure of the work, the so-called ontological status, became visible. In this respect the public understanding of the works was approached most effectively in Venice. Reconstructing "dematerialized works" may not be fully appropriate in terms of art historical authenticity, as art historians Helmut Draxler and Catherine Spencer have stressed, but it does come closer to the primary manifestation of the work than (the exhibition of) art documentation. The different historical layers which composed the exhibition, enclosed by a documentary framework that provided information about the context of the historical exhibition and many of the works included, can be regarded as a proposition to disclose the past in another manner than the writing of history.

19 Groys, in exh. cat. Venice 2013, p. 456.

The "recreational experience" of the Venice exhibition comes uncomfortably close to the Disneyfication of the contemporary art museum, and seems to conflict the (art historical) desire for authenticity—a problem Rosalind Krauss had already tackled in her 1998 critique of the contemporary late-capitalist, industrialized museum.[20] But as authenticity itself was something that the artists in the *Attitudes* show were explicitly trying to confront or dispute, the interpretation of the original show and the works in it should be reformulated. The historical context of the exhibition is represented in its documentation, and many works or artistic projects in it are merely conveyed in art documentation. These works, which are only knowable through their historical reference, have regained currency, or even "visibility," in the recreated context of the *Attitudes* exhibition in Venice that would otherwise be lost.[21] The inversion of the notion of aura, which, as Klaus Honnef suggested, is more present in the legend of the exhibition than the actual experience, is useful in this respect, while it also provides a key principle of the valorization of documentation and archives in which a sense of aura is captured. Although this type of "reproduced aura" cannot be effectively reactivated again, the reproduction, recreation, reenactment, or reconstruction of past events, performances, projects, and specific artworks can reevaluate the legendary status that is represented in their documentation and generate new formats of exhibition to show conceptual art.

In the 1960s and 1970s the direct collaboration between conceptual artists and curators/dealers instigated discursive practices in the arts—commonly acknowledged as the "linguistic turn"—which frustrated (traditional) institutional methods of acquisition, preservation, and exhibition (i.e., the display of works in a spatial configuration). However, when works of

20 Krauss 1998.

21 See also Chuz Martinez, "The Politics of Attitudes," in exh. cat. Venice 2013, p. 516. "The aspirations of writing on art have far more to do with the theory of knowledge than with traditional metaphysics. The notion of 'quality' has been displaced by another category: relevance. What really ought to have a bearing on writing is the specter of interaction between the mental conceptions with which art works, the attempts to represent these, and the cognitive systems that make structuring and communication between source and receiver possible."

conceptual art are consigned in a public collection (i.e., have become the commodities that conceptual artists were essentially trying to avoid), their initial, open-ended status has been renegotiated. The complexity of conceptual works of art today is that the "original" works are dead in terms of exhibition. In order to publicly disclose these works, the remaining art documentation can be translated, interpreted, or refabricated, but this also endangers their "authenticity" in a strict, art historical perspective. Unlike other art disciplines, visual art traditionally depends strongly on the originality or authenticity of artworks, and although these doctrines are frustrated within the case of conceptual art, the "original idea" still needs to be confined. That museums have to guarantee their boards of trustees and loaners that the works from their collections are handled with care and protected from possible damage or destruction makes it difficult to communicate the participatory aspect of many of these works, as the various ensuing problems described in the Paris case study demonstrate. Formats of reconstruction, reenactment, or reproduction are a feasible method to convey these works to a broader audience, but they need to be critically evaluated as well. This is the true challenge of the conceptual legacy that remains open to innovative or experimental forms of exhibition.

Before and after the Venice exhibition, many exhibitions on conceptual art have been organized in various places around the world.[22] The complexities of the "works, concepts, processes, situations, and information" that were produced in the 1960s and 1970s, however, are repeatedly unaddressed within museum exhibitions of conceptual art. As Charles Esche stressed, modernist tenets prevail within museum practices, and even support market tactics. Without a doubt, the market value of reproducible documents of conceptual art

22 Issues of stretching the canon of conceptual art were, for example, addressed in *Global Conceptualism: Points of Origin, 1950s–1980s* at the Queens Museum of Art in New York in 1999. Expanding conceptual practices in contemporary art have been addressed in several exhibitions at the Generali Foundation in Vienna, like *Concept Has Never Meant Horse* in 2006 and a series of exhibitions that resulted in Folie, Holz, and Lafer 2013.

complicates experimental methods in its (museum) curation, preventing the establishment of a more public understanding of the historical works in their spatial-temporal context. Traditionally, the museum curator's role was supposed to safeguard, analyze, and present cultural heritage, and perhaps also to enrich this heritage by acquiring contemporary works.[23] Today, driven by generating their own income and addressing diverse audiences, museums rather provide, as Krauss has pointed out, "a kind of intensity of experience, an aesthetic charge that is not so much temporal (historical) as it is now radically spatial."[24] Preferably, contemporary museum curators should combine these two objectives in order to accurately address historical works of conceptual art.

The Venice exhibition is exemplary in this respect, since Celant and his team, while providing a "recreational experience," or rather a "relational experience," at the same time gave a precise and correct art historical account of the works within the exhibitionary setting. The exhibition was organized in close collaboration with several external researchers, archival institutions, artists' estates, and the artists themselves, where possible. The idea that the continued exhibition of conceptual art implies a sort of "shared responsibility," as Jean-Marc Poinsot proposed, becomes a fact within this approach. It urges the current museological praxis to become more aware of the exhibition histories of works from the 1960s and 1970s in order to properly and effectively communicate these. Within this format of the remembering exhibition a certain method of art historical research becomes manifest, which assumes that the (making of an) exhibition becomes a form of research. This extends the practice of curating to a more academic undertaking, and requires museums and public art institutions to invest in the development of curatorial knowledge in regard to their collections—

23 See Nathalie Heinich and Michael Pollak, "From Museum Curator to Exhibition *Auteur*: Inventing a Singular Position," in Greenberg et al. 1996, p. 233. See also Groys 2009.

24 Krauss 1998, p. 431.

inviting specialized scholars or providing curatorial fellowships to participate in exhibition and collection programs—thereby bringing together art historical research and curation.

While copyright legislation to protect the authorship of artists' works in collections remains an issue to address, and artworks cannot always be easily reconstructed or reexecuted, various positions can nevertheless be taken, as the Venice case study illustrates. Consequently, the possible refabrication of conceptual works of art is something that obliges an extensive exchange and collaboration with artists, artists' estates, and other parties that should guarantee authorship protection.[25] Such a point of view obviously requires a substantial research and production budget, the means for which public museums do not always possess. Noteworthy in this respect is that the exhibition in Venice was organized by a wealthy private institution, which in various ways can make bolder decisions when it comes to the loan and security of artworks from museums and private collections, as well as the exchange with artists and artists' estates. Fondazione Prada managed to bring together works in the cramped environs of the reconstructed Kunsthalle Bern that are now in the custody of public museums, regulating both the protection of various historical works and the reexamination of others with respect to the artists' will (i.e., adhering to prescribed museum ethics). The productive collaboration with public institutions indicates that they, too, are able to find ways to approve of inventive exhibition designs to convey works of conceptual art and take responsibility in the continued disclosure of works that are in their allocated care.

At the press opening of *Seth Siegelaub: Beyond Conceptual Art* at the Stedelijk Museum in Amsterdam in 2015, I discussed the roles that artists and curators apply in the reexamination of works of conceptual art in an

25 See, for example, Nathalie Zonnenberg, "Ik heb de conceptuele kunst nooit als gedematerialiseerd beschouwd. Interview met Ann Goldstein over het Temporary Stedelijk en het voortbestaan van de conceptuele kunst," *De Witte Raaf* no. 152 (July/August 2011). <www.dewitteraaf.be/artikel/detail/nl/3658> (23-7-2018).

exhibitionary setting with participating artist Mario García Torres. García Torres is often invited by museums and art institutions to "anticipate retrospect" in regard to the histories of (artworks from) their institutions, and revisited the work from conceptual artists in various engaging projects.[26] According to him, there are two ways of looking at the legacy of conceptual art. On the one hand, as a collection of written, black-on-white letters that might be considered as something boring; on the other hand, it could be regarded as something really romantic—works that can circulate around the world for ever and ever.[27] In these both simple and inspiring terms, the artist pointed out the problematic nature of conceptual art and, at the same time, its possibilities in terms of continued exhibition. I admire but also envy the imaginative projects that artists can develop with respect to the re-exhibiting of works of conceptual art. For curators who wish to concurrently address the current ambiguous status of works of conceptual art in collections and anticipate the curatorial possibilities for the future public conveyance of these works, a creative approach that is also art-historically verified is preferable. The academically grounded curatorial perspective on the (continued) exhibition of conceptual art and its collected material outcome examined in this book provides a preliminary chart mapping the way forward.

26 See Smith 2012.

27 Mario García Torres, in discussion with the author, Amsterdam, December 11, 2015.

Summary

Within art history, conceptual art has gained importance in its radical break with modernist traditions of art production, distribution, and reception. At the end of the 1960s conceptual artists focused on criticizing the autonomous and aestheticized status of the artwork, as well as the broader implications of the general art system that lacked sociopolitical engagement. This resulted in an artistic practice that appealed to the "dematerialization of the art object." Although this positioning of the conceptual artists essentially challenged both traditional institutions and the art market, it would soon be included in the same system the artists were trying to dispute. Due to the use of contracts, certificates, and other documents containing information about artworks that were physically inaccessible, conceptual art, ironically enough, could be commodified and sold, and eventually ended up in many public art collections. Whereas many of the first collectors of conceptual art were private persons who entered into agreements with the artists mainly to support their work, the public disclosure of these works was not important and the documents were to be regarded as the artworks themselves, which in turn created problems for their continued exhibition.

In this book the dilemma of exhibition within conceptual art practices is analyzed and set against its theoretical discourse, as well as its historical ascription, in order to gain insight into the strategies and methodologies that conceptual artists applied to show their work. Anticipating Michael Newman's suggestion that the remaining documents of conceptual art contain some sort of "open-ended assignment" of conceptual art as a movement, the main question pursued here is how historical works of conceptual art should be handled within a contemporary exhibitionary context. What should be considered the "original artwork," and to what extent does the continued exhibition of such work—which is, after all, the task of public collections—conflict with the intentions of the art historical "movement"? Would it be better to accept the documentary status of many works of conceptual art and present them in books and publications, as was initially thought to be the proper place for this type of art? Or, if the exhibition in a spatial configuration is nevertheless compulsory, what other formats of display would be appropriate to effectively convey these works?

While the historical exhibition of conceptual art appears to be an opportunist endeavor in many aspects, the analysis of this history provides an understanding of the complexities and paradoxes of conceptual art's "ontological condition," as well as the artistic and curatorial strategies that guaranteed the survival of conceptual art as a movement. Exhibitions do not only represent artistic or aesthetic strategies, but also—and even more so—institutional or socioeconomic strategies, and it is in this regard that a curatorial perspective reveals the public or even "promotional" program of conceptual art, rather than its theoretical affirmations—although these aspects cannot entirely be separated within conceptual art. The historical development of conceptual art within an exhibitionary context is outlined in three case studies of this kind of art in museum exhibitions, which serves to both explain and unravel its state of preservation within the collections of public museums of contemporary art. Within this development a principle of "recuration" has recently entered the field, which offers perspectives and methodologies of exhibition-making that are perhaps more considerate of conceptual artworks and therefore also appropriate for their continued exhibition. The argumentation shows that the approach of recuration can encourage innovative and experimental forms of exhibition with respect to conceptual art's critical attitude towards the "art object"—despite the fact that it conflicts with modernist tenets of originality and market value—within contemporary museum practices.

Bibliography

Acconci, V., and B. Mayer, eds. *0 to 9: The Complete Magazine, 1967–1969*. New York: Ugly Duckling Presse, 2006.

Alberro, A. "The Turn of the Screw: Daniel Buren, Dan Flavin, and the Sixth Guggenheim International Exhibition." *October* no. 80 (1997), pp. 57–84.

——. "Conceptual Photography from the 60's and 70's." *Artforum* vol. 37, no. 3 (1998), p. 116.

——. *Conceptual Art and the Politics of Publicity*. Cambridge, MA: MIT Press, 2003.

——, and S. Buchmann. *Art after Conceptual Art*. Vienna: Generali Foundation/Cologne: Buchhandlung Walther König, 2006.

——, and P. Norvell. *Recording Conceptual Art: Early Interviews with Barry, Huebler, Kaltenbach, LeWitt, Morris, Oppenheim, Siegelaub, Smithson, Weiner*. Berkeley, CA: University of California Press, 2001.

——, and B. Stimson. *Conceptual Art: A Critical Anthology*. Cambridge, MA: MIT Press, 1999.

Alloway, L. "Artists and Photographs." *Studio International* vol. 179, no. 921 (April 1970), pp. 162–164.

——. "'Reality': Ideology at D5," *Artforum* 11 (October 1972), p. 31

Altshuler, B. *Salon to Biennial: Exhibitions that Made Art History, Volume 1: 1863–1959*. London: Phaidon Press, 2008.

——. "A Canon of Exhibitions." *Manifesta Journal* no. 11 (2010–2011), pp. 5–12.

——. *Biennials and Beyond: Exhibitions that Made Art History, 1962–2002*. London: Phaidon Press, 2013.

Andersen, H. "Exhibition: When Attitudes Become Form: From Bern 1969 to Venice 2013." Berlin Art Link, October 8, 2013. ‹www.berlinartlink.com/2013/10/08/exhibition-when-attitudes-become-form-from-bern-1969-to-venice-2013/›.

Andriesse, P., and M. van de Berg, eds. *Art Gallery Exhibiting: The Gallery as a Vehicle for Art* Amsterdam: Galerie Paul Andriesse/De Balie, 1996.

Anon. "Jan Dibbets." *Studio International* vol. 180, no. 924 (1970), pp. 41–44.

Antin, D., et al. "Book Supplement." *Studio International* vol. 17, no. 6 (July/August 1970).

Armleder, J., M. Copeland et al., eds. *Voids: A Retrospective*. Exh. cat. Paris (Centre Pompidou)/Zurich: JRP/Ringier, 2009.

L'art conceptuel, une perspective. Exh. cat. Paris (Musée d'art moderne de la Ville de Paris) 1989

Ashton, D. "Marketing Techniques in the Promotion of Art." *Studio International* vol. 172, no. 883 (1966), pp. 270–273.

Atkinson, T. B. M., et al. "Status and Priority." *Studio International* vol. 179, no. 918 (1970), pp. 28–31.

Aupetitallot, Y., and M. A. Brayer, eds. *Wide White Space: Achter het museum 1966–1976/Wide White Space: derrière le musée 1966–1976*. Düsseldorf: Richter, 1994.

Baere, B. de, and S. Klein Essink. "Op losse schroeven: Een gesprek met Wim Beeren." *Kunst & Museumjournaal* vol. 6, no. 6 (1995), pp. 42–51.

Bainbridge, B., et al. *Art-Language: The Journal of Conceptual Art* vols. 1–4, nos. 1–4 (1969–1978).

Beer, E., and R. de Leeuw, eds. *L'Exposition imaginaire: The Art of Exhibiting in the Eighties/De kunst van het tentoonstellen in de jaren tachtig*. The Hague: SDU Uitgeverij/Rijksdienst Beeldende Kunst, 1989.

Beeren, W. A. L. "De 33e Biënnale van Venetië." *Museumjournaal* vol. 11, no. 6 (1966), pp. 144–155.

——. "Het museum voor morgen." *Museumjournaal* vol. 11, no. 9/10 (1966), pp. 303–311.

——. "Tussen de polen van theorie en practijk: Het museum." *Museumjournaal* vol. 14, no. 6 (1969), pp. 281–288.

——. "Kunst als regeringszaak in de 20e eeuw in Nederland." *Museumjournaal* vol. 20, no. 6 (1975), pp. 251–256.

Beijeren, G. van, and A. van Ravesteijn. *Art & Project Bulletin* no. 1–156. Amsterdam: Art & Project, 1968–1989.

Belting, H. *The End of the History of Art?/Das Ende der Kunstgeschichte?*, trans. Christopher S. Wood. Chicago and London: The University of

Chicago Press, 1987/1983.
Benjamin, W. *Illuminations*, trans. Harry Zohn. London: Fontana, 1992.
Berndes, C., et al., eds. *Ian Wilson: The Discussions*. Eindhoven: Van Abbemuseum, 2008.
——. *Free Sol LeWitt*. Eindhoven: Van Abbemuseum, 2010.
Bezzola, T., R. Kurzmeyer, et al. *Harald Szeemann with by through because towards despite: Catalogue of all Exhibitions 1957–2005*. Zurich/Vienna/New York: Voldemeer/Springer, 2007.
Blok, C. "Gaat Sonsbeek buiten de perken?" *Museumjournaal* vol. 16, no. 4 (1971), pp. 169–177.
——. "Kopers, critici en de consequenties van de nieuwe kunst." *Museumjournaal* vol. 16, no. 3 (1971), pp. 126–130.
Blotkamp, C. "Conceptual Art in boeken: Ideeën als kunst." *Vrij Nederland* (December 6, 1969), p. 9.
——. "Sculpture at Sonsbeek." *Studio International* vol. 182, no. 936 (1971), p. 70.
——, et al., eds. *Museum in Motion? Het museum voor moderne kunst ter diskussie*. The Hague: Staatsuitgeverij, 1979.
Bochner, M. "Excerpts from Speculation (1967–1970)." *Artforum* vol. 8, no. 9 (1970), pp. 70–73.
Boettger, S. "The Lost Contingent: Paul Maenz's Prophetic 1967 Event and the Ambiguities of Historical Priority." *Art Journal* vol. 62, no. 1 (Spring, 2003), pp. 34–47.
Bongard, W. "When Rauschenberg Won the Biennale." *Studio International* vol. 175, no. 901 (June 1968), pp. 288–289.
Boomgaard, J., et al., eds. *Als de kunst er om vraagt: De Sonsbeek-tentoonstellingen 1971, 1986, 1993*. Amsterdam: Stichting Tentoonstellingsinitiatieven/Arnhem: Gemeenschap Beeldende Kunstenaars, 2001.
Bosch, P. van den, ed. *The Collection Visser at the Kröller-Müller Museum*. Otterlo: Kröller-Müller Museum, 2000.
Bourriaud, N. *Relational Aesthetics*, trans. Simon Pleasance and Fronza Woods. Dijon: Les presses du réel, 1998/2002.
Brock, B., "Documenta 5 en het kunstbedrijf." *Museumjournaal* vol. 17, no. 4 (1972), pp. 107–112.
Bryan-Wilson, J. "Hard Hats and Art Strikes: Robert Morris in 1970." *The Art Bulletin* vol. 89, no. 2 (2007), pp. 333–359.
Buchloh, B. H. D. "Conceptual Art 1962–1969: From the Aesthetic of Administration to the Critique of Institutions." *October* vol. 55 (Winter 1990), pp. 105–143.
——. "Benjamin Buchloh Replies to Joseph Kosuth and Seth Siegelaub."

October vol. 57 (Summer 1991), pp. 158–161.
——, et al. *L'art conceptuel, une perspective*. Exh. cat. Paris (Musée d'art moderne de la Ville de Paris) 1989.
Buren, D. "Beware!" *Studio International* vol. 179, no. 920 (March 1970), pp. 100–105.
——. "Standpoints." *Studio International* vol. 181, no. 932 (May 1971), pp. 181–185.
——. 'Where are the Artists?' In *The Next Documenta Should Be Curated by an Artist*, edited by J. Hoffmann, pp. 26–31. New York and Frankfurt: Revolver, 2004.
Burnham, J. "System Esthetics." *Artforum* vol. 7, no. 1 (September 1968), pp. 30–35.
——. "Real-Time Systems." *Artforum* vol. 8, no. 1 (September 1969), pp. 49–55.
——. "Alice's Head: Reflections on Conceptual Art." *Artforum* vol. 8, no. 6 (February 1970), pp. 37–43.
Burns, A., and J. Lundh. "Review When Attitudes Become Form Bern 1969: Venice 2013." *Kaleidoscope Web Specials*. <http://kaleidoscope-press.com/web-specials/reviewwhen-attitudes-become-forms-bern-1969venice-2013words-by-aileen-burns-johan-lundh/>.
Buskirk, M. *The Contingent Object of Contemporary Art*. Cambridge, MA: MIT Press, 2003.
Butin, H. "When Attitudes Become Form, Philip Morris Becomes Sponsor." *Kunstforum International* vol. 136, no. 8 (1997), pp. 342–349.
Butler C., et al. *From Conceptualism to Feminism: Lucy Lippard's Number Shows 1969–74*. London: Afterall Books, 2012.
Celant, G., ed. *Book as Artwork*. London: Nigel Greenwood Inc Ltd, 1972.
——. *When Attitudes Become Form Bern 1969/Venice 2013*. Venice (Fondazione Prada) 2013.
——. Hand-out *When Attitudes Become Form: Bern 1969/Venice 2013*. Venice (Fondazione Prada) June 1 to November 3, 2013.
Cherix, C., ed. *In & Out of Amsterdam: Travels in Conceptual Art 1960–1976*. exh. cat. New York (Museum of Modern Art) 2010.
Claura, M. "Comment (on Buren's text)." *Studio International* vol. 179, no. 920 (March 1970), p. 105.
——. "18 Paris IV. 70." *Studio International* vol. 179, no. 921 (April 1970), p. 179.
——. ed. *Paris 18 IV 70*. New York: Seth Siegelaub, 1970.
Clay, J. "Art Tamed and Wild." *Studio International* vol. 177, no. 912 (1969), pp. 261–265.
Corris, M. *Conceptual Art: Theory, Myth and Practice*. Cambridge:

University Press, 2004.
Cotter, H. "Art's Future Meets Its Past: Prada Foundation Remounts a 1969 Exhibition." *New York Times*, August 13, 2013. ‹www.nytimes.com/2013/08/14/arts/design/prada-foundation-remounts-a-1969-exhibition.html?pagewanted=all&_r=1&›.
Crosby, T. "The New Museum." *Studio International* vol. 171, no. 878 (June 1966), pp. 280–281.
Crow, T. "Head Trip: When Attitudes Become Form: Bern 1969/Venice 2013." *Artforum* vol. 52, no. 1 (September 2013), pp. 320–325, 432.
Cuvelier, P. "Une certain idée de l'art." *Libération*, December 8, 1989, p. 45.
Daalen, P. van. "Uit de dossiers van A379089 te Antwerpen." *Museumjournaal* vol. 19, no. 1 (1974), pp. 20–28.
Dander, P., and U. Wilmes, eds. *A Bit of Matter and A Little Bit More: The Collection and Archives of Herman and Nicole Daled 1966–1978*. Munich (Haus der Kunst) 2010.
Davidts, W. *Bouwen voor de kunst? Museumarchitectuur van Centre Pompidou tot Tate Modern*. Gent: A&S Books, 2006.
Denizot, R. "Exposition of an Exhibition: A Backward Look at Documenta 5." *Studio International* vol. 185, no. 953 (March 1973), pp. 98–99.
——. "A Serious Exhibition: Backward Look at Documenta 5 II." *Studio International* vol. 185, no. 954 (April 1973), pp. 15–152.
Derieux, F., et al., eds. *Harald Szeemann: Individual Methodology*. Zurich: JRP/Ringier, 2007.
Desaive, P. Y. "When Attitudes Become Form: Bern 1969/Venice 2013." *Flash Art* vol. 46 no. 291 (July/August/September 2013), p. 74.
Douglas, S., "Bad Attitudes: Harald Szeemann's Landmark Exhibition Was a Scandal in Its Day." *New York Observer*, June 1, 2013. ‹http://observer.com/2013/06/bad-attitudes-harald-szeemanns-landmark-exhibition-was-a-scandal-in-its-day/›.
Djuric, D., and M. Suvakovic, eds. *Impossible Histories: Historical Avant-gardes, Neo-avant-gardes, and Post-avant-gardes in Yugoslavia, 1918–1991*. Cambridge, MA: MIT Press, 2003.
Dufour, G., ed. *Dan Graham*. Exh. cat. Perth (Art Gallery of Western Australia) 1985.
Eichhorn, M., ed. *The Artist's Contract*. Cologne: Verlag der Buchhandlung Walther König, 2009.
Ekeberg, J., ed. *New Institutionalism Verksted #1*. Oslo: Office for Contemporary Art Norway, 2003.
Fanelli, F. "In Fruitless Search of Lost Time." *The Art Newspaper* vol. 22, no. 248 (July/August 2013), p. 25.
Filipovic, E., et al., eds. *The Biennial Reader*. Ostfildern: Hatje Cantz

Verlag GmbH, 2010.
Fischer, D., ed., *Ausstellungen bei Konrad Fischer: Düsseldorf, Oktober 1967–Oktober 1992*. Bielefeld: Edition Marzona, 1993.
Fischer, K., ed., *Prospect '69*, exh. cat. Düsseldorf (Kunsthalle Düsseldorf) 1969.
——, K., and R. Wedewer, eds. *Konzeption–Conception: Documentation of a To-day's Art Tendency*. Exh. cat. Leverkusen (Städtisches Museum/Schloss Morsbroich), 1969.
Folie, S., G. Holz, and I. Lafer, eds. *A Book about Collecting and Exhibiting Conceptual Art after Conceptual Art*. Cologne: Verlag der Buchhandlung Walther König, 2013.
Fraser, A., and A. Alberro. *Museum Highlights: The Writings of Andrea Fraser*. Cambridge, MA: MIT Press, 2005.
Fuchs, R. H. "Een bepaalde code." *Museumjournaal* vol. 16, no. 3 (1971), pp. 118–125.
——, et al., eds. *Sol LeWitt: Wall Drawings 1968–1984*. Exh. cat. Amsterdam (Stedelijk Museum); Eindhoven (Van Abbemuseum); Hartfort (Wadsworth Atheneum), 1984.
Gauthier, M., et al. *Art & Language: Too Dark to Read: Motifs Rétrospectifs 2002–1965*. Exh. cat. Villeneuve d'Ascq (Musée d'art moderne de Lille métropole) 2002.
Gintz, C., et al., eds. *L'art conceptuel: une perspective*. Exh. cat. Paris: Musée d'art moderne de la ville de Paris, 1989).
Glueck, G. "Guggenheim to Sell 3 Works to Help Buy Others," *The New York Times*, March 23, 1990
Goldberg, R. "Space as Praxis." *Studio International* vol. 190, no. 977 (1975), pp. 130–135.
Goldstein, A., and A. Rorimer, eds. *Reconsidering the Object of Art: 1965–1975*. Exh. cat. Los Angeles (Museum of Contemporary Art)/Cambridge, MA: MIT Press, 1995.
Grabner, M. "Mel Bochner at The Art Institute of Chicago." *Frieze* no. 105 (March 2007). ‹www.frieze.com/issue/print_back/mel_bochner/›.
Graevenitz, A. von. "Daniel Buren en de myte van zijn grensoverschrijdingen." *Museumjournaal* vol. 21, no. 3 (1976), pp. 120–123.
Greenberg, R. "Remembering Exhibitions: From Point to Line to Web." *Tate Papers* no. 12 (2009). ‹www.tate.org.uk/research/tateresearch/tatepapers/09autumn/greenberg›.
——, et al., eds. *Thinking about Exhibitions*. London and New York: Routledge, 1996.
Gribling, F. T. "Chicago, een nieuw museum voor contemporary art." *Museumjournaal* vol. 13, no. 2 (1968), pp. 38–41.

Groys, B. *Logik der Sammlung: Am Ende des musealen Zeitalters*. Munich: Carl Hanser, 1997.

——. Über das Neue: Versuch einer Kulturökonomie. Frankfurt am Main: Fischer Taschenbuch Verlag, 1999.

——. *Art Power*. Cambridge, MA: MIT Press, 2008.

——. "Politics of Installation." *e-flux journal* no. 2 (January 2009). ‹www.e-flux.com/journal/politics-of-installation/›.

——. *History Becomes Form: Moscow Conceptualism*. Cambridge, MA: MIT Press, 2010.

——. "Global Conceptualism Revisited." *e-flux journal* no. 29 (November 2011). ‹www.e-flux.com/journal/global-conceptualism-revisited/›.

H., F. "Worte ohne Bilder: 'Conception-art in Leverkusen.'" *Mündensche Nachrichten*, January 30, 1969.

Haaren, H. van, et al., eds. *Wim Beeren: Om de kunst: Opvattingen van een museumman over moderne kunst, kunstenaars, musea en kunstbeleid*. Rotterdam: NAi Uitgevers, 2005.

Hapgood, S. "Remaking Art History." *Art in America* vol. 78, no. 7 (July 1990), pp. 115–122, 181.

——, and C. Lauf, eds. *In Deed: Certificates of Authenticity in Art*. Amsterdam: Roma Publications, 2011.

Harrison, C. "Düsseldorf Commentary." *Studio International* vol. 176, no. 905 (November 1968), pp. 204.

——. "Against Precedents." *Studio International* vol. 178, no. 914 (September 1969), pp. 90–93.

——. "On Exhibitions and the World at Large: Seth Siegelaub in Conversation with Charles Harrison." *Studio International* vol. 178, no. 917 (December 1969), pp. 202–203.

——. "In gesprek met Seth Siegelaub." *Museumjournaal* vol. 15, no. 1 (1970), pp. 12–15.

——. "Notes towards Art Work." *Studio International* vol. 179, no. 919 (February 1970), pp. 42–43.

——. "A Very Abstract Context." *Studio International* vol. 180, no. 927 (November 1970), pp. 194–198.

——. "Art on TV." *Studio International* vol. 181, no. 929 (March 1971), pp. 30–31.

——. *Essays on Art & Language*. Cambridge, MA: MIT Press, 1991.

Hefting, P. H. "Anny de Dekker over de Wide White Space Gallery." *Museumjournaal* vol. 16, no. 5 (1971), pp. 261–266.

Héman, S., J. Poot, and H. Visser, eds. *Conceptual Art in the Netherlands and Belgium 1965–1975: Artists, Collectors, Galleries, Documents, Exhibitions, Events*. Exh. cat. Amsterdam (Stedelijk Museum)/

Rotterdam: NAi Publishers, 2002.
Hess, B. "30 Jahre Ausstellungen bei Konrad Fischer 1967–1997." Sediment *Mitteilungen zur Geschichte des Kunsthandels* (Heft 2). Bonn: Zentralarchiv des Deutschen und Internationalen Kunsthandels e.V., 1997.
Hoffmann, J., ed. *Mario García Torres/9 at Leo Castelli*. San Juan: Instituto de cultura Puertorriqueña, 2009.
——. *Life in Your Head: When Attitudes Became Form Become Attitudes: A Restoration – A Remake – A Rejuvenation – A Rebellion*. Exh. cat. San Francisco (CCA Wattis Institute for Contemporary Arts) 2012.
Honnef, K. *Concept Art*. Cologne: Phaidon-Verlags-GmbH, 1971.
——. "When Attitudes Become Form." *Kunstforum International* no. 223 (October/December 2013), pp. 30–33.
Hoptman, L., and T. Pospiszil, eds. *Primary Documents: A Sourcebook for Eastern European Art Since the 1950s*. New York: Museum of Modern Art, 2002.
Jappe, G. "Revision in Sachen Konzept-Kunst? Eine Ausstellung im Schloss Morsbroich." *Frankfurter Allgemeine Zeitung* no. 268 (November 18, 1969).
——. "Konrad Fischer Interviewed by Georg Jappe." *Studio International* vol. 181, no. 930 (February 1971), pp. 68–71.
——. "Projection: The New Trend at Prospect 71." *Studio International* vol. 182, no. 939 (December 1971), pp. 258–261.
——. "What is Reality? The Theme of Documenta 5." *Studio International* vol. 182, no. 935 (1971), pp. 2–3.
Klapheck, A. "Ideen als Kunstwerke: Die Ausstellung 'Konzeption' in Leverkusen/Sol LeWitt in Krefeld." *Rheinische Post*, November 15, 1969.
——. "Leverkusen Exhibition of Conceptual Art: Is It a Swindle or Not a Swindle?" *The German Tribune*, December 9, 1969.
Klüser, B., and K. Hegewisch, eds. *Die Kunst der Ausstellung: Eine Dokumentation dreißig exemplarischer Kunstausstellungen dieses Jahrhunderts*. Frankfurt am Main: Insel-Verlag, 1991.
Kolb, L., and D. Fluckiger. "New Institutionalism Revisited." *OnCurating* no. 21 (December 2013). ‹www.on-curating.org/index.php/issue-21-reader/new-institutionalism-revisited.html#.VmNvvSjH221›.
Kölle, B. "Die Kunst des Ausstellens: Untersuchungen zum Werk des Künstlers und Kunstvermittlers Konrad Lueg/Fischer (1939–1996)." Dissertation University of Hildesheim, 2005.
——, ed. *Okey, Dokey Konrad Fischer*. Cologne: Verlag der Buchhandlung Walther König, 2007.

Kosuth, J. "Art after Philosophy." *Studio International* vol. 178, no. 915 (October 1969), pp. 134–137.

——. "Art after Philosophy: Part II: 'Conceptual Art' and Recent Art." *Studio International* vol. 178, no. 916 (November 1969), pp. 160–161.

——. "Art after Philosophy: Part III." *Studio International* vol. 178, no. 917 (December 1969), pp. 212–213.

——. "No Exit." *Artforum* vol. 26, no. 7 (March 1988), pp. 112–115.

——, and G. Inboden. *Joseph Kosuth: The Making of Meaning*. Exh. cat. Stuttgart (Staatsgalerie) 1981.

Krauss, R. E. *Passages in Modern Sculpture*. London: Thames and Hudson, 1977.

——. "Sculpture in the Expanded Field." *October* vol. 8 (Spring 1979), pp. 30–44.

——. *The Originality of the Avant-Garde and Other Modernist Myths*. Cambridge, MA: MIT Press, 1985.

——. *A Voyage on the North Sea: Art in the Age of the Post-Medium Condition*. New York: Thames & Hudson, 1999.

——, et al., eds. *October: The Second Decade, 1986–1996*. Cambridge, MA: MIT Press, 1997.

Kreuzer, S. *More Konzeption Conception Now*. Exh. cat. Leverkusen (Museum Morsbroich) 2015.

Kudielka, R., "Sociology of an Art Boom." *Studio International* vol. 179, no. 922 (May 1970), pp. 206–209.

Künze, W. "Die neueste Kunst gibt's nur als Entwurf." *Leverkusener Rundschau*, October 24, 1969.

Landry, P. "L'art conceptuel, une perspective: An Interview with Claude Gintz and Juliette Laffon." *Le Journal du Musée d'art contemporain de Montréal* vol. 1, no. 2 (July/August 1990), n.p.

Lange, C. "55th Venice Biennale: Do Attitudes Still Become Form?" *Frieze Blog*, May 30, 2013. <http://blog.frieze.com/55th-venice-biennale-do-attitudes-still-become-form/>.

Lazzarato, M. "Immaterial Labour." In *Radical Thought in Italy*, edited by P. Virno and M. Hardt, trans. P. Colilli and E. Emory, pp. 132–146. Minneapolis: University of Minnesota Press, 1996.

Leering, J. "De rol van de beeldende kunst in de vormgeving van de leefomgeving." *Museumjournaal* vol. 19, no. 4 (1974), pp. 50–55.

Leering-Van Moorsel, L. "De collectie Martin en Mia Visser, een interview met de heer en mevrouw Visser, verzamelaars te Bergeyk." *Museumjournaal* vol. 13, no. 2 (1968), pp. 59–68.

Levine, L. "The Information Fall-Out." *Studio International* vol. 181, no. 934 (June 1971), pp. 264–267.

LeWitt, S. "Paragraphs on Conceptual Art." *Artforum* vol. 5, no. 10 (Summer 1967), pp. 79–84.

——. "Sentences on Conceptual Art." 0–9 no. 5 (January 1969), pp. 3–5.

——. "Drawing Series 1968 (Fours)." *Studio International* vol. 177, no. 910 (April 1969), p. 189.

——. "Wall Drawings." *Arts Magazine* 44, no. 6 (April 1970), p. 45.

——. "Doing Wall Drawings." *Art Now* vol. 3, no. 2 (June 1971), n.p.

——. "Letter to the Editor." *Flash Art* no. 42 (1973), pp. 4–6.

Lippard, L. R., ed. "Time: A Panel Discussion." *Art International* vol. 13, no. 9 (November 1969), pp. 20–23, 39.

——. "The Art Workers' Coalition: Not a History." *Studio International* vol. 180, no. 927 (November 1970), pp. 171–179.

——. "Groups." *Studio International* vol. 179, no. 920 (March 1970), pp. 93–100.

——. 955,000*: An Exhibition*. Vancouver: Vancouver Art Gallery, 1970.

——. *Six Years: The Dematerialization of the Art Object from 1966 to 1972: A cross-reference book of information on some esthetic boundaries: consisting of a bibliography into which are inserted a fragmented text, art works, documents, interviews, and symposia, arranged chronologically and focuses on so-called conceptual or information or idea art with mentions of such vaguely designated areas as minimal, antiform, systems, earth, or process art*. New York: Praeger, 1973.

——. "Curating by Numbers." *Tate Papers* no. 12 (Autumn 2009), ‹www.tate.org.uk/download/file/fid/7268›.

——, and J. Chandler. "The Dematerialization of Art." *Art International* vol. 12, no. 2 (February 1968), pp. 31–36.

Marcar, A., ed. *Op losse schroeven: Situaties en cryptostructuren*. Exh. cat. Amsterdam (Stedelijk Museum) 1969.

Mays, J. B. "Conceptualism: The Legacy and the Lessons." *The Globe and Mail*, August 25, 1990.

McEvilley, T. *The Triumph of Anti-Art: Conceptual and Performance Art in the Formation of Post-Modernism*. Kingston, New York: McPherson & Company, 2005.

McShine, K. L., ed. *Information*. New York: Museum of Modern Art, 1970.

Meister, H. "Das Ende vom Lied." *Westdeutsche Zeitung*, November 20, 1969.

Meschede, F., and G. de Werd, eds. *Mit der Möglichkeit gesehen zu werden: Dorothee und Konrad Fischer: Archiv einer Haltung/With a Probability of Being Seen: Dorothee and Konrad Fischer: Archives of an Attitude*. Barcelona (Museu d'Art Contemporani de Barcelona)/Kleve (Museum Kurhaus Kleve)/Düsseldorf: Richter Verlag, 2010.

Messer, T. M. "Impossible Art – Why It Is." *Art in America* vol. 57, no. 3 (May/June, 1969), pp. 30–47.

Meyer, J. "Reconsidering the Object of Art, 1965–1975." *Artforum* vol. 34, no. 6 (February 1996), pp. 79–80, 109.

Meyer, U. *Conceptual Art*. Toronto and Vancouver: Clarke, Irwin & Company Limited, 1972.

Michelson, A. "Three Notes on an Exhibition as a Work." *Artforum* vol. 8, no. 10 (1970), pp. 62–64.

Mollet-Viéville, G. "L'art conceptuel, une perspective." *Galeries Magazine* October/November 1989, p. 100.

Morris, R. "Notes on Sculpture." *Artforum* vol. 4, no. 6 (February 1966), pp. 43–44.

——. "Notes on Sculpture Part II." *Artforum* vol. 5, no. 2 (October 1966), pp. 21–23.

——. "Notes on Sculpture Part 3: Notes and Nonsequiturs." *Artforum* vol. 5, no. 10 (Summer 1967), pp. 24–29.

——. "Anti Form." *Artforum* vol. 6, no. 8 (April 1968), pp. 33–35.

——. "Notes on Sculpture Part 4: Beyond Objects." *Artforum* vol. 7, no. 8 (April 1969), pp. 50–54.

——. "Some Notes on the Phenomenology of Making: The Search for the Motivated." *Artforum* vol. 8, no. 8 (April 1970), pp. 62–66.

Morschel, J. "Aus dem Zettelkasten, Conceptual Art im Leverkusener Museum." *Süddeutsche Zeitung*, November 18, 1969.

Moseley, C. *Conception: Conceptual Documents 1968 to 1972: A Norwich Gallery Touring Exhibition and Publication*. Norwich: Norwich Gallery/ Birmingham: Article Press, 2001.

Nehls, T. "Vor allem wurde viel gelächelt: Zur Ausstellungseröffnung gab's einen Film." *Leverkusener Anzeiger* no. 250 (October 28, 1969).

Newman, M. "Conceptuele kunst van de jaren zestig tot negentig: Een onaf project?" *Kunst & Museumjournaal* vol. 7, no. 1–3 (1996), pp. 101–112.

——, and J. Bird, eds. *Rewriting Conceptual Art*. London: Reaktion Books, 1999.

Obrist, H. U. "Interview with Seth Siegelaub." *24th International Biennale of Graphic Arts*. Exh. cat. Ljubljana (International Centre of Graphic Arts) 2001, p. 220.

——. "Schaars goed. In gesprek met Tino Seghal." *Metropolis M* no. 1 (2004). <http://metropolism.com/features/schaars-goed/>.

——. *A Brief History of Curating*. Zurich: JRP Ringier, 2011.

——, ed. *Do It: The Compendium*. New York: Independent Curators International, 2013.

O'Doherty, B., *Inside the White Cube: The Ideology of the Gallery Space.*

Santa Monica and San Francisco: The Lapis Press, 1986.

O.M.A., R. Koolhaas, and B. Mau. *S,M,L,XL*. New York: Monacelli Press, 1995.

O'Neill, P. "The Curatorial Turn: From Practice to Discourse." In *Issues in Curating Contemporary Art and Performance*, edited by J. Rugg and M. Sedgwick, pp. 13–28. Chicago: University of Chicago Press, 2007.

——, ed. *Curating Subjects*. Amsterdam: De Appel, 2007.

——. *The Culture of Curating and the Curating of Culture(s)*. Cambridge MA: MIT Press, 2012.

——, and M. Wilson, eds. *Curating Research*. London: Open Editions, 2015.

Osborne, P. *Conceptual Art*. London and New York: Phaidon Press, 2002.

Overduyn, H. "De samenleving in tentoonstellingen, tentoonstellingen als vorm van samenleven." *Museumjournaal* vol. 18, no. 3 (1973), pp. 109–113.

Oxenaar, R. W. D. "Stekelbaarsjes op sterk water: De Biënnale Venetië 1972." *Museumjournaal* vol. 17, no. 4 (1972), pp. 164–169.

Pingen, R. *Dat museum is een mijnheer: De geschiedenis van het Van Abbemuseum 1936–2003*. Eindhoven: Van Abbemuseum/Amsterdam: Artimo, 2005.

Plagens, P. "557,087." *Artforum* vol. 8, no. 3 (November 1969), pp. 64–67.

Poinsot, J. M. *Quand l'oeuvre a lieu: L'art exposé et ses récits autorisés*. Genève: Mamco/Villeurbanne: Institut d'art contemporain & Art édition, 1999.

Rattemeyer, C., et al. *Exhibiting the New Art: 'Op Losse Schroeven' and 'When Attitudes Become Form' 1969*. London: Afterall Books, 2010.

Reichardt, J. "The Democratization of Art." *Studio International* vol. 171, no. 875 (March 1966), pp. 86, 87.

Reise, B. "Sol LeWitt Drawings 1968–1969." *Studio International* vol. 178, no. 917 (December 1969), pp. 222–225.

——. "A Tail of Two Exhibitions: The Aborted Haacke and Robert Morris Shows." *Studio International* vol. 182, no. 935 (July/August 1971), pp. 30–39.

Reuther, H. "Die Ashe in Urnen aufbewahren? Das Museum Leverkusen zeigt die 'Dokumentation einer heutigen Kunstrichtung.'" *Frankfurter Rundschau* (November 8, 1969).

Richard, S. *Unconcealed: The International Network of Conceptual Artists 1967–77: Dealers, Exhibitions and Public Collections*, edited by L. Morris. London: Ridinghouse, 2009.

Rorimer, A. "Reevaluating the Object of Collecting and Display." *The Art Bulletin* vol. 77, no. 1 (March 1995), pp. 21–24.

——. *New Art in the 60s and 70s: Redefining Reality*. New York: Thames & Hudson, 2001.

Schön, W. "Etwas, das es nicht gibt: 'Konzeption' – eine Ausstellung im Leverkusener Museum." *Rheinische Merkur*, November 7, 1969.

Schroeder, H. "Es gibt nichts zu sehen: Konzeption – Conception im Schloss eröffnet." *Kölnerische Rundschau*, no. 250 (October 28, 1969).

Siegelaub, S., ed. *January 5–31, 1969*. Exh. cat. New York (Seth Siegelaub) 1969.

——, ed. "The Context of Art/The Art of Context." *Kunst & Museumjournaal* vol. 7, no. 1–3 (1996).

——, and R. Polansky. "Artists' Reserved Rights Transfer and Sale Agreement." *Studio International* vol. 181, no. 932 (April 1971), pp. 142–144.

——, and J. W. Wendler, eds. *Xerox Book: Carl Andre, Robert Barry, Douglas Huebler, Joseph Kosuth, Sol LeWitt, Robert Morris, Lawrence Weiner*. New York: Seth Siegelaub, John W. Wendler, 1968.

Smith, T. *Thinking Contemporary Curating*. New York: Independent Curators International, 2012.

Smithson, R. "Aerial Art." *Studio International* vol. 177, no. 910 (April 1969), pp. 180–181.

Stachelhaus, H., "Entwurf ist kein tragfähiger Wurf." NRZ *Neue Ruhr-Zeitung*, November 21, 1969.

Staniszewski, M. A. *The Power of Display: A History of Exhibition Installations at the Museum of Modern Art*. Cambridge, MA: MIT Press, 1998.

Steeds, L., ed. *Making Art Global: Volume 2: Magiciens de la Terre 1989*. Cologne: Walther König Verlag, 2013.

Spencer, C. "When Attitudes Become Form: Bern 1969/Venice 2013." This is Tomorrow, September 2, 2013. ‹http://thisistomorrow.info/articles/when-attitudes-become-form-bern-1969-venice-2013›

Szeemann, H., ed. *Live in Your Head: When Attitudes Become Form: Works, Concepts, Processes, Situations, Information/Wenn Attitüden Form werden: Werke, Konzepte, Vorgänge, Situationen, Information/Quand les attitudes deviennent forme: Oeuvres, concepts, processus, situations, information/Quando attitudini diventano forma: Opere, concetti, processi, situazioni, informazione*. Bern (Kunsthalle Bern) 1969.

Tegenbosch, L. "Op losse schroeven." *de Volkskrant*, March 14, 1969.

Tuyl, G. van. "Het werk van Jan Dibbets op de Biënnale van Venetië." *Museumjournaal* vol. 17, no. 4 (1972), pp. 158–163.

——. "Informatie en/of interpretatie." *Museumjournaal* vol. 18, no. 4 (1973), pp. 163–167.

Thwaites, J. O. "Katalog genügt: Ideenspuk im Schloss." *Christ und Welt*, November 11, 1969.

Verhagen, E. "Histoires de l'art conceptuel une rétrospective." *Perspective* no. 3 (2007), p. 508–511.

Vries Robbé, L. de. "Film als kunst of als beeldende kunst." *Museumjournaal* vol. 19, no. 5 (1974), pp 202–207.

———. "Het kunstconcept van Concept Kunst." *Museumjournaal* vol. 20, no. 6 (1975), pp. 241–250.

Weiffenbach, J. "PASTA MOMA, or the Strike-Bound Modern." *Studio International* vol. 182, no. 938 (November 1971), pp. 175–177.

Welchman, J. C., ed. *Institutional Critique and After*. Zurich: JRP/Ringier, 2006.

Winkel, C. van. "Dertig jaar buiten de perken: Gesprek over Sonsbeek 71 met Cor Blok, Judith Cahen en Lambert Tegenbosch." *De Witte Raaf* no. 91 (May/June 2001). ‹www.dewitteraaf.be/artikel/detail/nl/2289›.

———. *During the Exhibition the Gallery Will Be Closed: Contemporary Art and the Paradoxes of Conceptualism*. Amsterdam: Valiz, 2012.

Wulffen, T. "L'Art Conceptuel: Une Perspective." *Kunstforum International* no. 106 (March/April 1990), pp. 298–299.

Zepter, C. "Signatur um Mitternacht: Nicht-Mitteilbares soll mitgeteilt werden." *Leverkusener Anzeiger*, November 5, 1969.

Zonnenberg, N. "The Context of Art (Continued): An Interview with Seth Siegelaub." *Manifesta Journal* no. 9 (2009–2010), pp. 41–51.

———. "Free Sol LeWitt & In-Between Minimalisms." *Manifesta Journal* no. 10 (2009–2010), pp. 98–103.

———. "The Amsterdam Connection: In Conversation with Jan Dibbets and Ger van Elk." *Metropolis M* no. 4 (August/September 2010), pp. 52–62 and 112–115. ‹www.metropolism.com/magazine/2010-no4/de-amsterdam-connectie›.

———. "Ik heb de conceptuele kunst nooit als gedematerialiseerd beschouwd: Interview met Ann Goldstein over het Temporary Stedelijk en het voortbestaan van de conceptuele kunst." *De Witte Raaf* no. 152 (July/August 2011).

Other Sources

Archives MAMVP (Box 524/1–13).
Conversation with Claude Gintz, Paris, December 3, 2011.
Conversations (e-mail) with Chiara Costa (Fondazione Prada), December, 2014.
Conversation with Mario Garcia Torres, Stedelijk Museum Amsterdam, December 11, 2015.
Former West Conference, Utrecht, November 6, 2009: ‹www.formerwest.org/ResearchCongresses/1stFormerWestCongress/Text/ReportDay2›.
OMA Projects: ‹www.oma.eu/projects/1986/casa-palestra-the-domestic-project-/›.
Stadtarchiv Leverkusen (410.1302).
Stadtarchiv Düsseldorf (IV 29367).
The Panza Collection Initiative: ‹www.guggenheim.org/conservation/the-panza-collection-initiative›.
The Siegelaub Collection and Archives, Stichting Egress Foundation: ‹http://egressfoundation.net/egress/index.php?option=com_content&view=article&id=62&Itemid=307›.

Index

Acknowledgments

This book is a revised version of the PhD dissertation that I defended at the Vrije Universiteit (VU) in Amsterdam in November 2016. For the realization of this study I am greatly indebted to my promoters, Wouter Davidts, Katja Kwastek, and Jonneke Jobse, who gave me many helpful comments and suggestions throughout the course of my research. It was Jonneke who encouraged me to undertake this research in the first place, while Wouter guided me through the development and elaboration of my thesis with many inspiring conversations. Katja was especially supportive with constructive criticism in the last phase of the manuscript's completion. I am also indebted to Carel Blotkamp for proposing to me the idea to initiate a PhD and giving me the confidence to execute such a project. In addition, I would like to thank the members of the reading committee, Eric de Bruyn, Ann-Sophie Lehmann, Mia Lerm-Hayes, Terry Smith, and Diederik Oostdijk, for accepting the invitation to assess the thesis, as well as for their valuable comments and revelations.

I would furthermore like to thank Jan van Adrichem for being a stable point of reference in reviewing my writings from the very start, and for providing me with stimulating conversations and feedback. Many thanks also go to my former PhD colleagues at the VU University, Iris Burgers, Elise Noyez, and Rose Tzalmona, for being a pillar of support during the first years of my research and joining in many inspiring and humorous conversations about the tasks that we were all undertaking. I am grateful to have been able to work within the Department of Art History and Comparative Arts and Media at the VU, where I have always felt appreciated and supported by the former chair, Koos Bosma (†), as well as by departmental staff members Richard Bionda, Agnes Groot, Fieke Konijn, Sven Lütticken, Jos ten Berge, Paul van den Akker, and Ingrid Vermeulen.

Additionally, I owe many thanks to the professional staff of the museums and archives that I consulted in my research: Stefanie Kreuzer of Museum Morsbroich in Leverkusen; Kathrin Barutzki of the Kunsthalle Düsseldorf; Gabriele John of the Stadtarchiv Leverkusen; Elisabeth Schleeben of the Stadtarchiv Düsseldorf; Anne Dressen, François Michaud, and Florence Pustienne of the Musée d'art moderne de la ville de Paris; and Chiara Costa of the Fondazione Prada, all of whom helped me to find and access useful information in their archives. I would like to express special thanks to Claude Gintz, who shared with me his ideas and memory of the curation of the exhibition *L'art conceptuel, une perspective*, and Jan Dibbets, Ger van Elk (†), Ann Goldstein, and Seth Siegelaub (†) for the stimulating conversations about conceptual art's legacy.

In regard to the finalization of my PhD endeavor, special thanks go to my paranymphs, Sanneke Stigter and Sjoukje van der Meulen, for accepting to mentally as well as emotionally support me during the final hour of my defense. Lastly,

I am most grateful to my family and friends, who bore with me and supported me throughout this important project, and accepted recurring absences at social events and get-togethers. That the dissertation has ultimately become a book, I owe thanks to Astrid Vorstermans of Valiz, who believed it would be a valuable addition to the *vis-à-vis* series, and to the generous support of the Mondriaan Fund and the Prins Bernhard Cultuurfonds. I would also like to express thanks to Dutton Hauhart, Els Brinkman, and Sam de Groot for the English copy-editing, proofreading, and layout of the book.

About the Author

Nathalie Zonnenberg is an art historian and curator based in Amsterdam. She received a PhD in art history from the Vrije Universiteit (VU) in Amsterdam. Currently she is a lecturer in Modern and Contemporary Art at the Open University (NL) and in Curatorial Studies at the Royal Academy of Fine Arts (KASK) in Ghent (BE). Prior to this (2007–2017) she was a lecturer in the department of History and Art History at Utrecht University and at the VU in Amsterdam. As a curator she has worked for several art institutions, including Witte de With Center for Contemporary art in Rotterdam, the Kröller-Müller Museum in Otterlo (NL), and Beyond, a public art program in the public sphere of Leidsche Rijn, Utrecht. She has curated several exhibitions, such as *Size Matters: In Relation to Minimalism* at Kunstfort Vijfhuizen (NL) in 2014, REDONE. *Conceptual Art from the Collection* at the Kröller-Müller Museum in 2008, and *L'enfer c'est les autres* at the Stedelijk Museum Bureau Amsterdam in 2007. Zonnenberg was senior editor of *Manifesta Journal* (2009–2011) and has authored many publications and reviews on contemporary art in various catalogues, artist's books, and magazines, among them *Metropolis M, De Witte Raaf,* and *Afterall Journal.*

Author: Nathalie Zonnenberg
Copy-editing: Dutton R. Hauhart, Reitz Ink
Proofreading: Els Brinkman
Index: Elke Stevens
Design: Sam de Groot
Appropriated images on cover, pp. 10, 30, 78, 110, 146, 182: Sam de Groot
Typefaces: Eldorado (William Addison Dwiggins, 1953), Computer Modern (Donald Knuth, 1984), SKI DATA (Tariq Heijboer, 2014)
Printing and binding: Bariet/Ten Brink, Meppel
Publisher: Valiz, Amsterdam, 2019, ‹www.valiz.nl›

Distribution
USA: DAP, ‹www.artbook.com›
GB/IE: Anagram Books, ‹www.anagrambooks.com›
NL/BE/LU: Coen Sligting, ‹www.coensligtingbookimport.nl›
Europe/Asia: Idea Books, ‹www.ideabooks.nl›
Australia: Perimeter, ‹www.perimeterdistribution.com›
Individual orders: ‹www.valiz.nl›

This publication has been generously supported by Prins Bernhard Cultuurfonds and Mondriaan Fund

PRINS BERNHARD **CULTUURFONDS**

mondriaan fund

ISBN 978-90-78088-76-9
Printed and bound in the EU

vis-à-vis

The vis-à-vis series provides a platform to stimulating and relevant subjects in recent and emerging visual arts, architecture and design. The authors relate to history and art history, to other authors, to recent topics and to the reader. Most are academic researchers. What binds them is a visual way of thinking, an undaunted treatment of the subject matter and a skilful, creative style of writing.

Series design by Sam de Groot, ‹www.samdegroot.nl›.

2015

Sophie Berrebi, *The Shape of Evidence: Contemporary Art and the Document*, ISBN 978-90-78088-98-1

Janneke Wesseling, *De volmaakte beschouwer: De ervaring van het kunstwerk en receptie-esthetica*, ISBN 978-94-92095-09-1 (e-book)

2016

Janneke Wesseling, *Of Sponge, Stone and the Intertwinement with the Here and Now: A Methodology of Artistic Research*, ISBN 78-94-92095-21-3

2017

Janneke Wesseling, *The Perfect Spectator: The Experience of the Art Work and Reception Aesthetics*, ISBN 978-90-80818-50-7

Wouter Davidts, *Triple Bond: Essays on Art, Architecture, and Museums*, ISBN 978-90-78088-49-3

Sandra Kisters, *The Lure of the Biographical: On the (Self-)Representation of Artists*, ISBN 978-94-92095-25-1

Christa-Maria Lerm Hayes (ed.), *Brian O'Doherty/Patrick Ireland: Word, Image and Institutional Critique*, ISBN 978-94-92095-24-4

2018

John Macarthur, Susan Holden, Ashley Paine, Wouter Davidts, *Pavilion Propositions: Nine Points on an Architectural Phenomenon*, ISBN 978-94-92095-50-3

Jeroen Lutters, *The Trade of the Teacher: Visual Thinking with Mieke Bal*, ISBN 978-94-92095-56-5

Ernst van Alphen, *Failed Images: Photography and its Counter-Practices*, ISBN 978-94-92095-45-9

Paul Kempers, *'Het gaat om heel eenvoudige dingen': Jean Leering en de kunst*, ISBN 978-94-92095-07-7

Eva Wittocx, Ann Demeester, Melanie Bühler, *The Transhistorical Museum: Mapping the Field*, ISBN 978-94-92095-52-7